The Business of Billionaires & Superyachts

The only etiquette guide for succeeding in the fabulously hedonistic world of 7-Star yachting.

Written & illustrated by Christina Prince

Dedication

To my Mom and Dad
who gave me the faith and
confidence to know in my heart
that you can accomplish
anything in life.
You gave me the courage to
keep on doing
what brings
me joy.

Contents

This Is The Adventure Of A Lifetime That People Only Ever Dream Of

Pack your bags, take out half and you're ready!

Welcome to the secretive world of yacht stewardessing — the only career on earth, where you're hired to travel around the world, live the hedonistic life of the ridiculously wealthy, have all your expenses paid for, be fed like a superstar, hang with all the hot men and make millions. Darling, this is the glitz and glamour industry!

I'll explain everything that superyacht crews have been hiding for a very long time. Ten years ago you never would have gotten it out of anyone, or me, because the first rule of yachting is never talk about what happens in the yachting industry. I'm confessing everything now so you can successfully land a job on superyachts and shine as a yachting industry leader. The pages that you are about to read reveal everything you need to know about:

- ✔ Yacht stewardess etiquette expectations
- ✔ What you should look like
- ✔ Where the plum jobs are
- ✔ Who you are going to be living with.

I'm going to tell you how to:
- ✔ Deal with international UHNWI (ultra high net worth individuals) with 7-Star expectations
- ✔ The level of service required
- ✔ How to throw fabulous million-dollar parties complete with lions hanging from cranes
- ✔ Care for priceless interiors.

We're going to strategize how to:
- ✔ Survive the Mediterranean and Caribbean seasons
- ✔ Dealing with relationships in tight quarters
- ✔ Gain leadership skills to direct dream teams
- ✔ What to do with the tips you can make.

The world's billionaires purchase these mega yachts as the ultimate status symbol in luxury, privacy and freedom of travel. Owned and treated as the exclusive playground of the unlisted Forbes billionaires, the money to purchase, maintain, refuel, and pay crew will continuously astonish you.

These multi-million dollar yachts are managed to the level of a 7-Star boutique hotel with twenty-four-hour wait staff constantly on call. These are floating, self-indulgent palaces, opulent beyond belief and grand in all respects. This is the world where money is no object and nothing is too extravagant. It is the last untouched frontier in restricted access to the gilded world of the super wealthy. To sum it up, there's a reason why Tiger Woods christened his yacht *Privacy*.

The largest private yacht in the world is *Azzam* at 180 meters. It does not charter; as the owner is unwell and has never had the chance to use it. It's a shame because the yacht cost this Arab gentleman $600 million, and he had to build a marina to fit it in.

Not in the market to buy? The starting price to charter a mediocre sixty-meter boat superyacht starts at $350,000 a week, not including fuel, food, alcohol and tips.

Teams of professional crew maintain the standards and expectations of luxury yachting. Captains are in a role similar to hotel managers. First officers, bosons, and deckhands are in charge of the exterior of the ship. The most critical people on board – those who will make or break a guest's trip – are the stewardesses. We are the first impression guests are greeted with in the morning and the last contact at night. At all times we are required to exude a radiant, glamorous pulled-together image. Aside from looking polished, our duty is to deliver from the heart: discreet, first class service, exceeding the expectations of both owners and guests.

In this world of indulgence, it is essential for a happy crew to make all requests run as smooth as clockwork. The word *no* doesn't exist in our vocabulary. It just means you haven't tried hard enough. Copper Juliet roses delivered in three hours' time to the remote west coast of Corsica, "Easy." "Oh! Fourteen kilos of Beluga black caviar expressed to Antigua for appetizers, I got this." Guests arriving in an hour by private helicopter, "Sure, let's get moving!" Movie scripts can't begin to capture this world, and you're in it! While sometimes you'll think the requests are ridiculous — and trust me you will have stories — our job is to complete all tasks with a smile, even if it's four in the morning and you feel like you haven't slept in days. This career is definitely not a backpacking gig!

This book covers all you need to know about getting your dream job and keeping it with clear tactics. Immerse yourself in the 7-Star world of global UHNWI (ultra high net worth individuals), the level of service, fabulous million-dollar parties complete with lions hanging from cranes, caring for antique interiors and talking yachty lingo. You'll need to know what to pack, where all the plum jobs are and how to treat the imported hookers! Lady, we gotcha!

Yachting is a wonderfully fulfilling career. Learning how to run a superyacht is rewarded with bonuses that no land-based job can ever compete with. This is the beginning of your adventure.

VOCABULARY

MONTAUK 8·12 PriSSy

Success Is
Not Final
Failure Is Not Fatal
It Is The Courage To
Continue
That Counts.

- A-Z Of Ghetto To Top-Notch Yacht Lingo -

A

Adrift: Floating in the water without any propulsion. "We're adrift in the middle of the ocean," translates to every crew member's worst fear — unless you have attractive people on board, large quantities of food, plenty of alcohol and you're not floating around off the Ivory Coast of Africa.

Aft: Back of the boat. "Sarah, Sarah, Emily," "Go ahead, Emily," "What's your location, Sarah?" "Bridge deck aft " (the bridge deck, at the back of the boat) "Fabulous, meeting you there now." The opposite of aft is forward.

Aground: When someone has not been paying attention and the yacht has hit land — aground, unexpectedly ashore. Without a doubt, this is a disaster, but a good dinner party story worth repeating — later.

Agencies: After a couple of years in the industry and depending on what experience you have, these agents will be chasing you to fill prime positions. Call them up and tell them what you want: "Charter, sixty meters, six girls underneath me and permanent. Salary starting at *0000" and they will work magic. They will be the first to recommend you if they think you are worthy. No other industry has this ability to chop and change and have people scout jobs for them. Agents take a fee of fourty-one hundred percent of your first month's wages, paid by the owners of the yacht.

Allergies: Crew with pain in the arse allergies and intolerances are a nightmare. Refrain from giving the chef your weekly clean eating plan and lists of foods you cannot eat. More than likely you will not be acknowledged and will be referred to as a difficult bitch. For guests that express allergies, inform the chief stewardess and ensure the offending food is taken away from them. Criticizing, teasing and tormenting people about their intolerances is considered the height of bad manners.

APA: Advance provisioning allowance. Charter guests will wire money ahead for provisioning costs.

Ashore: "The guests are heading ashore." Ashore = land. This means you'll have to work harder than when they're on board, so upon their return, everything is showroom finish again.

Astern: The boat's bum is moored up to the dock. Can also mean looking behind.

B

Back to back charters: When there is minimal time between each group of paying charter guests. We dread this, as the whole yacht needs to be detailed from top to bottom in record time. It can be done with a fantastic team, lots of positivity and a whiff of a big tip!

Bank accounts: Before you leave home, inform your bank that you are no longer a tax resident for tax purposes.

Bare boat: When the boat has nothing on it and you have to buy everything.

Beds and heads: Term used for making beds and cleaning toilets.

Beam: The widest part of the yacht.

Boson: Is the leader of the deck team.

Boson's locker: Where the deck crew store their cleaning supplies and any equipment needed to maintain the deck department.

Bridge: Where the captain dictates his orders from.

Bilge: The storage space under the floorboards on the lowest level of a yacht. Accessed by lifting up the floor board panels.

Bow: The very front of the boat that comes to a pointy bit.

Bow thrusters: Propellers that are fitted on either side on the front bottom of the hull. Instead of using the rudder, the captain will depend on the bow thrusters to position the boat.

Bulkheads: Are the dividing walls that separate the compartments inside the yacht.

Bunkering: When you go into port to take on fuel.

Buzzers: OMG you caved and bought one (or several) out for the guests. Why would you terrorize yourself and stews with this? That annoying ring tone will send you crazy in a day! If you haven't seen one of these, it looks like a single (unmounted) handheld door buzzer. When pressed, the connecting bell will sound in the pantry, telling you the guests want service. Particular nationalities prefer them as staff can disappear and be summoned when they are needed.

C

Casting off: When you let go of the lines (ropes) that tie you to the wharf.

Charter: A yacht can choose to go charter as opposed to private. The owners rent out their yacht to other rich people for a fee.

Charger *(service plate)*: The largest plates (metallic or matching with the plate set) that are placed underneath the entrée *(starter)* and main course plates when setting a formal dinner table. They are only taken away before dessert is served.

Charter broker: Depending on whom you talk to these people are either trustworthy or not. Brokers are usually considered slimy as they will often say and do anything to close a deal. But before we start bashing them, this career path can potentially be an exit strategy out of yachting. They can receive twenty percent of any sale. If most yachts sell for around the eleven million $$$ mark, that can mean some serious cash. Some captains also have their broker's license and do a bit of sideline wheeling and dealing. There is nothing from stopping you from doing the same.

Chewing: By far the quickest way to alienate all those around you. Chew with your mouth closed. If people want to have a conversation during meal times, it is up to them to fill the silence while you are chewing. Swallow quickly to be polite.

Cleaning caddy: A basket that keeps all your cleaning supplies together. Put a cloth underneath to avoid spillage.

Cleat: The metal T-things on the boat deck, that tie off lines that hold the boat or sails in place.

Crewing agents: Individuals or global firms who headhunt, recruit and source crew to staff a yacht.

Cockpit: It's the area on the main deck that is hollowed out.

Copy that: Yes, I have heard and understood your request.

Courtesy flag: A small flag of the country that you are visiting is flown as a sign of respect.

Crew mess: Where the crew congregates to feed, watch TV and be social. It is all crew members' job — but mainly stewardesses — to keep this area tidy and clean. Golden rule, "Do unto others as you would like them to do to you," when it comes to noise levels and cleaning up after yourself.

Crew uniforms: No room for personalization here. I hope you like white polos and khaki bottoms. Everyone will be given a set with his or her number on it.

Cruising location: Where is this boat traveling to for the season? It better not be St. Tropez or St. Bart's again, because I'll be bored.

Cucumber: Not to be confused with zucchini. Know your vegetables as the chef will send you out for last minute supplies.

Crudités: Plate of sliced fresh vegetables served with dipping sauce. Guests will ask for this to snack midafternoon or before a meal.

D

Day head: Easily accessible head (toilet) for all guests to use that is not in a cabin. You will usually find one on each deck close to the guests' socializing areas. Day heads need to be checked after each guest use. Water drops in the sink need to be removed, toilet seats checked, and a neat toilet paper fold is required to complete this banal task.

Day worker: Pardon is that another word for shit kicker? When one picks up a temporary gig on a yacht as an extra set of hands in the ship yard, before or after a charter trip or as a trial period to see if the person fits in It's not a permanent position because the person does not live on the yacht. Day working helps prepare you for life at sea, instead of having the rude shock of what the job entails and what is expected of you.

Deck: The different levels of the yacht. Usually it refers to the wooden decks. "Meet me on deck" — meet me outside.

Dehumidifier: Found in all cigar boxes and is used to keep the air inside a certain temperature.

Detailing: Deep cleaning an area using cotton buds, toothpicks and toothbrushes. Bring the whole room back up to showroom finish by ensuring there is no dirt or dust around light fittings, switches, mirror corners, inside cupboard corners, edges of benches, tiny cracks, gaps, behind cabinets, underneath drawers, in-between sliding panel runners, air-conditioning vents, plugs, under things, over things and in things. Phew! Basically, make it look brand new by your cleaning efforts!

Dingy: Another term for a small tender that shuttles you back and forth to the bigger boat out on the mooring.

Displacement: The volume of water that is displaced by the yacht.

Ditch Bag: Same as a grab bag. Where you put all your essentials in case the boat sinks and you need to get into the life raft. See grab bag for difference.

Dock walking: We all have to do it. You get dressed in your finest makeshift yacht crew uniform and walk the docks handing out resumes or business cards. If a boat needs help, they could snap you up that day or call you later.

Draught/Draft: How deep the hull of the vessel is below the waterline. It is essentially the amount of water the boat needs to float.

Dragging: When the anchor did not catch or the captain did not let out enough chain and the boat drifts with the current.

Dry Boat: When the crew is not allowed to drink alcohol on board at any time. Tough for fun loving yachties. So the captain may come up with a few different versions. "Don't come back to the boat wasted," or "no drinking on charter or owner's trips."

DPA: Designated Person Ashore assigned by the yacht management company to ensure the safe operation of each ISM compliant yacht > 500GT.

Dusting: Dust is your enemy! The silly stories you hear of fussy madams and hormonal chief stewardesses checking for dust on ceiling ledges and places you didn't even know existed, are all true. If there is dust to be found, they will make your life hell. Heads up! Beware, just when you think you've done a good job and dusted the bananas out of that place. At certain times of the day, the light hits the room at different angles. Every speck of dust will be visible on every surface and window. You'll know it when you see it as it's embarrassing to us over-achieving stewardesses.

E

ENG 1: The medical exam that all yachties are required to have. Mandatory renewal every two years.

EPIRB: Electronic device that sends out a distress signal when it hits the water or is manually activated.

F

Fenders: Big grey plastic cushions filled with air, which stop yachts from hitting each other or the dock. Place one between objects that are getting too close to the yacht while in movement.

Fender kicker: Tire kicking but for yachts. Kick the fender and say, "Gee, she's a beautiful boat." The same as when you are shopping for a car.

Fly bridge: The top — highest deck — where the captain can drive the yacht in the fresh air.

FLIBS: Fort Lauderdale boat show

Freelance stewardess: When an experienced stewardess chooses to pick up random gigs instead of a permanent role on a boat. A higher amount of pay is expected, and yes, one can live off this income. Perfect for when you're noncommittal, burnt out or have found a lovely boyfriend in a port of call.

Forward: The front of the yacht. Opposite of aft - back of the boat.

G

Galley: Kitchen on a yacht.

Grab bag: Red medical bag. Kept in the bridge and one grabs it for medical emergencies.

Guests: The only reason you are here on this fabulous floating palace. If you break down what it costs to stay on a yacht for one night and compare it to the most expensive hotel in the world and the kind of service they deliver – this is the standard you should be aiming for.

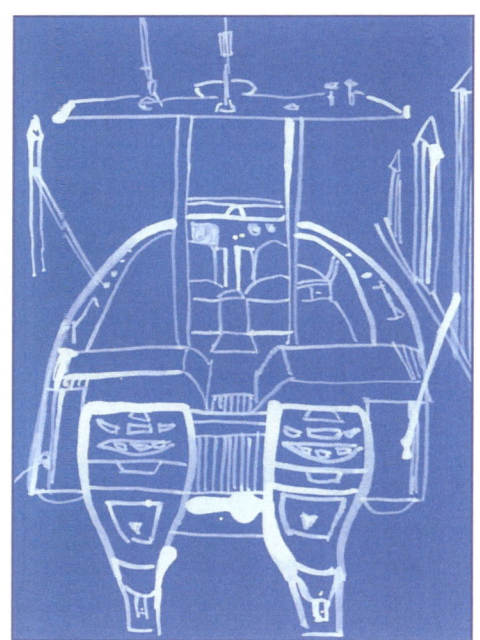

H

Hatch: A window that opens up on a boat.

Head: Boat term for toilet.

Heads & beds: See beds and heads.

Helm station: Duplicate control panels of the bridge, situated on the wing stations. This gives the driver a clearer view of placing the yacht when docking.

HOD: Heads Of Departments.

Hull: The super structure of the bottom of the boat.

I

Idiot proofing: After the guests' belongings have been packed, the stewardess goes through all the rooms and cupboards making sure they haven't left anything behind.

Inventories: List of everything on board and where it is stored. A bright idea is to place expiration dates on inventory logs, so you do not have to go through all the supplies.

"I'm just going to tidy my cabin": is code for "I'm going for a nap, leave me alone."

J

Jibing – A jibe or gybe is a maneuver where a sailboat turns her stern through the wind, tacking in the opposite direction.

K

Keel: The bottom structure of a ship's hull. On a sailboat, it's the long pointy thing that balances the yacht from keeling all the way over.

L

Lazarette: Bottom deck of the aft, where tenders, scuba diving rooms, jets skis and fun personal crafts are stored. Can be used to access the engine rooms. There are lazarettes on some yachts with guest spaces for lounging, showering and also open up to the *pool.* Other lazarettes are designed to drive your tender inside and park. The water is then drained out.

Line: Sailor's talk for rope used to moor the vessel. Amateurs use the term rope.

Leeward: The side of the boat facing away from the wind.

Length: The length of the yacht.

Log: The yacht's record of where it's been and what's been happening onboard.

Longitude & latitude: Memorize to impress people.

M

Master cabin: Where the *owners* or head charter guests sleep. It is the grandest cabin onboard.

Management company: An external company that is paid to take care of the financial state and the screening process of the yacht.

Mise en place: A French term for having everything prepared before service.

Mixer: Liquid added to liquor to form basic drinks. Examples are coke, juice or water. "Is there a preference for a perticular mixer Sir?"

Mooring: A mooring field is usually about a hundred yards out in the water away from the marina. They are recognized by evenly spaced buoys where boats are tied up if they are not in a slip or on anchor.

M/Y: Abbreviation for motor yacht

N

Networking: Making friends with people that appeal to you. Refrain from walking up to the most important person in the room and start reeling off your resume.

Nautical mile: One nautical mile is one minute of latitude (1,852m or 6,080ft). Sixty minutes is equal to one degree of latitude

O

Off charter: When guests are not on board the yacht.

On deck: If the captain says be on deck at 08:00, it means be ready to start working. Have your coffee or breakfast beforehand.

On board: "Be on board at 05:30 or else we're leaving without you" = BE. ON. THE. BOAT. "The guests are on board" means they are waiting for you to come serve them.

On the hard: When the boat is hauled out of the water for repairs in the shipyard.

Outboard: A small engine attached outside the tender.

Owner: It is common for yachties to refer to the owner of the yacht as my *owner.* There is truth in this statement as your *owner* basically owns you like a *slave* while you're onboard.

P

Painter: The line that is towing a boat.

Private: All yachts are private and they choose to charter out to people that are willing to pay the hiring fee.

Port: Left-hand side of the boat.

Provisioning: Spending other people's money to purchase groceries for the yacht.

"The Principal": The head charter guest that is paying for the trip.

R

Roger that: Same meaning as copy that.

Runners: After the guests have left we place down runners. They are tailor-made fabric covers for the floors, tabletops, and couches.

Rank: The hierarchy in any formal organization. Never give lip or attitude to those above you. Yachts are run like the military.

Revenge on a boat: The most satisfying way to seek long-term revenge is fake tan product. Throw out the sun-screen lotion and replace it with a strong fake tan with no pigment in the white cream. Watch your victims slowly turn orange and wonder out loud if they are dying from jaundice. Alternatively ruin their laundry to let them know not to mess with you.

Rudder: The paddle under the boat that moves to change the direction of the vessel.

S

Scuppers: On every deck, where the teak finishes at the sides of the boat, are gutters to direct the off flow of water. On boats, these are referred to as scuppers.

Scented towels: Face towels soaked in mystical, expensive scents and pure water, then chilled to the perfect temperature. Serve to guests on a silver platter and handed out with tongs upon arrival, before meals and after eating messy foods. Scented towels are a must-have in the yacht stewardesses' arsenal of tools to impress.

Seacock: A valve sealing off a pipe opening to seawater, black water, grey water, etc.

Seaman's discharge book: A log book that records the seafarer's qualifications and movements on and off boats. Use it as a backup travel document to justify your extensive traveling like a drug dealer. Get one as soon as you can as there are many benefits. Two of them being excess luggage and easily changeable air flight tickets.

Showing: A showing is the abbreviation for boat/yacht showing. It is the same as a house showing or open house. The occasions of showings arise when potential buyers of the yacht are invited on for an inspection. After the yacht is ready for viewing, the agent prefers that you be out of sight. If they are trying to close the deal and this is the third or fourth time the potential buyers have come, the buyer may ask you to stick around and serve champagne/tea/coffee/water. This is all, of course, as per captain's request.

Show room finish/ Showroom standard: Making the yacht look like it is brand new, ready for a photo-shoot or buyer's viewing. All the runners are taken up, prints and fingermarks removed, flowers are put out and sometimes the tables are elaborately set.

Shelia shine: The go-to product for shining all metal work on appliances.

Silver service: White gloved formal service.

Sky lounge: Top deck of the yacht where an outdoor living space is created and enclosed.

Slip: The parking space where the yacht is tied up on the dock.

Smoking: We all lie on our CVs about this. If you smoke, give up now. It will make your life hell.

Son of a gun: Old term for a child born to a military man who couldn't obtain verified paternal parentage. It's now used as a positive term for when one does well.

Spring lines: Two lines that are crossed in the mid-section of the boat, holding the boat in place next to the dock.

Starboard: Right-hand side of the boat.

STCW: A necessary course that all yacht crew must have for them to be considered seaworthy. Renewable every five years.

Stern: The rear of a ship. The opposite of the bow.

Stern thrusters: Mini propellers on either side of the back of the boat that propel the boat into position.

Swim platform: The lowest deck of the yacht where you can enter the water.

S/Y: Abbreviation for sailing yacht.

Sun deck: Top deck of the yacht where an outdoor living space is created.

T

Tender: Small watercraft used to transport passengers from a larger yacht to land.

Tacking: or "Get ready to tack," when the sailboat is facing one direction and swings so that the same wind direction is hitting the other side of the boat. The boom will swing over to the opposite direction as well — beware, it's always a courtesy to scream "heads." This sailing tack is used when one is heading upwind. Because you cannot head straight into the wind you tack making a zigzag pattern up the wind.

Toilet folds: Part of the stewardess's arsenal to show off how experienced she is.

Topside: The opposite of below deck. The main outside spaces of the boat.

Transom: The flat vertical part of the back of the boat.

T/T: "*Tender to*" labeled on the tender before yacht's name. E.g. T/T Sublime. All tenders need to be labeled like this or else you risk receiving a fine.

Turndown: A procedure to getting a cabin ready for guests to retire.

U

Underscore plates: No fingers in bowls please! Always serve bowls with a doily and plate underneath.

V

Vacuuming: Is a task that is required to be done daily. Don't be surprised if this is your allocated job if your the latest addition to the crew.

VIP: Every guest on a yacht is a VIP, including the hookers, drunks and mistresses. Treat them with the utmost respect at all times.

Visas needed: To enter the USA: Captains won't even look at you without a B1B2 visa. South African countries also need certain visas for traveling to Europe.

W

Watchkeeping: Ensuring there is a clear path when the boat is moving. The term is also used when the boat is stationary and then you are watching to make sure that everything is running smoothly.

Waterline: Where the water surface levels off on the ship's hull.

Watch schedule: A crewmember has to be present on board at all times for insurance purposes. You're watching for alarms, foreign persons on board, lines and fenders. Additional chores include tidying up the crew mess after meals and restocking drinks.

White gloves: Fancy white cotton gloves used to stop fingerprints from appearing on glasses and cutlery. Wear them when setting the table or serving.

Windward: Side or direction from which the wind blows. Opposite of leeward.

Y

Yacht: Big white, immaculate floating palace where one has their every wish and desire taken care off.

Yachtie: Term given to any person serving on a yacht — we all deny it, but we're one of them!

Another $$ Another Day Red

Too much rain thrns the water green.

If its meant to be blue.

1.

ARE YOU
READY
FOR
THIS?

Be The
Person You
Could Have
Been
Now.

12 Essential Questions Every Wannabe Stewardess Needs To Ask Herself

Before you pack your bags and throw yourself at the nearest yacht ask yourself these questions:

1. Do I honestly want this?
2. Can I handle being a paid housewife?
3. Can I handle putting my life on hold for weeks at a time? (Am I willing to swap my life for money?)
4. Is getting married and having a boyfriend a huge priority?
5. Can I handle traveling regularly and living out of a suitcase?
6. Am I happy and fun to be around, with an easygoing personality? (Because no one wants to live with someone who is miserable)
7. Do I enjoy making others happy and providing excellent customer service?
8. Can I handle being told what to do all the time?
9. Do I have a can-do personality?
10. Do I like cleaning? Am I clean?
11. Am I honestly organized and keen to put objects in a methodical order?
12. Am I capable of saying, "Yes I will," constantly with a smile and not punch anyone in the guts?

No lying!

What desirable skill set should a potential stewardess have?

1. A background in hospitality
2. Superb guest service skills. Have an "As you please" or "It's my pleasure" mentality
3. A well-organized methodology with administration expertise
4. The ability to take orders, work in a team and manage co-workers
5. Excellent interaction skills — you need to be a people person
6. The capacity to deal with difficult personalities in a trivial environment
7. Professional etiquette in communication, personal hygiene, appearance and attitude
8. The capability to think and act quickly under pressure while multitasking!
9. Discretion and confidentially
10. Housekeeping skills with an eye for detail
11. Multi-lingual
12. Floral arrangement abilities.

- International Stew Courses -

Yes, we recommend you have stewardess courses under your belt. There's a fine art to managing these multi-million-dollar floating homes. That's why they pay us the big bucks!

Courses We Recommend:

STCW 2010

Standards of training, certification and watch-keeping.
This five-day course covers basic safety training in fire prevention: firefighting, personal survival techniques, social responsibility, first aid and CPR. It is considered the minimum entry requirement into yachting and all captains will request it. The rough price is $900 to $1300 USD and is due for renewal every five years.

ENG 1

Seafarers' medical certificate for all persons crossing open seas. Inquire first with your local medical centers as only certain doctors are licensed to perform this medical.

Stewardess Courses

These courses run from three days to two weeks. You receive hands-on training in the world of yacht stewardessing with emphasis on silver service and guest care.

Basic training courses are recommended to get your foot in the door. It shows dedication to your new career and knowledge of what being a yacht stewardess entails. Undertake a correspondence course every year as qualifications matter. Stewardesses with courses under their belt tend to get picked sooner, snap up the quality jobs, progress faster and earn more money. Captains and chief stewardesses look for stewardess-related credentials on your resume. If you don't have qualifications, it tells us either you think you know everything or you can't be bothered committing to your new career. You've got to play the game.

An outstanding stewardess is always polite, well mannered, immaculately groomed and happy. She eats with her mouth closed at the dining room table. There is no burping, sculling of drinks or swearing. She sits with her legs together and has only one helping from the massive buffet. She holds herself like a princess and saves her naughtiness for behind closed doors.

2. THE ROLE OF A YACHT STEWARDESS

- The Excellent Stewardess Download On Crew Tasks -
What's expected of you? Where do you start?

The interior aspect of managing a yacht is divided into three different departments. Service, housekeeping, and laundry. Stewardesses are either separated into teams to complete job lists or allocated a specific department to work under the direction of the HOD (Head of Department.)

This is the delightful job of a yacht stewardess:

Service

✓ Guest service of all meals and every snack-y whim in between
✓ Drink service
✓ Creating table settings and event management on the highest-end scale imaginable
✓ Possibly light cooking duties. When requested, help in the galley with food preparation and washing up

Housekeeping

✓ Detailing guest and crew accommodations
✓ Beds and Heads: Making beds, cleaning toilets and detailing showers
✓ Inventories
✓ Polishing/detailing: interior metal work, decorative ornaments, platters and cutlery
✓ Crew provisioning and re-stocking
✓ Loading and unloading the dishwasher. Funny, this is always a big deal!
✓ Helping with docking and fenders

Laundry

✓ Washing of crew uniforms, guest laundry, guest bed linens and towels. Laundry is required to be completed at a professional level as guest laundry is worth more than a deposit on a large house. Italian hand woven and hand embroidered bedding can run in excess of $12,000 (made by half-naked virgins!) and sixty-five gram Egyptian cotton with double-rolled, hand-sewn, scalloped edged towels are easily priced at $400 bucks apiece.

OFF CHARTER/GUESTS OFF

- Will You Pass The Test? The Daily Grind On The Grandest Assets In The World -

This will never be your normal nine-to-five office job

A typical day running a yacht will look like this:

07:00	Wake up. Call dibs with your cabin mates for shower/bathroom times
07:30	Eat breakfast. Place used dishes in the dishwasher and tidy up after yourself
08:00	Interior meeting in the crew mess with the chief stew. Discuss priorities, job list, guest arrivals, maintenance and time scheduling. Commence duties
10:00	Fifteen-minute break
12:00	Lunch break. After lunch, pack away food and stack dishwasher. Wipe tables and tidy crew mess
15:00	Fifteen-minute break
16:45	Wrap it up interior meeting
17:00	Finish for the day, ensure your station is cleaned up and put away Hit the gym, head down to the beach, read a book, call home...
19:30	Watch duties commence if it's your allocated night.

Friday afternoon – Group interior meeting and service training (Masterclass)

PRE-CHARTER/ANTICIPATION OF GUEST ARRIVAL

- The Absolutely Need To Know List Before Guests Arrive -

Print it out & sleep with it under your pillow

The month before or as soon as you join the yacht

1. Uniforms cannot be last minute. Distribute crew uniforms and double check that all crew have a full inventory of 'guest on' day uniforms, night uniforms, matching belts, socks, shoes and hats. If you're short of stock, order a.s.a.p. Complete all alterations now. Emphasize to the crew that last minute is too late and you're not here to baby them
2. Begin training crew. Have a schedule in place for training and stick with it. Laundry room ethics, guest cabins expectations, drink service and silver service. Training will significantly increase the confidence of the crew. Get the boys involved too!
3. Take inventories of supplies needed at sea. Crew and guest provisioning, guest toiletries, table decorations, items required for theme nights, linens, gifts for turn downs and guests' gifts such as caps and t-shirts
4. Run coffee machines to check they're working. Order coffee pods if the boat is outside of the USA. They are exhausting to source last minute.

Two weeks before

1. Take inventory of all liquor and wines on board. Place your order, stockpiling as much as you can. The greatest tragedy on a boat is running out of alcohol
2. Complete provisioning lists and double check with chefs. Don't over order food — space is limited.

The week before

1. Catch up on all the sleep you can plus some. I'm begging you not to burn the candle at both ends and party hard. You'll be coming down with guests on. The team needs you fresh, well rested and vibrant. Let's start the season off with positive vibes!
2. Place the order for fresh flowers for each guest area, including guest bathrooms. When ordering, give the florist vase dimensions and visuals of your theme and a basic color scheme to follow. Remember to order extra fresh loose flowers, greenery and roses.

Provisioning & service

1. Start taking provisions on board
2. Double check dry store has all provisions, stock is organized and there is enough
3. Check silver items for tarnish and polishing. Bring all silver trays to the pantry and prepare for service
4. Check all glasses for labels and smears. Wash and dry ready for guest use
5. Wipe out all fridges. Make sure each fridge has two types of milk, butter, waters and sodas

Guest cabins and guest areas

1. Check the vertical herb garden and plants on the back deck have been trimmed and watered
2. Thoroughly vacuum all upholstery and cushions with the brittle-haired upholstery brush
3. Check all toiletry baskets are full, set up in the correct order, refilled and smear free
4. Are all the guest bathroom towels evenly stacked? Are the face towels perfectly rolled with the logos evenly spaced on the vanity?
5. Check toilet paper. Do all rolls have a diamond fold and toilet paper decoration? Do the rolls in the storage closet have the ends folded over in the same direction and stacked neatly?
6. Check all curtains and blinds are in a uniform shape with the gathering evenly spaced
7. Make up each bed with flat sheets, duvets, and a day cover
8. Put out bathrobes, slippers and laundry bags. Pay attention to concealing all labels
9. Check all cabin glasses and water jugs for watermarks
10. Check every light in cabins, in wardrobes, in cupboards and bathroom is working
11. Detail lazarette day head and sun deck day head. Inform deck crew these areas are no longer to be used as storage for exterior
12. Prepare the helicopter and tender areas for guest welcome reception
13. Check the fireplace on the back deck aft is cleaned and restocked for guest use
14. Walk around the boat, checking for any irregularities. A maintenance list should be handed to the engineer with adequate time to complete.

The evening before/morning of the day of guest arrival

1. Dust, vacuum and wipe the entire boat from sundeck to the main deck
2. Flush all toilets with dolphin friendly bleach. Check all faucets (taps) in the bathrooms for pressure and temperature
3. Place Valrhona chocolates and decadent imported snacks into custom made boxes and place in guest areas
4. Put out spa water trays in the entertainment areas (including sparkling and natural water) with glasses
5. Place flower vases in the appropriate places with a piece of clear rubber protector underneath
6. Set up bar ready for guest arrival
7. Have the welcome canapés ready to roll at the back of house (pantry)
8. Set a silver tray with rolled & chilled scented hand towels for each expected guest. Cover with cling wrap and place in the fridge
9. Prepare a table setting for the appropriate time of guest arrival and add extras
10. Print out menus
11. Put out sun lotion baskets
12. Put out shoe baskets with Ceder Milano handmade, roe deer-antler shoehorns
13. Have a pile of laminated luggage tags ready, with the names of each cabin printed on them, ready

for the storage of guest luggage

14. Be in 'guest on' uniform and ready to have the last soothing cup of tea with the interior crew one hour before guest arrival

15. Try not to neglect other boat duties whilst preparing for a visit. Be responsible for making your allocated department run smoothly.

- The Quickest Way To Know Who You Are Serving -
Preference sheets - Guest habit profiling

A preference sheet is a detailed document that covers every aspect of your guest's lifestyle. It will specify food intolerances, likes and dislikes, preferred activities and all guest wishes. The captain will request preference sheets as soon as charter guests lock in dates, via the charter broker or the principal guest's PA. If the yacht is private, there will be a folder of well-documented particulars of the family and guests.

When creating a faultless preference sheet, ask open-ended questions. Go through the sequence of the day onboard to check that you haven't missed anything. Ask vital questions such as:

✓ How many are guests coming aboard? Adults + Children? Ages?

✓ Will there be any additional guests or plans to entertain during the charter?

✓ Can we offer restaurant/nightclub reservations to you?

✓ Daily habits or activities planned? Swimming, paddle boarding, reading, relaxing?

✓ Can everybody swim?

✓ What kind of drinks will be consumed?

✓ Do you prefer a particular kind of food?

✓ Are there any special dietary requirements or allergies?

✓ At what time should we expect you for breakfast?

✓ Do you have a preference for continental (fresh bakery goods and local cold cuts) or hot buffet breakfasts? What kind of cereal do you like?

✓ How do you drink your coffee and tea?

✓ What kind of milk do you like? (Full cream, half-and-half, skim, lactose-free, almond?)

✓ Lunch: Plated (how many courses) or family style?

✓ What are your favorite snacks?

✓ Would you enjoy canapés before lunch and dinner?

✓ Dinner: Plated (how many courses) or family style?

✓ Cheese plates? Desserts? Both?

✓ Petit fours? Dark, white, milk chocolates?

✓ Do you have a fondness for any particular flowers or colors?

Have the following items well stocked for all charter trips:

✓ A variety of sugars: brown, white, agave, honey, sweet & low, stevia and coconut sugar

✓ All condiments: mustards, ketchup, mayonnaise, sweet chili, hot chili sauces and BBQ sauce

✓ A variety of organic jams, peanut butter and tons of nutella

✓ Ice-cream toppings for random requests

✓ A selection of mixers. Tonic, cokes, soda, back-up juice in every flavor you can lay your hands on

✓ A backup supply of snacks.

After reading the preference sheets, use your intuition and common sense to take the guest experience to another level. If guests are ultra-healthy, go the extra mile by dehydrating fruits, creating designer smoothies-of-the-day and serve kombucha as an aperitif. For buck's parties, our guests are here to let loose and drink. Surprise them with a make-your-own Bloody Mary bar and grilled BBQ brunches. Keep the hot canapés coming throughout the day and always keep the beer on ice. The ability to anticipate all guests' needs should be easily forecasted with preference sheets. You must be able to know they want it, even before they knew it.

- How To Take The Headache Out Of Making It A Successful Trip -

It's about them, not you

At the beginning of every guest trip, discuss expectations for making this the perfect guest trip. What will make our guests exceptionally happy? From there, set clear goals to measure the team's success. This is my beginning checklist:

1. Promise that we, as a team are going to give this trip 1000%
2. As a team we are going to be consistent in delivering perfect service. Everything will go out the same way
3. We're always going to smile, no matter how tired or miserable we are
4. Quiet. The guests came for peace, not to hear us ye-haring out the back
5. Place petit fours on the table, after dinner or when they sit down to watch a movie
6. Know the times of sunrise and sunset and what the weather is doing
7. Know where all light switches are. We will turn them on for guest arrival and every day one hour before sunset
8. We promise to put out the massive amounts of candles in glass vases with no fingerprints and not break matching sets.

The audiovisual system will make or break a trip!

9. We must know how to use all the audiovisual systems and what the system is capable off
10. How strong is the wifi and where are the signal points? What is the password?
11. Do all areas have airplay? How many devices can we connect?
12. Know what satellite channels we have before suggesting guests watch television. Make sure it's all working and ready to go before guests ask. They will be disappointed if it doesn't work
13. If you know they want to hook something up or watch something, get it ready beforehand
14. Can you stream a movie from a laptop?
15. Does everyone know how to use the remote controls? How do you switch off the TVs in the guest rooms?

The AV systems are always our biggest problem. The biggest gauge on every trip is our ability to keep going above and beyond the call of duty. Have passion for the job and take responsibility for creating a positive experience for all those around you. Plan, research and get super organized. When in doubt, change your lipstick shade to change your attitude!

ON CHARTER/GUESTS ON

- When The Real Fun Begins -

And the real world ceases to exist

With guests on board, the routine follows this basic outline:

1. The service team wakes before guests and takes over from the night girl
2. Check there is enough chilled champagne, vodka and caviar in stock and then set up breakfast
3. If you're not begging the chef for a bacon sandwich while waiting for guests, then you're vacuuming and dusting in main guest areas
4. The housekeeping team begins their day before the first guest awakes. They start off by

detailing guest areas that the service team has not completed, continuing onto vacated guest cabins

5. When serving guests, the service team is to inform housekeeping if a guest leaves the table. Unless the crew member is on service, if a guest enters a particular space, crew are to vanish

6. The service team packs down after breakfast, which includes the clearing of pantries. Afterward, they begin setting up for lunch

7. The service team serves and cleans up after lunch. The service team will coordinate breaks amongst themselves after lunch, before the dinner service begins

8. During guests' lunch, the housekeeping team will tidy up cabins and guest areas. Everything will be put back to a showroom finish before they have their afternoon break

9. All hands on deck for the commencement of dinner service. Service girls are with guests and the housekeeping team is to complete bed turndowns

10. Housekeeping team finishes when all cabins are completed and guest areas are tidied up

11. The service team knocks off when guests have finished dinner and they have cleared most of the back pantry. The guests are now left with the night girl

12. The laundry girl has completed her day when the laundry room is cleared or has done a handover with the night girl.

AFTER CHARTER/GUEST DEPARTURE

- The Guests Have Left, What Happens Next -

No, we don't sit around working on our tan and drinking beer!

Ah, now, big exhale! Open the fridge and drink straight from the leftover Krug 1928 champagne. Hide the Almas beluga black caviar behind the jams to eat later. Shake out the 24-karat gold leaf Beyond Gourmet jellybeans from the handmade crystal guest snack jar and take them down to the crew mess for the deckhands. Finally, they can stop stealing them and eat as many as they want. Duck off to your cabin to put your hair back into the messy bakery bun that it was pre-charter and get out of those stockings. On the way back up to the main deck, poke your head into the galley to tell the chefs, "Well done, the food was delicious, the guests loved it! Great job, let's get loose tonight!"

After a demanding and excessive trip, we need to get a few martinis into us a.s.a.p. until we can book ourselves into counseling sessions. We've all experienced hectic trips with crazy, high maintenance Madams, wives of the owners. They can make our lives hell, by shitting in the shower, leaving filthy used tampons around, and by complaining because they don't receive enough attention. Husbands and friends are not much better. They can spend the week downing six-thousand-dollars-a-bottle, fifty-year-old Appleton rum and smoking Cohiba Behike cigars that we couldn't source for less than twenty-thousand-a-box. Normal.

This is not an excuse for our loose and excessive behavior off charter. We've all picked up the crew's bar tab at Buddha bar in Monaco and had weekend benders at Fontainebleau Miami that only end because we've spent our month's pay that was deposited yesterday. It happens. Yachting is all about being surrounded by so much hedonism and self-gratification, that at the end of the day you either go hard and get in with the action — or you go home.

All right, pack down. We hold off turning over cabins and getting wasted until we've received confirmation that the guests have boarded their private Gulfstream planes and left the country. There is nothing worse than stripping the place, only to find out the guests didn't take off due to bad weather, and they're coming back!

After the guests have left, we are called collectively to the bridge by the captain to discuss the trip. This meeting is our chance to find out how much money they tipped us. Hopefully, they didn't overspend the APA (advanced provisioning allowance) and we get the rest of that too.

From here on in, our time can go two ways. If there are no guest trips booked for a couple of weeks, we will have prepared beforehand to enjoy the freedom. This usually ranges from renting villas in St Martin, eating in expensive restaurants, and day drinking on the beach. The rest of the time, we'll be in dirty ports, middle-of-nowhere shipyards, or on anchor up the creek.

- Common Attitude Problems Stewardesses Don't Know They're Making -
The best stewardesses are calm, discreet, happy, a little remote and extremely decisive

Do's:

1. Have a POSITIVE ATTITUDE. Positivity and being happy go a long way in getting results
2. Remember you are representing the yacht, the owners and your fellow crewmembers at all times
3. Respect the chief stewardess and your superiors. They are responsible for you, the interior and the jobs that need completion. Your job is to listen to your manager and follow orders. Know your place. If the owners, captain and chief stewardess ask you to do the most outrageous, nonsensical task, just say yes!
4. Always strive to be a team player. Everyone is different; no one is perfect, and that includes you. There is no place for gossip or drama on board. If you have issues, talk to that person and try and sort it out. The whole boat does not need to be part of it. If speaking with that person doesn't resolve your issue, your last resort is to go to the captain
5. Bite your tongue when you see or hear something crazy
6. Be willing to help without being asked
7. Every boat is different. You're going to have to adjust and make changes to suit every boat
8. There is no problem with asking. If you don't know, ask. Be willing to learn and ask intelligent questions
9. Stay organized and keep on top of everything. Finish one job before moving onto the next. Always strive to complete given jobs by the end of the day. Or work till you are finished
10. Stay out of the liquor cabinet. It cannot be replaced. The wine is upwards of $500 a pop
11. A lady should never burp or fart! Ever. Rude!
12. Be true to your word. When you sign a confidentiality agreement, don't be a fool and post away on social media
13. Keep your Russian in check. If you know Russian, don't flaunt it or tell anyone. Russians dislike eavesdropping on their private conversations, and will disembark you rather than have you aware of their sordid details
14. Only do the owner's friends or children when you're ready to be terminated.

Don'ts:

1. Don't be late. Get up and show up, no matter how hung over and tired you are
2. GET OFF YOUR PHONE. Do not be on your mobile while working
3. If you smoke, don't smell like a chimney
4. No gum or eating while working
5. Don't let the decorations in your cabin undermine your workplace professionalism
6. Don't throw a party on the boat and especially on the sun deck where other crew from yachts can see you. There are secret cameras and security guards watching you twenty-four-seven
7. Refrain from using guest areas, guest cabins, and guest resources without prior permission from the captain. Have the mentality that you're a guest in someone's home
8. **Never complain about anything.**
9. **Never complain about anything.**

3.

THE GIFT WRAPPING IS EVERY THING

Dress Shabbily &
They Remember The
Dress;
Dress Impeccably &
They Remember
The Women.
- Coco Chanel

Darling, some of the best days are unexpected. You've just got to say yes.

- I Am What I Wear -

The art of successfully packing for yacht life

Our backyard changes more than the wind. Last week it was the French Riviera, drinking rosé with the sexy first officer from two boats down. This week we're doing Antigua Charter yacht week, and next? St. Barts of course! Drama, what does one wear to fit in?

Here is how we pack lightly: Choose items in a single color-way that are complimentary for your complexion and one that works for every occasion. This way you'll always looked pulled together and the outfit can be quickly repurposed with accessories. Read on for our refined twenty-piece capsule wardrobe for the traveling goddess that you are:

Three dresses:

1. The perfect party dress that instantly makes you the center of attention. You'll need this for random invitations to the Buddha Bar in Monaco or Christmas balls in Cannes
2. A multi-functional dress in a natural fabric. Cut at thigh length with a full skirt, nipped in at the waist, buttons up the center front, sleeveless with a collar will be perfect
3. A long, black, loose-fitting dress. Donna Karen does glamorous clothes that are perfect for covering up at crew dinners and for looking delish while traveling long distance.

Four tops:

4. Pack a dark-colored, long sleeved blouse that works for the transitions of seasons
5. A short sleeved blouse in a light color. We love everything Givenchy
6. Only one T-shirt. You'll get sick of them quickly as your new uniform will be T-shirts and polos
7. A sweater that highlights your tan for the spring and autumn seasons. Think vibrant saturated colors in hues of turquoise, Barbie pink and coral red. Stay away from tacky nautical stripes and hoodies, which are bulky to carry.

Bottoms:

8. Pack a pair of expensive designer jeans that look like they were made for you. Ideal for scooter riding in the Hamptons
9. Leggings: essential for lounging in the crew mess, doing watch duty and for chilly nights
10. Shorts for when you're going to the beach, sailing with friends or ducking out for a Saturday morning coffee.

Skirt:

11. One perfect stretchy skirt for sightseeing lunch dates in Malta.

Accessories:

12. The impeccable collapsible handbag
13. A belt to match all outfits and pull in those outfits to accentuate your waist
14. Bikinis, they are versatile outfits in themselves. Pack as many as you can fit in!
15. A large scarf that you can double as a dress with a belt and a cover-up for plane rides. The 140 cm Hermes scarves in cashmere are the best
16. We're going to count this as one because you want to keep it all together in one mesh bag: Gym gear — only shorts, the places you're going to are too hot — sports bras, lightweight tops, underwear & socks. All machine washable only.

Shoes:

17. Running shoes
18. Flip flops or Birkenstocks, for the ease of getting on and off the yacht (constant wearing will cause callouses)

19. A pair of high heels that say I'm not paying for my own drinks tonight
20. Shoes that are easy to walk in that match your job interview outfit

N.B Shoes for the boat are unnecessary. The boat will provide snappy uniforms with matching shoes and sunglasses.

Toiletries:

21. Pack miniatures of everything that you need. Once onboard to can help yourself to their supplies, including tampons and hairdryers.

Check off the essentials:

1. Passport with at least one year's validity
2. Spare passport photos that are the correct size and resolution to your country
3. Medical insurance. Take it out for as long as you think it will take you to get a job. The boat insurance will cover you once you have moved your stuff on board
4. An eye mask for sleeping
5. A padlock to lock your gear up in the crew house and for random gyms you'll be visiting along the way.

All of the above, plus toiletries should fit into **one soft, collapsible suitcase with wheels.** The suitcase needs to be stowed into tight storage areas and weigh no more than 20 kg. Budget airlines are capping this as the weight limit. Most of the time you will be living in uniforms AND at any moment you might have to pack in a hurry and leave. Only if you misbehave and there are no warnings.

Packing for an 'I'm getting the fuck off the boat' weekend:

1. Cake
2. Condoms
3. Champagne
4. After sun lotion that instantly makes everyone fall in love with you
5. Eye drops (for stepping back on board).

- How To Turn Heads In The World Of Stewardess Presentation -
No one wants to play with the fat kids

It all starts with the first impression

Yo, princess, this is an image-based industry. Hit the gym, lay off the pizza, and rock that *Giselle hair*

✓ Aim for the polished air hostess look. Hair needs to be combed and pulled back. French rolls, the Emirates cabin crew bun and fishtail braids work well. Well-coiffed hair will set you apart from all the misfits trying to get into the industry

✓ Don't go overboard with the make-up. Aim for a bright natural look. You don't want to be ridiculed because you looked like a Crayola box attacked you

✓ Don't show too much skin like strippers beginning their dance. No thongs, miniskirts or cleavage-baring tops

✓ Wear only minimal jewelry — it's considered unhygienic. Your jewelry will get trashed anyway with the excessive hand washing. Save it for people who will appreciate it more

✓ Apply very light perfume. Guests want to smell the food, not the Victoria Secret scent you picked up on sale in Fort Lauderdale

✓ Use clear nail or basic polish. Always have your toenails painted too as you never know when you have to be presentable

✓ Be ready to work, play the part and dress the part. Good quality clothing and perfect lipstick open all doors.

STOP!
WISHING.
START
DOING.

4.

Your Soul Is
Screaming For You To
Fulfill Your True Purpose.
You Cannot Make
More Time.

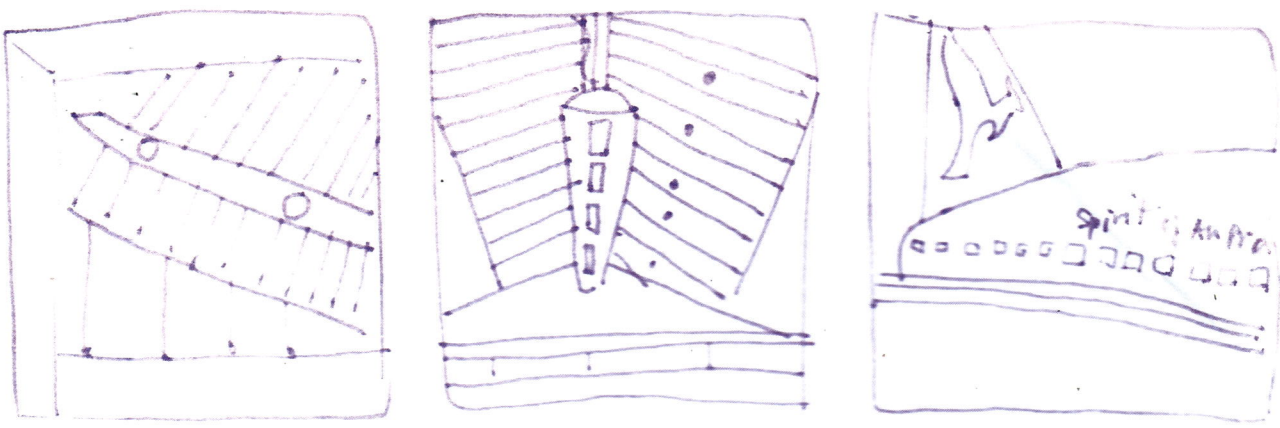

- A Clear Strategy For Potential Yachties -
The step-by-step guide to getting the most legendary job in the world

1. Organize a B1/B2 visa with the United States Embassy before leaving home. This is vital as all captains request it and you will need it for entering and exiting the States on a yacht

2. Complete the prerequisite for all seafarers — the STCW 2010, five-day course. Book early, as the most popular schools run this program every week during peak season and it can be hard to get in

3. Be in favorable yacht hotspots to interview for jobs

4. Looking for a new job is a full-time career. Be consistent. Sign up with crew placement agents, online crewing agencies, and online job boards. Post your CV in places where captains and HOD's look for them

5. Be proactive. Create an online website with your resume that potential employers can view. Print the web address on your business card. It will save you the hassle of tripping around with a stack of resumes

6. Have professional business cards made up with an appropriate email. Give them to everyone!

7. NETWORK. This industry is all about who you know. Everyone knows everyone, and after years of being in the industry, you'll be surprised how small it is

8. Be on your best behavior at networking events and gatherings of industry members

9. One cannot afford to be selective. Be inclusive. Invite everyone when doing any activity

10. Get as much experience under your belt as you can. Every day of work is another day learning

11. Go to interviews, show up and be present. Be ten minutes early for everything. You're on sailor time now.

- The Six Quickest Ways To Find Day Work -
The step-by-step guide

1. Make friends with everyone in your crew house without being over-bearing and needy. You are not the stewardess bible either

2. Dock walk every single day

3. Network at the local bar. Be friendly and talk about everything else but yachting to make a memorable impression. Once you've been friends for a couple of hours and there's a lull in the conversation, you can casually drop the hint that you are seeking work

4. Check local notice boards daily at marinas, online agencies, and in a few select uniform shops

5. Be persistent. Continue being sociable and meeting people. Hang around marinas so people know you're looking and enthusiastic. Treat day working and looking for the next dream job as a profession. We like to keep the hours of eight am to one pm Monday to Friday. You're then free in the afternoons and weekends to head to the beach and relax

6. Apply, apply, and apply. Who are these people to say no to your dreams?

- Nailing The CV -
Bring it to the plate girl!

Make your resume standout with a winning profile picture, a clear yachting CV layout and good references. Let's work our way down your CV together. Read my comments below regarding the profile picture. In the following order, list: your name, personal details, objectives, qualifications, skills, yachting experience, professional experience, hobbies (closely related to the job at hand) and references. Keep all sections brief and to the point. Think about each word costing you a hundred dollars to print. Employers can put two and two together and know what your work experience means just from looking at your job title. You may have a ton of prior relevant experience, but information overload means your resume gets chucked. If it's short and well written, we'll continue through and read the first three lines of each previous position held. Ensure each job description details the following:

✓ How many people did you lead and train?
✓ How many crew on the boat?
✓ What big events did you take part in?
✓ What skills/departments did you specialize in?
✓ Cruising locations of the yacht?

When you have finished writing it, check and re-check your sentence structure and spelling. This industry is all about your attention to detail and your resume is your marketing banner. Consider getting your resume professionally done as the results will be succinct, to the point and will make you shine even brighter as an industry leader.

- 8 Proven Techniques For Perfecting The Money Shot -
This is the glamour industry

The yachting industry is the only profession that demands your mug shot on the first page of your CV. There is no doubt that this is the deal breaker in building a connection with the reader. If the reader finds you attractive you will quickly get put on the YES pile; if not, you end up on the NO pile. The time you spend preparing for your CV photo should be equal to the time it takes to write your resume. You need to make yourself stand out from the hundreds of other candidates. Here's how to do it right:

1. Choose your background carefully. A plain white background presents a professional portrait look. The current trend is to have boats or the ocean in the background. Steer clear of using the fence or a palm tree in the garden of the crew house

2. Lighting makes all the difference. Flash settings are excellent for over exposing skin and removing imperfections. No shadows on the face, especially under the eyes. Sagginess and double chins will not be tolerated. Darling, look sparkly! There is quality magical, free studio lighting at dusk, one hour before the sun sets. Dusk light is in the red spectrum as opposed to morning light, which is in the blue. This red glow of evening gives people a rosy complexion and will enhance your radiant tanned look

3. Use make-up to your advantage. Cover imperfections, blush rosy cheeks, highlight eyebrows, cheekbones, and wear a complimentary lipstick.

4. Well-maintained hair is an asset. Blow-dried, straightened and styled but not too glamour-princess.

You want to portray the look of easy maintenance, not high maintenance. We've debated this – the ruling vote states hair out, not done up in a bun/ponytail.

5. Iron that shirt! This is your first impression

6. IN: Crew uniforms with epaulets and white business shirts. Pined in the back if necessary to give your waist definition. OUT: Colored T-shirts, anything with graphics or wording

7. The ladies' breast cleavage is not to be on show. Save it for your Facebook feed where we'll stalk you later

8. Smile! We want to know you're happy and we can live with you from the get-go.

- Make Friends With Crewing Agencies -

Crewing agencies are an excellent way to land incredible jobs. They know everyone and every yacht and can be your best bet for matching you with a suitable boat. Go ahead and create an online profile on their website before you get into town. Show up to interview with crew agents as if you are interviewing with a captain. Dress appropriately and be on time. Crewing agents are the people who are going to sell you and will not put anyone forward who is not up to scratch as their reputation is on the line. They also work on a commission basis, the longer you're on board, the larger the cut they receive. It's always in their best interests to get it right the first time. Captains and HODs prefer crewing agents due to the many benefits:

✓ The crewing agency has reference checked the potential employee

✓ If the new crew member decides to leave or gets fired before their trial is up or mid-way through the season, the crewing agent is obliged under contract to replace that crew member within two to three days with no extra monetary cost. This is dependent on the agreement between the crewing agent and the boat.

The dirty gossip on crew agents: Some boats only use them when the captain has a reputation for being a terrible leader who can't give clear objectives to save his life, and treats his crew like subjects in a tadpole experiment. Yes, you'll have the opportunity to work with captains like this and say what has been repeated many times behind their backs, "I wouldn't piss on him, even if he was on fire." These captains keep their jobs only because they receive low wages and depend on crewing agents to supply them with a constant stream of unsuspecting victims to torture.

On the flip side there are lovely captains out there. Loved by both owners and crew; their followers cannot do enough for them. These guys tend to have an even temperament, an unlimited budget and only use crewing agents because they're the best source of worldwide A-team players.

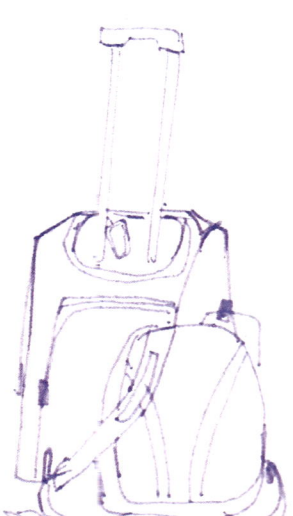

Get to know your crewing agent. Be nice. Send them flowers or gifts when they land you the dream job. Reply immediately to their emails. Always let them know your whereabouts and if you take another job. Crewing agents crack the shits when negotiating your placement in the Maldives and you disappear onto a larger yacht for more money and an intense charter. How were you to know they switched off the internet on the charter yacht to make it faster for the fat New York guests thus burning a bridge with your new crew agent?

Heads up: Crewing agents are like the rest of the industry leaders in yachting. They love to place the prettiest, skinniest, more experienced girls first. For the interview, it wouldn't hurt to purchase a new dress that screams, "I'm easy to live with, yes, I'm polished and yes, I know how to use cutlery. Hire me!"

- What Is This Dock Walking? -
It's kind of scary walking up to these big boats

If it's not illegal and you want a job, walk the docks. Yes! All of us started off in the crew houses, grabbing a couple of friends and convincing them to go dock walking with us because we were too shit scared to do it by ourselves. It can be quite intimidating at first, walking up to those mega yachts, asking them if they're looking for crew. We can all remember how much we wanted to be on the other side of the fence, handing out resumes and business cards. We wanted to be them, living on board and tripping around the world.

But once you're in, you're in! Make it a game of catching the deckhand's eye or one of the stews coming off. Introduce yourself, ask if they are looking for any day workers and pass them one of your business cards. Don't ask for the captain, first mate or chief stewardess. You'll just annoy them, calling them away from their work.

The trick with dock walking is to suck up all that nervousness; pretend that you're the most confident person that you know, and go for it! I like to pretend I'm Beyoncé, she's fierce, and have you noticed how she can do no wrong? It's easy, once you get chatting with the crew, you'll find most are friendly and will give you pointers as to which boats are looking for crew and a little pep talk to boost your confidence.

The 3 secrets to being a fabulous dock walker is:

1. Start out early. The perfect time is 08:00 when crew are raising the aft deck flag and having their deck meetings on the aft deck. Conversation on the aft deck with the deckhands and in the crew mess with the interior crew, usually goes like this, "Man, I wish we had some help today," and boom! You ring the passer rail call button

2. Girls: dress to fit in with the girls on board. White polos, smart shorts or a smart non-revealing summer dress. Have an appropriate change of clothes. Look presentable and approachable to the interior crew and yet girly enough to get the attention of the deckhands

3. Be consistent: hit the same docks every day at the same time. If yacht crew sees you consistently, it shows commitment to genuinely wanting to work! How could you not want to help someone who wants it that badly?

- 10 Steps To Take Networking To A Professional Level -
Mate, it's about making friends

You'll hear it repeatedly. Network! It used to be such a dirty 80s word but honestly, it's the only way to get ahead in this industry. The yachting world works on personal recommendations and word of mouth referrals. Exceptional people recommend exceptional people. The larger your networking circle, the greater your chances are of job opportunities. Begin networking by creatively working the room:

1. Turn up to as many yachty social events that you hear about with as many friends as you can muster

2. Don't neck all the free alcohol. Captains actively look for potential crew with a water bottle in their hand at networking events

3. Make a pact with your buddies that whenever you meet someone, you will introduce them to the rest of the group. Trust me, the other person will be as grateful as your friends to enlarge their social circle

4. When chit chatting in a large circle, stand so that your body invites conversations with people. No crossed arms, looking down your nose or having your back to anyone. Invite people to stand in your space. As people come into your space, introduce everybody with their name and a one-line bio of what they do. "Hi, this is Emilija, she's amazing and is looking for a nursing gig."

5. For your opening question refrain from asking, "so which boat are you on,"... "what position are you looking for?" or "how long have you been doing this?" Avoid talking yachting and the position that you're currently seeking. After you've been doing this for a while, you're sick of hearing these

questions. Refrain from telling everyone about how well suited you are to this industry and how you love cleaning — beyond dull. Try to ask the other person how their day was, what they love in life, where they're from, what sports they play and what they're drinking

6. Your brain can only do one thing at a time. If you're talking, you're not listening; therefore, you're not learning. Listen to what the other person is saying and repeat it back to them

7. Before beginning the evening, make a pact with yourself and your mates in the crew house of how many people you're going to meet that night. Do not leave the event until you've reached that number

8. No resting-bitch faces. Smile, look friendly and approachable

9. When in doubt, systematically walk around the room and pick off the strays. They'll be grateful to meet new friends

10. The next day follow up with the people you meet via email or FB, tell them how great it was to meet them. If you found common ground, invite them out for a drink, or better still, a sports activity.

INTERVIEWING

- What To Look For When Taking Your First Job -

1. Crew
2. Cruising location
3. Money
4. Size of boat

My best advice when starting out is: Always take a position where the crew, cruising locations and yacht are to your liking, over money. It'll be more fun with a great crew and boat. Remember it's about the adventure not the money. Money always follows when you love what you do!

- BOOM! Sick, Dude, First Interview! -
How exciting, betcha didn't sleep last night

How to give a great first impression! Know what position you're going for, what's expected of you and what kind of yacht it is. The interviewer is going to be precise with their questions. After all, you are going to be living with each other twenty-four hours a day.

Checklist of questions that you're going to be asked. It's OK if you don't know all the answers, you're new, remember!

✓ How does this job fit in with your overall personal & professional goals?

✓ What made you decide to join yachting?

✓ Do you have any previous restaurant and housekeeping experience? Tell me about it...

✓ How would you rate your decorative abilities? Table settings, place card production, napkin folds, and preparations?

✓ How would you describe your administrative/organizational skills?

✓ How do you feel about working long shifts/hours? What hours do you consider to be normal, with and without guests onboard?

✓ Would you consider yourself best at working behind the scenes or in front of guests, on show? Why?

✓ What kinds of work teams have you managed previously?

✓ How did you get along with your previous manager?

✓ Please describe your least and most favorite tasks/responsibilities performed in previous stewardess

roles? (Or management role if no previous stewardess experience)
- ✓ What keeps you motivated at work?
- ✓ Tell me about a time that you had to go above and beyond to get a job done
- ✓ Please explain how you would deal with conflicts between your team members and other crew?
- ✓ What makes you a good team player? (give me some examples)
- ✓ What are your worst habits?
- ✓ Why did you leave your last position?
- ✓ Have you completed your STCW 2010, hold a current B1/B2 USA Visa and ENG1? What dates do they expire?
- ✓ Are you a smoker?
- ✓ Do you have any tattoos or body piercing? If so, where are they?
- ✓ Do you suffer from motion or seasickness?
- ✓ Do you have any commitments during the next twelve months?
- ✓ What salary and benefits package would make you happy?
- ✓ Define your perfect day off.

Be honest during the job interview. The truth always comes out.

- Boss Lady Questions To Ask For A Successful Interview -

Let's arm you with a few choice questions

Is the yacht:
- ✓ Private or charter?
- ✓ Private usually means more down time. Charters, less money in monthly wages but more chances of making it up in tips
- ✓ Size? The smaller the yacht, the more flexible the captain and crew are with working hours
- ✓ Make, model, year of the yacht and/or building?
- ✓ Older yachts tend to need more maintenance
- ✓ Cruising location? Summers and winters in?
- ✓ Yard periods? Where?

Owners:
- ✓ One or multiple owners? Multiple owners tend to do back-to-back trips and wear out the crew. As there is minimal down time, it increases the rate of crew turnover
- ✓ Does the owner have a family that joins him? Children?
- ✓ How often are the owners on board? Is it heavily used?
- ✓ Do the owners bring the same guests?
- ✓ Late nights? Big drinkers? Is it a party crowd?
- ✓ Are they fussy? What kind of style of service do they prefer? Are they particular?

Crew:
- ✓ How many crew are there?
- ✓ What is the nationality of the crew?
- ✓ Are there couples on board?
- ✓ Who will I be sharing my cabin with?
- ✓ Will there be an opportunity to further my career onboard?

✓ What did the last stew do that made her successful?

✓ Why did the last stewardess leave?

✓ What's my biggest priority in the next three months?

✓ Do you love your job? Do you love working on this yacht? What do you enjoy the most?

✓ What is the working week?

✓ What hours do you consider a normal working day?

Salary:

✓ Usually, it's not polite to ask about pay during your first interview. Wait until they offer you the job first, before asking

✓ How are my wages paid? Cash, check or bank account?

✓ Does the yacht cover health insurance?

✓ Food? Is there a chef?

✓ Are the crew fending for themselves, and if so, is there a food allowance on top of pay?

✓ Bonuses? After three months? What about at the end of year?

✓ Vacation time? Annual holiday?

✓ Is there paid time off for my annual leave?

✓ Are my return flights covered to go home?

✓ Will the yacht reimburse me for any training and courses undertaken?

✓ Does the yacht offer a contract? (Be wary of yachts and captains that don't do contracts. It's their way of diddling you out of money.)

Termination Period:

✓ Upon termination, is there a month's notice period written into the contract?

Uniforms:

✓ Am I supplied with all uniforms? (If a yacht cannot dress you, they cannot afford you).

Be prepared. Articulate what you are going to say. In the real world, you would be hired for your skills. Here, they can teach you everything you need to learn. The captains and heads of departments want to know if the crew can live with you.

- Peak Times To Find Yacht Jobs In The Busiest Locations -

Be in the right place at the right time

Fort Lauderdale

January: It's quiet and a tad chilly this time of year, but a few yachts are kicking around. The crew hired for the Christmas/New Year trips that don't work out, make a bee-line back to Lauderdale. Some yachts have already wrapped up their Caribbean/Bahamas season and have returned to Florida to see the rest of the season out.

February, March & April: Yachts (mostly smaller) are busting balls to get ready for the Miami boat show. Larger ships are doing their yard period and getting ready for the Med season and New England. Work can be found helping out with refits.

May & June: Yachts are starting to leave to cross over to the Med and head north for the New England summer. Jump on a yacht to begin the season! Now is not the time to rest your breasts on the bar. Get cracking.

July & August: Not much is happening here. It's bloody hot working outside. Crews are getting bored of seeing each other at the same places and doing the same things.

September: Yachts are starting to arrive back from the New England summer to wallop it on the refit. Potentially this could be a favorable time to gain yard/maintenance/refit experience.

October: Mega yard period. Yachts are getting ready for the big one: The Lauderdale Boat Show. Passer rails are being sanded and varnished, engine rooms are pulled apart and boats are hauled out. This is the time to get experience detailing yachts since there are only a few guest trips around.

November: November is the perfect time to be in Fort Lauderdale. Dude! Everyone's in town! All your mates have arrived back from the Med and New England season, all cashed up and ready to party! Beware this is also a prime time to lose your job as there are only so many tomfooleries captains can take. Captains and crews see this as a prime time to jump ship because there's an abundance of yachts. If you're working, it's crunch time. Long hours will be had getting the boat ready for the FLIBS boat show and the Caribbean season.

December: Yachts are crewing up for the Bahamas and Caribbean winter trips and taking off. Get onto it!

Fort Lauderdale Vibe:

Fort Liquordale is the place to be for crew downtime. You're here because you've just had a slamming season, about to pack up for one or looking for the next dream gig. So while we're here and our friends are too, we gotta cram in all the fun.

Get ready to socialize. There is nothing to do here that doesn't involve copious amounts of drinking. $5 burgers @ Tap 42 on a Monday night, midweek networking events, and ladies drink for free on Wednesdays and Thursdays at choice venues. Weekends are spent downtown and on the beach. Don't forget Miami is only forty minutes down the road.

Getting there and around:

Taxis are about twenty bucks from the airport to the crew houses around 17th street. Once settled in, hire a bike for your stay. Beware of scooters — Florida drivers are the most careless in the world. The rule is no drinking and no boys on the back.

St. Maarten

January: The marinas are packed shoulder to shoulder in between guest trips. After the Christmas/New Year's trips, the crew that don't work out due to personality clashes are being offloaded and flown back to the port where they were picked up from. Due to the high crew turnover, positions need filling and there is day work to be had. Get in there!

February, March, and April: Prime opportunity to network and get on a mega yacht.

May: The last of the boats are packing up and heading elsewhere. It's the beginning of the hurricane season and insurance prices have started to skyrocket. Owners, even as rich as they are, like to penny pinch, insurance being the first item.

June, July, August: Middle of summer. It's hot here in winter but summer is just unbearable!

October & September: The nights and people's temperaments are starting to cool down. It's safe to venture out!

November: Start of the season. Large super yachts will start making their way here from the Med and Fort Lauderdale. Time to arrive, get your face seen by all the crew and introduce yourself.

December: High season! Last minute crew changes are made and temporary day work can be found.

St. Maarten Vibe:
Beautiful beaches, cheap drinks and gorgeous men with their shirts off make this a destination in itself. St. Maarten is not dangerous as far as Caribbean islands go, there are worse places with poorer economies. Be wary though: no walking home by yourself at night, don't flash your hard-earned money and keep your belongings on you. Be respectful and don't be another rich yachty flashing your wealth in front of locals who are trying to make ends meet.

Getting There & Around:
Taxis are priced at €12 from the airport to Mullet Bay and €30 to Philipsburg, the other side of the island. For a cheaper ride, flag down one of the taxi/minivans that regularly circumnavigate the island for €2. Bring coins and no shiny valuables.

Antibes

The world capital of super/mega/gigantic yachts — all the big boys are here!

January and February: Dude, it's the middle of winter. You can give it a shot. A few yachts are kicking around Europe in sheds doing full refits. If you want work, you'll find it.

March: The very beginning of the season. People are getting in early, registering with crewing agents and claiming their beds.

April: Everyone is starting to pile in for the season. There's an influx of people as yachts arrive for the Med season and professional crews are flying in now to pick up jobs. The days are warming up and getting longer. Perfect time to get out there and start networking.

May: High season is kicking off. Antibes is filling up fast with crew and northern Europeans coming down for vacations. Lines for crewing agents are a nightmare and crew houses are full with waiting lists. The dissatisfied crew that was picked up in the Caribbean and the States are now taking the opportunity to jump ship. At the last minute, there's always a rush to finalize crew manifests and get the boat up to scratch for the Cannes Film Festival and the Monaco Grand Prix. You could interview for one job and be on board, just like that!

June: Game on! You want to be here, right now. Get out, be sociable, network and day work like nobody's business! All the yachts doing the Med season should be here by now.

July: Mid-season – babe, it's hot. Yachts are out cruising different locations such as St. Tropez, the Croatian coast, south of Italy, and Spain. There are some boats looking to crew up for short-term guest trips.

August & September: Most yachts are still back-to-back with charter trips and others are returning to port for some down time before the next guest trip. Monaco boat show is commencing at the end of the month. Yes, we'll need help for that!

October: Season's over. The weather will change suddenly in two days indicating the season is over. One day you'll be sunbaking and the next, all rugged up, digging out trackie daks and stealing beanies. Larger yachts are winterizing and returning to skeleton crew. Others are making the crossing to catch the Fort Lauderdale boat show or heading to the Caribbean to begin the season.

November: Where did everyone go? You'll start to see the same faces at the bars. Go on! You might as well make friends.

December: Either you're loving life using your weekends to go skiing or you're miserable wishing you were in St. Maarten soaking up the sun.

Antibes Vibe:
"I love France, the wines, foie gras, oysters, all the French woman made up, and the shoes… are to die for." Yes, the French do it better and are the last word on refinement. They have natural food, passionate lovers, and stylish clothing. All the exceptionally good-looking crew are found here, more than anywhere else in the world. Drinks are expensive in Antibes, the only other port being more expensive is St. Tropez. If you get here pre-season, everyone is conserving cash until they get onto a boat. Get here after season and there seems to be a more relaxed party vibe.

Getting There & Around:
Catch the bus service from Cote D'Azur Airport, (Nice) one-way fare is €11 and €17 for an open return. It will drop you off outside Antibes train station where you can walk anywhere. The town is small and many taxi drivers will refuse to take you. Beware if you're not traveling light. Once there, Antibes is easily walked around to reach all of the crew agents and bars. One-way tickets in the SOF are €4.50 for the train service that runs up and down the coastline. This makes all the marinas squished full of big boats easily accessible. The odds are in your favor as this area is more densely packed than the marinas in Florida.

Palma de Mallorca

Capital of the Balearic Islands
NB. Heads up, Palma is predominantly sailing boats. There are a few motorboats but not as many as Antibes.

January, February: The weather is not too bad and if find yourself here during these winter months then you'll be doing refits in the shipyard or babysitting boats in the harbor. There are a few yachties kicking around, so you will make friends!

March & April: Good time to arrive as it's starting to warm up. How late the Caribbean season runs will dictate when the Mallorca season starts. It takes two to four weeks to cross the Atlantic, conditional on weather.

May: You'll find during this month there's a mad dash for yachts to get their crew list finalized. Towards the end of May, boats start leaving Palma for the Monaco Grand Prix, France, Turkey, and Greece. Please don't freak out if you hear the rumor, "If you don't have work by the thirty-first of May, you've missed the season." Crew chop and change all season, be tough, don't give up!

June: The Palma Super Yacht Cup, the longest running regatta in Europe starts mid-June. It attracts sailing yachts 90 to 150 ft, which means the town is packed with handsome sailing crew in tight T-shirts and professional jobs.

July & August: July is the peak of the European summer and August is the holiday month for Mallorcans. The whole place shuts down as it is simply too hot to work! You'll find everyone at the beach or nearest romantic terrace. Don't let this deter you. Get your skort on and keep on dock walking.

September: Busy racing month in Palma with good winds and regattas. Yes, snap up the invitations to go sailing with a few bottles of Miraval Côtes de Provence rosé and pinchos.

October, November & December: Boats are crossing over, but there is still day work to be found in the shipyard. Don't be disheartened that the beach has shut down. Head to the hills to go hiking, climbing and horse riding.

Palma Vibe:
The week starts off with Tapas Tuesday. Bars fill up fast with cheap meal and drink deals and this is the

perfect time to mix with the locals. Friday nights is the big ones here and you'll find delicious looking Spanish men on holidays, hunky professional sailing crews and cheap wine. Sounds like the start of the most talked about love affair to me!

Yachting and professional race crews tend to begin the night in Santa Catalina around the Cuban bar area. Begin here to scope out who's in town and head off to mingle with the Spanish. Does it help to be forewarned? The Spanish know how to party, and the party doesn't start until after dinner (22:00), then it's a world of choices with all the big nightclubs, and Magaluf is just around the corner. You might have heard of Magaluf: it's a loose English holiday destination with cheap alcohol. Brits here just can't avoid getting themselves on the front page of the international newspapers for giving fellatio in bars and falling off balconies.

Getting There & Around:

There's a bus directly outside the airport that goes to the center of Palma for €2. Taxis are priced at €20 for the same distance. Stay around the marina areas as this is the area where all the bars are, therefore your new friends will be too. If you have a skateboard, Palma and Spain are the skateboarder's dream. Endless smooth bike paths are yours to ride on!

DECIDING FACTORS

- Charter Vs. Private -

High pressure and go, go, go vs. chilled

Private yachts are reserved for the owners and his friends. Charter yachts are used by the owners, his friends, and then rented out for a fee to the rich and famous.

Private yachts have a lot of benefits. Private owners tend to dislike change and expect to see the same faces. They want the yacht to be your home! To do that, they will care for their crew in the hope you'll be around for years. The private yacht owners invest in their crew's health, education and well-being plus bonuses/perks. The stories you hear are true. Crews on sole owner yachts have far more down time and actually have a life. The owners are too busy making money in New York to come onboard. Often the crew will only see them for one month in the year. For crews, last minute business deals can see trip cancellations, which means you get to enjoy the best parts of the world, while the owners are busy in the office. Can't make it to the Mardi Gras in Brazil? I'll take that ticket!

On the flip side, yacht owners hope that by chartering their boat out, they can see a return on the money spent for the upkeep of owning a yacht. Charter guests will have high expectations for 7-Star service and are not overy concerned with the crew's wellbeing. Yacht charter guests love keeping the crew up all night, bringing their friends, sleeping all day and requesting breakfast at three in the afternoon. Get ready to work crazy hours.

The difference:

There's a good and bad to every story and you never really know what you're going to get until the guests are on board.

- Why Chief Stewardesses Love Bigger -

Small boats vs. the mega yachts

Big is always better, no matter what they say to your face. But sometimes too big hurts. Gain some experience to find the size that suits you and stick with it

To obtain a larger amount of yachting experience in standards and procedures, it's recommended by everyone in the industry that you start off on larger yachts first. The chief stewardesses and interior team members have a wealth of knowledge to be shared for the benefit the team. The other girls will teach you cool tricks of the trades and sneaky little short cuts! Such as how to get blood out of sheets (medical grade hydrogen peroxide), the quickest way to remove water spots from glasses (steam over a kettle) and how to handle late night drunk guests (if they can't walk to the bar for another drink, they don't get another one). Not only will the girls above you give you invaluable knowledge, they will also guide you in the intricate ways of yachting etiquette. If you're lucky and the recruitment process is up to scratch, most of your team members will be about the same age, same ethnicity and hopefully the same height to swap clothes with.

Working on larger yachts is great. There is always a crewmember to keep company with, and someone is always doing something cool on the weekends. Tender rides, kite boarding, wine and food at the best eateries, weekends away on the next island or just chilling at the beach.

Small yachts also have their rewards. Smaller yachts offer a certain amount of freedom that big boats can't compete with. Potentially finishing early, long weekends and flexibility with your schedule. There are also fewer personalities to deal with.

- Permanent VS. Freelance Positions -
So many options

When you're a greenie, it's a mine field out there. Private, charter, Bahamas or St. Bart's, permanent or freelance positions — where do you begin? Take the permanent role, as it will get you the plum jobs in the end. Permanent jobs also have added bonuses such as medical cover, holiday pay and vacation time. For your first job, you need to commit long-term. Boat-hopping or excessive freelance screams warning bells. Too many yachts on your resume make the potential employer question your ability and/ or personality. We wonder if you're crazy, aggressive or just an asshole.

To get your foot in the door, any experience is better than nothing. Yes, accept all the day work that you can find and short trips to the Bahamas. After you've been doing this for a while, and you can't do permanent roles, switch over to freelance gigs. They are the cherry on top of the ice-cream sundae. Freelance gigs can last from one day, a weekend to two weeks. Expect a higher rate of pay and the potential of a tip if it's a charter trip. Freelance gigs can be picked up when:

1. The yacht has minimal guest use and the captain only hires interior crew for guests' trips
2. To increase crew numbers if they run with skeleton crew when owners are not on board
3. You may be hired on a trial basis before being offered a permanent position
4. You're recruited to help turn over the yacht quickly for the next charter, boat show, brokerage showing or after a shipyard refit.

Temp gigs end up being a short sprint with a bright light at the end of the tunnel. Guests arrive tired and cranky, want to stay up all night, get up early, cram in as much as they can and fly out. You'll be run off your feet for few days, but who cares, they'll leave soon, and you can go back to drinking frozen Patron pineapple margaritas on the beach. Permanent positions mean you'll just have to wait for your time off like the rest of the world, but at least you know a consistent paycheck is coming in.

YACHTING 101
Co-habituating with random people who are not your family and friends. Breathing the same air twenty-four hours a day, 365-days a year. Living in a space no bigger that a one-bedroom apartment, under stressful conditions and occasionally working with no sleep. Then, getting up every day with a smile, being friendly without letting anyone know that you want to stab them.

- LOOONNGGEEVVVIIITTYY -

They say longevity counts for a lot, but is it worth staying on a boat if you're miserable? People get sick from that. Misery erodes your soul. However, if it's your first job, everyone will say that you need to be on that boat for a year, minimum. It's true. Captains and crew agents want to see longevity and the ability to work well with others, handle the job and stick it out. Commitment. No matter how fucked up you think that first boat is. No boat is always professional or perfect, the other crews are lying if they say it is.

If you feel like enduring your first year, the aim of the game is not to boat hop and have a million yachts on your resume. Yachts and crews dislike crew turnover. It gets painful, the re-training, seeing crew members leave who are like family and different faces every time you come back from holidays. You have to suck it up boss lady, like the rest of us.

- Player With A Passport On Rotation -
You mean a holiday from the living-the-dream program?

This is the heaven of yachting. The gods have blessed the term rotation. Three months on, one month off, or five months on and one month off. PAID TIME OFF. Whatever your rotation schedule is, it sure beats the crap out of working all year and begging for two weeks off. These blessed souls, on top of their salary, receive medical insurance and all living expenses taken care of and have paid-flights home to their chosen port. Can you imagine the possibilities! You're free to travel wherever you want in the world. Live in one tropical paradise and then head to another mind-blowing part of the world.

Some are us are blessed like my friend, Azza, who is exceptionally good looking with a Peter Pan complex. His yacht owner (who is the finance minister to an oil-producing Arab country) is splendidly generous and covers his FIRST-CLASS flights home twice a year. All that is available to you too, open for negotiation when confirming your pay package before starting.

Player with a passport: where do you go on your time off? Forget about heading back to the ports you only saw out of the laundry room porthole. Enjoy those places on the next milk run in the safety of the all-expenses-paid yacht. We're talking about the other places:

Belize: Amazing game fishing, cheap as chips to live (approx. $500 a month) and endless sun and beaches. Winner!

Berlin: Rent a full apartment here for €600 a month and pretend you're a local. This city is known for its art scene, kicking nightlife and contemporary architecture. Join a local cross-fit club, make friends and immerse yourself in the party culture.

Barcelona: By far one of the most underrated cities for yachties. The marina is being re-modelled to accommodate larger yachts. This city is amazeballs. Smooth bike paths for your skateboard, kite boarding, dirt-cheap wine/beer, hormone & additive free fresh food and hotties down the beach. It's a city with a thriving, international night scene and friendly locals. What more could you ask for? I think this could be the new base for yachties as its an overnight ferry to Palma and a day trip on the train to Antibes.

Utila and Roatan, Honduras: Got some time off and want to make some friends quickly and have some fun? Got it. These islands are beautiful, laid back, filled with adventure, cheap and easily accessible. Come here to go diving, hang with down-to-earth people, enjoy the stunning beaches and be surrounded by the lush tropical paradise. Heaven!

Nicaragua and Costa Rica: Sorry to lump these two beauties together but with cheap flights ($120 return) from Lauderdale it always makes it hard to choose. Here you'll find affordable living, surf and yoga schools, giving you the ability to breath out and relax. Make it happen and the perfect spot to camp out for a couple of weeks will present itself.

When in doubt and when the owners don't cover your travel expenses, take this advice: Book flights on a Tuesday or Wednesday morning (prices are higher the rest of the week). Book three weeks out or three days. The prices will be the same and bring a designer packed lunch on the plane from the yacht.

Take advantage of your time off. Don't book a hotel next to the yacht to save money. Yachts are not tied up on budget destinations. Get. Out. There. Even if the gods have not blessed you with rotation … yet.

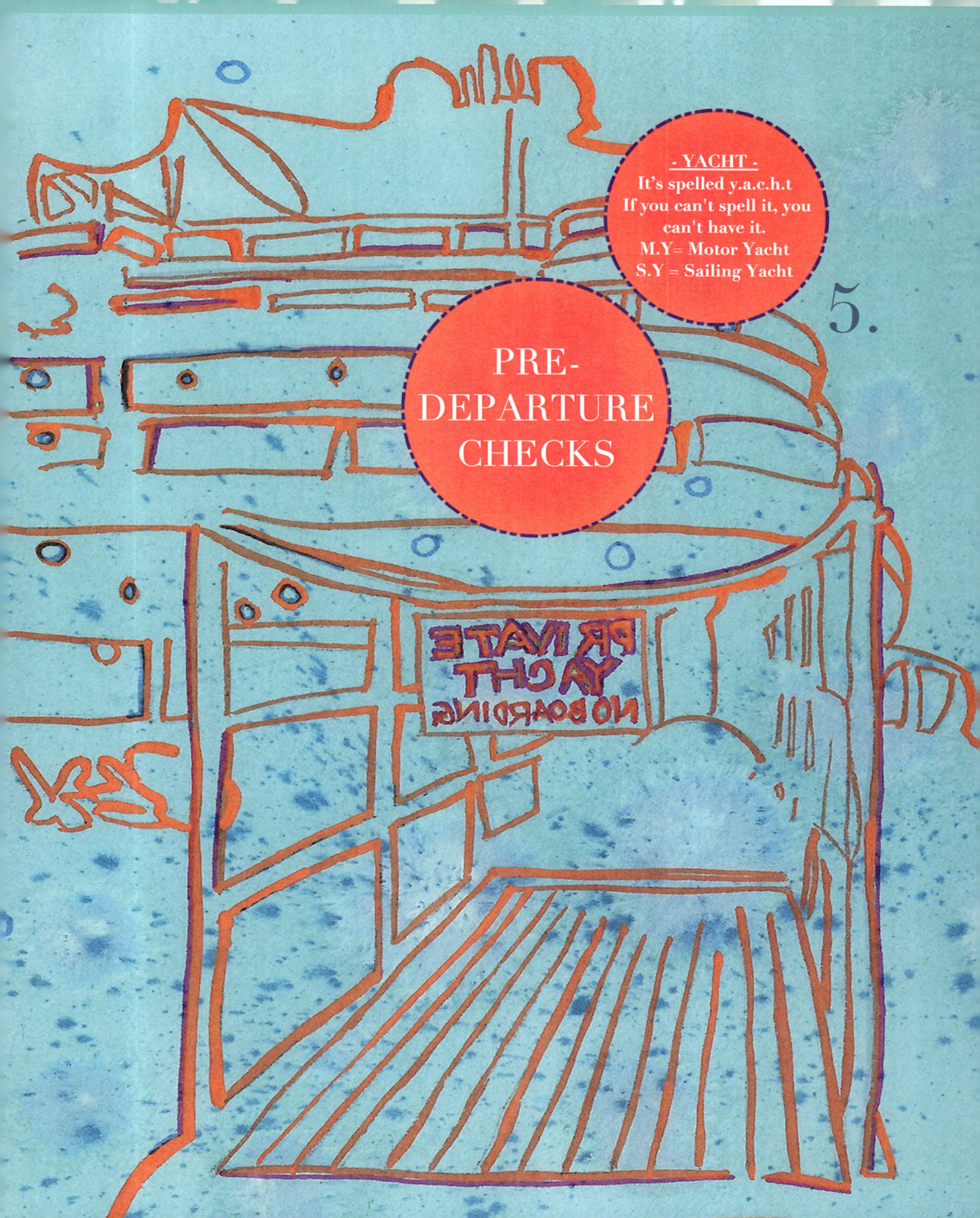

- YACHT -
It's spelled y.a.c.h.t
If you can't spell it, you
can't have it.
M.Y= Motor Yacht
S.Y = Sailing Yacht

PRE-
DEPARTURE
CHECKS

5.

- Understanding Common Mistakes Yacht Owners Make When Buying A Yacht -

Just because you're mega wealthy does not mean you make good choices

If you have to ask how much a yacht is or if you need purchase on finance, you can't afford it. The minimum price for a small boat is a million bucks. Contemporary yachts cost money. The rule is: a million per a meter. You may try and purchase something stingy, but it will end up costing a fortune in maintenance and replacement. Anything earlier than the 1980s is outdated. It doesn't matter how much metallic paint you use on the hull or gut the interior, no one is going to be impressed. Let me tell you, refitting is ridiculously expensive if you want the best-of-the-best luxury finishes.

When buying a yacht, consider the crew spaces, as they are the people who are going to be spending the most time on your baby. Crew live and work fifty-two weeks a year in this space while most owners come on board for three months max. Our rule is: if all the crew can't sit around the crew mess table then you will have no crew longevity.

The purchase of a yacht is the cheapest expense that you will ever incur as a yacht owner. The yearly running cost is ten percent of whatever you bought it for. Let's break it down together in US dollars, it's still the strongest currency around as they just keep printing it like crazy.

Let's say you drop a cheap $50m, which can get you anything from a 150 ft. to 200 ft. yacht.

✓ Docking fees are $300 to $2200 a day and $4000 in exclusive ports such as Capri in Italy. During the Monaco Grand Prix, you might tip the dock master $150,000 to get a slip for one night. Please don't think of sticking your crew on anchor for months on end. They will lose their minds

✓ $1 million in insurance

✓ $1 to $ 3 million for food, beverages and flowers

✓ With a boat that burns 300 liters an hour, fuel costs can easily add up to $500,000 over twelve months

✓ Roughly $100,000 pay package per crew member. As a general rule, captains make approximately $1000-a-foot, per month. Nine to fifteen crew = two million dollars a year

✓ Maintenance and replacement parts will eat up the last of the budget and will easily burn owners.

To average it out, give or take five million to run a mega yacht for just one year. Be prepared to allocate one accountant for tax write off purposes and to account for all the money being thrown into this never-ending pit. There will always be something breaking, needing replacement or feeding. Understand that boats rapidly decline in value, you will never make a profit on the final sale. It's the newbie fender kickers who get in trouble when they listen to yacht brokers. Please don't try and tell us that you'll make money back in charters either. You have to secure the charters and factor in the wear and tear on the yacht, machinery and crew. But what do we know? Give it a shot!

- Safety Of Guests -
If anything happens, it's our fault. Shit rolls down hill

It is your responsibility, as a crew member, no matter what rank you are to ensure the safety of the guests on board. If you have any doubts as to how to proceed with a situation, use common sense and seek advice from the person above you in the chain of command.

AT ALL TIMES OF THE DAY YOU SHOULD KNOW WHERE YOUR GUESTS ARE AND WHAT THEY ARE DOING

The stewardess on duty should always be on the radio reporting the location of guests. On charter, information is king. The more the crew knows, the more we can anticipate guests' needs. Sharing information guarantees the whole crew looks professional and keeps the guests herded together, preventing accidents from arising. Situations that you need to pay close attention to:

- ✓ Upon guest arrival, let the deckhands take their bags and offer to help them up on the passer rail. It's an embarrassment to our industry if one of our guests fall in

- ✓ After leaving the dock and mooring, shut the pool gates to the swimming platform

- ✓ Upon boarding, brief all guests about the out-of-bounds areas. No-go areas are: structures and surfaces that are slippery, the non-skid slope from the bridge deck to bow and the bow when underway in rough weather

- ✓ These people come to party. Don't be surprised to find them dancing on the superstructure that holds the spinning radars, on glass tables and jumping off the sun deck. If it's high and dangerous, guests assume it's a dancing podium. There's a chance the boat could move due to wake. Introduce alcohol into the mix and hello, broken bones! Prevent the medevacs from coming in, get the guests off the dangerous bits

- ✓ No riding jet skis while under the influence. You'll find it's common for guests to ride the wave-runners completely wasted. Put your foot down the first time and stop accidents happening on your yacht

- ✓ To avoid the excessiveness, have bottled water in ice buckets on the pool deck and keep offering water throughout the day

- ✓ Know what your role will be if the following scenarios arise: fire, a sinking ship or a man overboard.

Be confident in the role that you're playing. Seconds could mean the difference when saving lives.

- Educate Yourself To Be The First Aid Giver -
Providing the kiss of life to the rich and famous

Should any medical emergency arise on a yacht, the guests will grab the closest crew member to take charge of the situation. Be prepared, have a contingency plan in place for all circumstances. High-risk guests are the elderly, the disabled and the overweight. Keep yourself up to date in administering CPR and the use of defibrillators. Before the start of the season or when joining a new boat, clarify what your role is in the following situations: drowning person, overweight person unable to get out of the water, heart attacks, elderly people having accidents in their cabin, deceased guests, injured crew, the treatment of alcohol and/or food poisoning. You may also be called upon to treat cuts, stings, bites, and mysterious rashes. Preparation is essential. Know where the first aid kits are and the location of local emergency phone numbers. Have a clear plan. These are the usual situations we've dealt with over the years:

- ✓ A man flying off a jet ski at sixty MPH. It resulted in a severe concussion and a fractured leg. He'd been drinking and needed to be taken to hospital for immediate care. This didn't stop the fiftieth birthday celebrations, however!

- ✓ Jellyfish stings and coral cuts. Marine injuries can get severely infected when not treated properly. Be careful if you don't know what you're treating. Vinegar can sometimes have an adverse reaction to the stinging cells. When in doubt about marine bites and stings, immerse the area in the hottest water the victim can stand to relieve the pain. The young and elderly have an increased risk of having a medical grade reaction. Seek medical treatment as soon as possible

- ✓ Broken toes: guests and crew hitting their toes on protruding deck fixtures

- ✓ Large, overweight and non-swimmers that insist on going swimming. You can never say no, but you can help make it less stressful. Get in the water with them to keep them calm. Bring all the floatation devices you can find. Life rings, lifejackets, and noodles

- ✓ Be prepared for dog bites, severed fingers, cuts, concussions, sprains and deathly hangovers

One of your priorities when joining a yacht is to familiarize yourself with the first aid kit. Know what you have, dates of expiry and medication to be purchased. Once guests are on board, you may be at sea for weeks at a time with no access to large amounts of drugs. Ignorance is not bliss. If this stuff frightens you, educate yourself and remove the fear.

- Not Wanted! Seasickness On My Yacht -
The worst holiday feeling apart from being too high on drugs

Seasickness tablets should be handed out to all guests and crew one to two hours BEFORE LEAVING DOCK. After swallowing the first pill, you will need to keep taking them and follow directions on the packet. They work as a preventative and not a cure. If guests/crew tell you, "I never get seasick," always insist. Every boat has a different momentum in the water, and even the most hardened crew will feel a little queasy for the first few days of traveling.

Symptoms of seasickness:
- ✓ Generally feeling unwell
- ✓ Yawning and drowsiness or feeling giddy or restless
- ✓ Nausea or vomiting, or both
- ✓ Headache
- ✓ Cold sweat, which means you sweat even though you're not overheated
- ✓ A pale appearance
- ✓ Eructation (the medical term for belching and burping).

After working years as a professional dive instructor taking seventy people a day to the Great Barrier Reef, this is our short-term cure for seasickness. Quietly let the guest know that the worst place they could be is the head (the loo) in the guest room. Confined space, no air is ALWAYS a recipe for disaster. Take the guest outside to the steadiest part of the boat, main deck aft, away from the diesel fumes. Bring them to the side of the yacht where the wind is hitting their back. If they spew, you don't want that spew coming back in your face. Now, pick a spot on the horizon, focus on it. Breathe through your nose and out through your mouth. Repeat. Keep focus on the same point on the horizon. This is also good for people who have drunk too much liquor and need to get steady on their feet. Repeat after me, "In through your nose, out through your mouth."

Apologies to the many poor, unsuspecting people we've experimented with to test out our seasickness theories. We've learned our lesson. Do not give seasick people any soda pops or juices with acid. Ginger tea or candies always help with nausea. Chilled water and dry crackers are the way to go. People also seem to crave plain, salted, potato chips and chocolates. Wristbands with the hard plastic bubble that applies pressure on the wrist nerve work. Keep them on hand.

- OLD WIVES TALE FOR CURING THE INABILITY
TO HOLD DOWN WATER AND CONSISTENT VOMITING -

In a mug mix together two tablespoons of apple cider vinegar and two tablespoons of honey.
Add hot water and sip.

CHILDREN

- Caring For Children -
They want to know everything and touch it too. Hello, finger prints everywhere

The level of interaction a crew member has with owners'/guests' children depends on the size of the yacht. Please don't take a job on a small boat if you don't like children. You'll be expected to play with them and keep them entertained. Larger yachts tend to bring a full-time nanny to watch the kids, but be aware these nannies think they're on holiday too!

Kids are fun! They're going to want to play games with you and want your attention. This will provide opportunities to teach them how to skateboard, play in the park and read bedtime stories. Fishing rods and catching fish is a must do on any boat. All the fun stuff!

Before guest arrival, check the preferences sheets. Don't be surprised to learn these little kids are fussy. They are into kid food — mac and cheese, pizza, chicken nuggets, French fries, hot dogs, broccoli and Nutella in hard to source organic brands. Keep the cupboards full of a good supply of favorite snacks as well. Raisins, apples, bananas, goldfish crackers and chocolate chip cookies. These kids are hilarious with their you've got to be kidding requests. Be prepared for four-year-olds demanding salmon sashimi with brown rice, hold the mayo and Belgium white chocolate ice cream with peanut butter brittles, marshmallows with salted caramel topping for dessert.

Pass on any information you receive relating to children's sizes to the deck crew, to ensure the yacht has the right-sized life jackets, fins and masks on board. It pays to check all gear for leaks and fittings. Kids freak out when they get a little bit of water in their mask. Make sure you have enough life rings and noodles onboard as these can help to pull children around when snorkeling. Kids who are heavily laden with floatation devices will put the most overbearing parents at ease.

Children are to be briefed upon arrival of the yacht rules:

1. No one is allowed in the water without an adult
2. No one is allowed on the swim platforms when the aft deck gates are closed
3. No roaming the yacht by yourself, ever
4. If it doesn't come out of your body or is the associated paper, it does not go in the toilet. Explain that the plumbing is no bigger than their wrist. If they put anything bad in the toilet, they have to get it out as they have the smallest hands
5. No eating anywhere except the dining table. Hopefully you will have parents who are respectful of this.

The most important thing to remember is:
When having children on board, know where they are at all times and ensure they have constant adult supervision. If they are in the water, a constant head count is needed. Never let them out of your sight!

- Tricks For Getting Kids To Fall Asleep -
Yachting is all about being multi-talented

It's not unusual for parents, rich or poor, to palm off their children to whoever will take them. It is never your place as hired help to refuse requests of child minding. Be expected to keep them entertained and occasionally put them to bed if the nanny has chucked in the towel and the parents are out for dinner. These are tried and tested methods for getting the little monsters down:

1. Teach them to tell the time and give them half-an-hour warning before bedtime
2. Bedtime stories. Calm, peaceful
3. Definitely no sugar, ice cream, or chocolate before bed. Why would you want to hype them up?
4. Crank up the air conditioner as cold as possible without freezing the kids. Freezing temperatures = snuggling under the blankets = sleepy = sleeping
5. Sleep in the same room as them. It may be tight; squeezing in-between the bunks, but it's worth it
6. Walking and cuddles are a given for toddlers
7. Thank the children for a gloriously fabulous day. Tell them all the things they have to look forward to tomorrow. Surely they'll need sleep for all that!
8. It's a bit naughty, but sleepy time tea. New York kids will ask for it, but others can't stand it.

Just remember they are not your kids, so you have to treat them with respect. They will remember everything and will dob you in. If all else fails during their tantrums (normal), lie down on the floor next to them. Kids love it when you are submissive.

WATCH KEEPING

- Long Watches. Long Nights -
…Watch keeping…there's a course about this…

Adventure! Lines have been thrown and the first officer comes down and tells you which watch you're on? WTF is a watch?

Translation: we do watch keeping on long passages as the yacht continuously runs and the crew need to keep a lookout. We also keep a watch schedule with a different set of duties when the ship is tied to the wharf.

While the yacht is moving and you're on watch, you are using your eyes and radar system, to look out for:
✓ Ships that are on a collision course with you
✓ Debris in the water
✓ Containers floating just below the surface
✓ Rocks
✓ People lost at sea
✓ Whales
✓ Anything out of the ordinary that potentially has the risk of colliding with the yacht, or risks the safety of those on board.

While keeping watch you need to:
✓ Recognize navigation lights
✓ Keep an eye on the engine revs
✓ Update the log every hour
✓ Observe the fuel intake
✓ Monitor channel sixteen for important messages or other boats hailing you
✓ Regularly watch the radar **and** be on the lookout with binoculars.

Most importantly DO NOT FALL ASLEEP. The first officer will kill you.

✓ Watches are split into two, three or four hour stints depending on the size of the crew
✓ Highly experienced crew members are paired with those with less experience
✓ Be fifteen minutes early for your watch shift so your eyes can adjust
✓ Keep a large flashlight on deck that can be used to shine outside on objects that catch your attention. Smaller torches can also be utilized in the bridge for filling in the logbook, plotting charts and checking for crumbs.

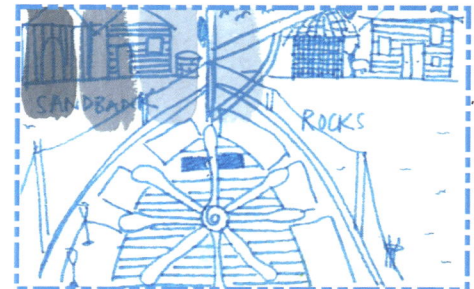

> **Watch keeping is a serious act. You have the lives of those on board, asleep, in your hands.**

- Watch Keeping With No Guests On Board At The Dock -
Anything, and it usually does, can happen

At no time are these bad-boy yachts to be left alone; they need constant supervision, much like four-year-olds with paint. A watch rotation schedule starts at 07:00 and finishes the next morning at 07:00. You will find a list of duties to be completed posted in the crew mess and it will read like this:

1. Raise flag at 08:00
2. After lunch and dinner, pack away all leftovers neatly in fridges. Wipe down all crew mess benches. Restock crew mess. Take out the garbage
3. Turn on outside lights; sidewalk ways, aft deck and fly bridge lights
4. Turn off any interior lights except for side door crew entrance, bridge, stairwells, and crew mess area
5. Check in/out board. If everyone is on board, raise passer rail before going to bed
6. Walk around the whole boat before retiring for the night. Check to see if fenders are in place and if there is anything unusual
7. Call engineer: +44 00000 Captain: +44 111111 if any alarms go off.

RADIO USAGE

- Radio Etiquette -
Big kids with walkie-talkies

Want to know what the definition of crazy is? Imagine someone talking in your ear all day and not talking properly, mumbling, only speaking in half sentences and talking too loud! That's what it's like being yacht crew and wearing earpieces twenty-four-seven for weeks on end. Get this wrong and you'll infuriate everyone. Here's how to properly transmit:

1. First take a deep breath and relax. Yes, we're all in a rush, but it doesn't help. If two people talk over each other, it creates an ear-splitting static, and everyone has to rip out their earpieces from sheer frustration
2. To begin: press transmit button and count one, two…
3. Introduce the conversation with pro-words such as "ah" … "hmm," like you're thinking about what you're going to say next
4. Say the name of the person you are calling twice, then yours, "Yulian, Yulian, Christina." The first part of the conversation tends to drop out, that's why we say it twice
5. Wait for the response, "Go ahead, Christina." If there's no response, wait awhile and try again
6. Wait until they finish transmitting and count one, two, before pressing the transmit button to reply
7. Start your conversation with a greeting and keep your sentences short and sweet, "Morning, Yulian, may I please borrow one of your deckhands to help me lift up the bilge hatches?"
8. Take your finger off the transmit button and wait for a response
9. Let the other person talk, "Ben will be free after morning tea, is that OK?"
10. To end conversation reply with a, "copy that" or "roger that" or a "thank-you."

THE WORLD OF MIND BLOWING 7-STAR SERVICE

6.

Assumption Is The Mother Of All Fuck Ups
#yachtlife

- Defining 7-Star Service -
Always going above and beyond society's expectations

7-Star service is the art of anticipation. It is knowing what guests want before they even knew they wanted it. To provide 7-Star service is to execute their demands effortlessly, seamlessly and to marry their expectations with their reality. To bring 7-Star Service to the table, you need to blow their minds at every opportunity.

- The Art Of Providing 7-Star Service -
"We're here to make this the best day of your life"

In need of creating a memorable impression and upping your game? Going above and beyond the call of duty is the expectation. Here's how to impress:

1. Address all owners and guests as Sir & Ma'am, Mr. & Mrs. or Miss, followed by their surname. Always. The better-quality yachts in the Med tend to refer to their guests as Mr. (insert last name here) and Madam (insert first name here). Memorize all of your guest names before their arrival. Certainly do not refer to them as anything else (especially over the radio) ...Names such as the fat one or the spoilt princess will be overheard, and you will get caught!

2. Excellent service is quiet and unobtrusive. Refrain from instigating long, in-depth conversations with your guests. They don't have the patience for it! You are NOT considered to be on their level. Listen and learn. They don't give a fuck. If you're in the line of service, politely listen to what their needs are and make those requests happen immediately. Yacht guests just want to be left alone, to chill out from their busy lives, for you to read their minds and have things magically appear

3. White gloves all the way, unless otherwise requested

4. Always welcome guests with ice-cold drinks. Start off with a pop from the get go! Pour champagne cocktails for initial arrival and afterwards we prefer: elderflower cordial topped up with soda water, a spring of mint, a couple of slices of cucumber and a lime wheel. A refreshing and mysterious taste

5. If guests are uptight or stressed out, serve them calming fresh plant herbal iced teas. Fresh herbs such as lavender, lemongrass, mint, mugwort and hibiscus flowers have a high vibration than dried. You can feel the energy when drinking it

6. Present chilled scented towels with bergamot on a silver platter for guests' arrival and return

7. Print theme meal introductions and guest names on the dinner menu for example: Mr. and Mrs. Flannigan's 4th of July Celebration Dinner. People nick these as mementos

8. With guest permission, take photographs during their trip. Print and display in picture frames placed around the yacht for a sense of the ownership feel

9. Take it a step further and present them with an iMovie of their trip on their last day

10. Move sunscreens closer to guests, you don't want them to lift a finger. Not sure about applying it? Don't offer, but if they ask and they're good looking, it's not our job to say no

11. Create a playlist of their favorite bands

12. Make turn down cards with handwritten messages from the crew

13. Leave postcards with stamps on the bedside table from the place visited that day

14. Know where their stuff is. They will ask you for their phone, camera, sunglasses and random things when they are feeling lazy.

Make it a home run every time.

- How To Amaze And Charm The Fussiest Crowds -
Without taking off your clothes to be charismatic

It takes all sorts to make the world go round. Yacht owners and charter guests are the fussiest bods in the universe. Their standard environment is a 5-Star hotel and mansions with full-time live-in staff. It's easy for them to expect the best of the best at all times. Beware of treating them all the same though; their traditions, beliefs, and expectations may differ. Read on to avoid fire-able faux pas.

Russians

Out of all the kooky bunch of internationals, Russians are our favorite. They just want to relax, eat and have a few drinks with friends. I have never found them to be rude, only happier as they get drunker. Occasionally on a boys' only trip, one might try and kiss you, but take it with a sense of humor. If they like you, they won't hesitate to leave a jaw-dropping tip!

Russians are known for being particular and demanding. It is not their wish to appear rude; it's the way they communicate with each other. If they ask for something, drop whatever you're doing and make it happen. They hate to wait and wanted it last week. Upon arrival offer and expect to unpack their belongings. Always offer to press/steam clothing. Do not take anything from their wardrobe without being asked. Please handle everything with care, as their clothing is pricey.

Always serve champagne on arrival, white wine at lunch and red with dinner. Purchase top quality wines in the high-end dollar bracket. Even if they don't recognize the label, they want to drink the expensive stuff. Obviously, always have chilled Russian vodka on hand. Easy to get Belvedere gold label and Grey Goose have had no complaints so far.

Keep the food coming! Russians enjoy large, long meals where everyone comes and goes. They wander around, return to the table, keep on drinking, picking at the food and then continue snacking throughout the day. Start the day off right. Always double check if they prefer their oatmeal cooked with water or milk, as they're quite particular. Serve the tastiest, biggest organic tomatoes you can find for lunch and dinner. You must know they die for watermelon. They dream about it! It symbolizes the freedom of summer. Serve it after meals, as a snack or when the sun is setting. Cube the seedless watermelons (if not they will ask you to remove the seeds) and present it with fashionable toothpicks. Keep the fruit bowls topped up with the choicest cherries, sun-ripened organic strawberries, peaches, grapes and honeydew melon you can find.

Once they have requested assorted chocolates after dinner, the party begins. Have cards and gaming chips within easy access, as they'll want to play poker and smoke. These guys are big smokers, so make sure you have backup cigars and cigarettes, the cigar cutter is sharp, have extra lighters and the Baccarat crystal ashtray is polished to a high shine.

Russians, like the Asians, are a superstitious lot. They believe if you whistle, you're whistling your money away. So no whistling while you're working. No white Casa Lilies on board either, it's a symbol of death and divorce. When ordering bouquets of flowers, have odd numbers. Even is bad luck.

United Arab Emiratis & Saudi Arabians

Formalities first: Do not look royalty in the eye and always be polite, smiling and helpful to the surrounding entourage. Their guests will be diplomats, prime ministers, directors of billion dollar companies and fellow Arab royalty.

Arabs are polite, well-mannered and well-spoken. They speak multiple languages and are educated in the best schools in England and the USA. Thus, they are well traveled; know their locations, food and wine. Therefore, your service standards have to be up to snuff and regarding food, PRESENT ONLY THE BEST.

On arrival serve a variety of non-alcoholic drinks such as freshly squeezed juices and spa water. Their all-time favorite is rosewater, mango and watermelon. After the refreshment drinks, move on to thick, black Arabic coffee, served with milk, cream and sugar on the side. It's quicker if you learn the proper technique of brewing coffee and etiquette from the butlers and palace staff. After watersports, along with scented bergamot and orange chilled towels, they'll be impressed by iced lemongrass-infused, fresh coconut water and rose water. Garnish with a colored orchid and present with a matching coaster.

Arabs/Emeriti will feel cheated if they don't see an abundance of food in sight at all times and for every mealtime. For them, an abundance of food is a status symbol of their wealth. Fly in the best lobsters, oysters, caviar, foie gras and canapés your suppliers can source. Don't feel ashamed to order outside catering to keep up with the demand.

Keep snack platters and chocolate jars topped up. They like a selection of massive macadamia nuts, cashews, dried hazelnuts, pistachios, dried chickpeas, and the largest, fattest dates and figs you can get your hands on. Dried mangos, pineapples, cherries and strawberries will make a memorable impression. Another way forward in this quest for perfection is to invest in a dehydrator and dry your own organic fruits. Be warned, if there's no food available, one person will order something from the galley. Another will see it, and then all of a sudden the galley has an order for twenty fish and chips. The chefs will not be happy campers if they have to stop prepping for dinner to make twenty extra meals!

To ensure this high standard is always maintained, keep a stewardess in sight of guests at all times. They may not call on you, but they expect to see you there in anticipation.

Our golden points for serving United Arab Emiratis and Saudi Arabian nationals:

1. They go crazy for tissues and need to see them everywhere, in every room. Not sure why
2. Handout (serve on a silver platter with tongs) hot or cold towels as guests sit at the table, before the meal
3. Chilled water is served with all coffee and juices by default
4. Make cereals and muesli from scratch
5. Keep a constant eye on the bathrooms. They will use the bidet and the towels supplied instead of the toilet paper. This can get messy. Bring gloves
6. Never show any emotional/moral judgment or scowl. Instant dismissal. The girls they bring are not relatives.

Asians

Wealthy Asians are a nightmare to work for. They want the most bang for their buck and will work you till you have nothing left. If you can overcome this by always showing the utmost respect, dignity and composure, you're a better person than I will ever be.

As Asian guests are coming on board, do not ask them to remove their shoes. Bare feet are unsightly for them and they're never seen without a pair of outdoor/indoor shoes on. Bypass this potential faux pas by leaving monogrammed slippers (with the yacht's name) next to the guest entrance as they remove their shoes. Shoes are to be removed on board, not on the dock, but at the top of the passer rail. This is beneath them!

You should know Asians find it offensive to place shoes on a table or bench. Think about it, you walk on the street then put the streets' dirt directly onto the surface where you eat! This is instant dismissal. When helping them settle in, never set an Asian woman's handbag on the floor or the table. Unlike European women who throw their expensive handbags around, an Asian lady's accessories are treated with respect and placed its own seat or couch.

When doing the final touches to the yacht and ordering flowers, consider this — white is a funeral color. Red and gold are deemed to be auspicious. You'll notice gifts are packaged in red and all the Asian women have red wallets and bags. This means you won't lose it and it will bring you good luck.

Let's begin service:

1. Hired help are expected to be invisible. Pour, serve, refill, be precise, disappear and reappear as needed
2. Begin by serving the elderly first, all the men — oldest to youngest, then females
3. Pour wine and teas/drinks with both hands. Offer a selection. Oolong is standard, jasmine, plus a variety of green and herbal tea to keep them happy. Purchase loose leaf tea over teabags. Always ask to top up the teapot with hot water, instead of changing out the tea. Tea, for them, is a way of

life. Take careful notes

4. To set the table: have small individual rice bowls, side plates, teacups, chopsticks and chopstick rests for each guest. Place platters of food in the middle of the table, preferably on a lazy Susan (a spinning round table.) Guests will share amongst themselves. Serving dishes are not to be picked up and passed around. You'll notice as per their tradition, one does not help themselves first, that is considered rude. They will pick out the choicest pieces from the platters and serve those on either side of them first. Throughout the meal, they will continue doing this as a sign of respect.

After the main meal serve a variety of exotic fruits. They love mangos, lychees, and watermelon. Finish the meal service by offering un-scented hot towels. Afterwards, many of them will smoke. When lighting cigarettes and cigars (indoors as well) always cup the flame to protect it as sign of respect. Funny superstition: Asians believe that sweeping the floor at night is sweeping money out the door. Try and get all the housework done in the morning.

Europeans

Don't expect Europeans to be all enthusiastic and jumping around early in the morning. They know how to relax and you'll find they're late to rise and late to bed. Upon waking, their preference generally is a continental breakfast usually around 11:00. To follow, lunch is around 15:00 to 17:00 with the typical request for a variety of salads and fresh seafood. They love to eat healthy. Afterwards, they'll wander off for a nap or a swim. Dinner will be served around 22:30. This tends to be the most formal meal of the day with the meal service potentially ending around 01:30 Guests will stay up for a while then crash around 02:00 or 03:00. Yes, you do have to stay up with them!

Our big things when serving Europeans is:

1. Do not clear the table until everyone has finished eating
2. Fresh bread, butter, olive oil and balsamic vinegar are to be served with every meal
3. A variety of salads are expected with lunch and dinner
4. Forget about talking wines. They'll tell you what they want.

Americans

Americans recognize exceptional service and will reward it. To please them, never wipe the smile off your face and be super quick in fulfilling orders. Blame it on the American servers (waiters) depending on tips for their livelihood. Better service equals better tips.

Most of the American charter guests are self-made millionaires. The USA has the more billionaires per capita in the world than any other country. For the most part, they're non-traditional and grateful for everything you do that's above and beyond the call of duty. An exception is made for New York Jews. Never will you be worked so hard. They are raised in the most powerful, cutthroat environment on the planet, and they will load you up with non-stop demands. These uptight guys take weeks to chill out. If you can get your hands on Valium, gently sprinkle it on their coffee in the morning. It's the only way they can decompress.

Americans love status-symbol consumer goods. Being early adaptors to trends, the yacht, furnishings and the wines are all about image. To impress them, buy European and explain why it's so sought after and exclusive to them.

United state nationals are on a constant health kick or diet fad to compensate for all the pharmaceutical drugs they take. Their bathroom drawers are filled with bottles of pills for every ailment. They seriously can't poo without them! Americans, healthy or not, are very un-experimental plain eaters. It has been said more than once in our galleys, "These people have palates like babies." Mac and cheese, steaks, ribs, coleslaw, prosciutto, salami meats, truffle cheeses are pretty standard. They freak out when they see the heads on fish or anything that gives a clue as to where the meat has come from.

It is true what they say. Americans survive in this fake bubble. Remember they grew up on a steady diet of trashy TV. Just because they have no class does not mean you need to come down to their level. It's not uncommon to have the stewardesses more refined than their owners. Be it!

Euro-Indians

If they're hiring a boat, they're out to impress but forget about the tip if someone along the way promised you one. It's not in their culture. These people want their money's worth and have no hesitation asking and making you run continuously. Watch them double and triple up on drinks with requests to bring more food! Keep them smiling by keeping them well fed, drinks in abundance and ensure a throbbing stereo system is working. If they can't play their music everywhere, you're dead meat!

Meal times can be a real pain if you only have one chef. Multiple separate dishes are served that are spilt into vegetarian and non-vegetarian. When delegated to arrange the wine list, converse with your wine supplier to choose the trendiest wines for your price bracket. The show-off wines with recognizable labels will speak louder than a good-year vintage from a boutique vineyard.

When planning your Euro-Indians and Asian charter guests' activities, be aware that most of them can't swim. They'll also want to wear lifejackets in the tenders.

Whatever you do with this crowd, the biggest no-no you can make is to touch the top of the head. This is sacrilegious and applies to little children as well.

Brazilians

There seems to be a trend with Brazilians hiring/owning yachts, more so than any other South American country. Enjoyable bunch they are! Educated overseas, well-traveled and worldly. The men of the family take care of the alcohol and music while the women look after the delivery of food. Listen to what they want and go out of your way to make them happy. There's something about them – there are super generous, calm and well-mannered. They have respect for their staff and will always have a smile for you!

Meals are healthy with an emphasis on individual portion control. Bring out a variety of salads with roast vegetables and legumes, grilled meats and well-done fresh seafood. Healthy, homemade food goes down a treat with these guys. To wrap up meals, offer natural, homemade ice cream and sorbets. Fresh vanilla, chocolate, mango and banana are on the top of the list.

*Brazilians are the happiest when the beers and wine are always on ice and super chilled.

Everyone Else International

Whoever they are you have to remember they're paying your wages. Before opening the pantry door to outdoor guest spaces, put on a fresh swipe of lipstick, plaster a smile on your face, pull your shoulders back and think happy thoughts. We're here on yachts to provide guest service that is beyond 7-Star and whatever it takes, we'll do it!

- Dealing With Multiple/Divorce Owners That Share The Yacht -
A different version of hell on the high seas

If they're fifty-five and sharing the expense of a yacht, they're cheap! Stay away from these people. Shared owners, like people who rarely go to restaurants, will expect everything for nothing. Heed our warning when taking a position on a yacht with shared owners that charter out as well. The season will be scheduled with back-to-back owners' use while squeezing in charters in between trips. Our version of yachting hell! Be prepared to work harder than you ever have in your life. Be organized. Take obscene over the top, highly detailed it's a sickness guest preference notes. Pull your shit together, focus. You're going to get superb at this:

1. After the guests have packed up all their belongings but are still on board, idiot-proof the cupboards. Open all cabinets in the cabin and check for any items left behind

2. While the trauma is still fresh in your mind, update preference sheets as soon as the guests leave

3. After guests have departed, pack up the belongings they've left behind with clearly attached labels stating who it belongs to and what it is. Check and double check that all their stuff is labeled. Stow luggage in bilges, out of sight

4. Turnover cabins. Change sheets, wipe down all surfaces and detail all nooks and crannies to get rid of any evidence that someone has ever occupied the room. Be aware of the other woman being naughty and hiding her stuff in random places, like her panties in the bathrobe for the wife to find

5. Consult preference sheets for the next lot of millionaires returning to the yacht

6. Prepare for the next set by unpacking, ironing and organizing all their belongings. Ensure all their belongings look new or as close to perfect as possible. This is to make your life easier down the track by giving them less to complain about

7. Finish off this saga off by displaying all framed family pictures. Have the personalized snorkeling gear ready to go and their favorite flowers perfuming the air

8. Repeat. For as long as your sanity lasts.

- Guests Trust You Like God With Their Deepest Secrets -
The millionaire wife's wellbeing is your hands

Given the close nature of living and working in confined spaces, it's only natural that you bond with your guests. After all, you're in a service industry, you're a people person, and you've already found common ground and connected. You'll find after being in contact for a few days, or even after a few drinks, some guests feel that it is OK to unload on you. Don't let this relationship go any further. Be polite and listen, offer a sympathetic ear for a short period of time. Don't hang around to hear their venting. Make your excuses, clear the room and let them call their psychiatrist. It's not our place to offer advice or get involved. Whatever you're told, trust that everything is said with the greatest confidence. Let them save face and do not run back to fellow crewmembers or paste it all over Facebook!

To The Top Darling. Nothing But The Best.

7

7-STAR FOOD & BEVERAGE SERVICE

I would like to dedicate the following section to Peter from The Belsize in Hampstead Heath, London. He took me on as a naive nineteen year old from Hicksville, Australia and taught me everything I know today. Before I got there I was a rum & coke drinking scuba instructor. He introduced me to the wonderful world of wines and cocktails and didn't complain when I drank all the imported red wines and green melon cocktails with my girlfriends.

- Introduction To Millionaire's Mega Yacht Service -

To deliver immaculate, non-intrusive, quietly classy service is all crew's primary goal on all yachts. The object of the game is to read guests' minds and fulfill their desire before they even knew they desired it — have their favorite fruit juice freshly squeezed, presented at the breakfast table as soon as they sit. Catch on early (the first day) that the Madam enjoys cold drip iced coffee with home-made skinny almond milk and a secret shot of Firestarter vodka, with whipped coconut cream after her afternoon skinny dip, and follow up with the same, day after day. Be consistent with your service, always smiling and completing each task in the same way.

Service is an art form. There are certain ways to flip out and place a napkin on a diner's lap, an etiquette to presenting wine and a particular way of clearing the table. People are trained in this profession, take it very seriously and make a full-time career out of it. Don't be scared, follow the ground rules and do yourself a favor. Take yourself out to the most expensive restaurant you can find — with proper white tablecloths, full sets of cutlery, and glasses — and take notes.

- THE 6 RULES OF YACHT SERVICE -

BE A TEAM
BE PEDANTIC
BE PRECISE
THE GUEST IS ALWAYS RIGHT — AGREE
STAY CALM DURING SERVICE WHEN SOMETHING GOES WRONG
CLEAN AND TIDY THE PANTRIES AFTER EVERY SERVICE

- The Different Types Of Service In The Dining Room -

Silver Service
Considered to be serving food from platters held by the server during formal meals with white formal gloves. Always present the dish to the host before serving and announce what it is: "The Australian lamb, Sir, served with baby roast carrots and English potatoes." Start serving the first female guest on the host's right. If not, the guest of honor is served first, then it ends with the host. Service continues clockwise.

American
Of all the service styles this is the most common. The food is plated in the galley and served to the seated guests. Plates are brought out two at a time and placed before the guest, with the plate facing up as the chef requested e.g. garnish in the right-hand corner. Sauces are presented in a serving dish, or gravy boat, placed on a white saucer and the waiter either pours or ladles it to each guest. Sauces and condiments are then left on the table for the guests to help themselves.

Russian (silver service)
Food is plated in the galley on large silver serving platters. The platters are staggered as they are brought out, unlike French service where the food is brought out altogether. Food is then presented and announced to the host first, and then served to the woman on his/her right-hand side. Standing to the left of the guest, use the silver serving spoon and fork in your right hand to form a tong. Transfer the food from the serving platter to the guest's dinner plate with no drips. Proportion the food equally and plate each guest the same way. Meat is placed at the top of the plate (twelve o'clock), and vegetables around the clock face (fanning out from six o'clock.) Do not overcrowd the plate, as the platters are left on the table for you to offer again, or for the guests to help themselves.

French
Same as the Russian service where food is plated in the galley but instead serving the guest with a silver spoon and fork, they help themselves off the serving platter as you hold it on their left-hand side. More servers are needed for this style of service as the dishes come out altogether. The platters are then placed on the waiter's station and are offered again when appropriate.

English
English service when done properly is impressive. All the food is plated on silver serving trays in the galley and placed before the host. The host will then carve the meat and will plate each guest with the meat and vegetables from the serving dishes. The waiter, standing to the right of the host will take the plate from the host and place it in front of each guest. All sauces and side dishes are placed in the center of the table and passed around by guests.

Family Style Service
The food is prepared and elegantly presented on silver platters in the galley. The server will then introduce the food as he places the platters artfully on the table. Guests will then help themselves. Clear and refresh platters if need be.

Gueridon
Gueridon service is considered a moveable service or trolley from which food can be carved, filleted, flambéed or prepared and served. It's a theatrical show for the guests. Think of filleting a large fish, carving a turkey or putting together a fancy Caesar salad. Other examples are guacamole, pineapple flambé, banana au Rhum, steak Diane and shucking fresh oysters.

- Successfully Deliver Different Meal Services -

Breakfast

Breakfast is set up by the first service stewardess on duty and more often than not served on the aft deck or bridge deck aft. Wait until the deckhands have wiped down the area and given you the green light to go ahead for set-up. The table needs to be set and everything ready to go before the first guest rises.

The night before, the night stewardess will leave the following in the galley or waiter's station for you to set up:

1. Breakfast plates, bread plates and breakfast bowls
2. Cutlery (fork, knife, dessert spoon for yogurts, teaspoons for coffee and bread knife plate)
3. Water and juice glasses
4. Placemats, napkins, napkin rings. Table runner and table decorations
5. Serving platters: fruit bowl, cheese plate, breadbaskets and a large bowl for holding individual yogurts. If serving buffet style, include platters for eggs, bacon, sausages, vegetables, etc
6. Under plates for all serving bowls plus serving tongs for all serving platters
7. Have condiments ready to go: honey, maple syrup and sugar in ramekins, salt and pepper
8. 2x coffee thermos for stand-by percolated coffee
9. 2x milk jugs (full fat and low fat)
10. Labels for all cereals, juices, milks, coffees if the guests are helping themselves.

You will need to set the table up with placemats and plates: breakfast plates and cereal/fruit bowls, knives, forks and cereal spoons. Napkins, water glasses, juice glasses, butter and jam ramekins plus salt and pepper shakers.

On the sideboard, depending on what hand over notes are given to you, set up — with place mats underneath — a breakfast buffet with:

1. Three different types of cereal
2. Toast, freshly baked pastries
3. Fresh fruit plate/salad
4. A savory dish with beautifully sliced ham and various cheeses
5. Yogurt — if in separate containers, place in a large bowl with ice in the bottom
6. Juices, water and milk in glass jugs
7. Coffee and tea should be made to order and prepared according to guest preference.

Guests can help themselves from this buffet, but usually don't! They'll point to what they want and expect you to get it for them, and they'll also order á la carte (cooked to order) from the chef. Make sure you bring the chef a plate to serve it on to avoid getting screamed at.

Lunch

Lunches are usually served family style, depending on where you are in the world. Condiments in ramekins corresponding with lunch should always be placed on the tables before diners start their meal. Always present freshly baked bread, olive oil and balsamic vinegar placed on the table.

Hors d'oeuvres (also known as starters, appetizers or finger food)

Anything more than two bites are known as hors d'oeuvres and anything smaller is considered a canapé. These food items are served at cocktail hour, before the main part of a meal or served on their own at receptions and events. These miniature food items (the idea is that they are to be picked at) are served on platters for guests help themselves, or can be individually plated. Either hot or cold, use appropriate cutlery and napkins. Aim to serve four per person.

Examples of hors d'oeuvres: mini mushroom/tomato/goats cheese tarts, fresh shrimp with dipping sauce, mini spring rolls, Thai chicken skewers, crunchy crab parcels, mini fish tacos, pulled pork steamed buns, and mini brioche hamburgers.

Canapés (served during cocktail hour)

These are one-bite samplers that can be taken with one hand. Ideally, the other hand is holding a glass of champagne. One bite, designed so as not to intrude in ongoing conversations. Canapés are to be served on a platter and taken around the room, presented to every guest and placed on the table closest to them. Trays are to be taken back to the galley to be replenished and re-served as necessary.

How to serve canapés:
1. Hold the platter with your right hand placed flat underneath. In your left hand have serviettes placed on a plate. Fingers are commonly used and are acceptable
2. If cutlery is needed, place a toothpick, small spoon or fork in food
3. Continue making the rounds with the canapés untill everyone has had their fill or loses interest. Place the platter on the closest table or bar for guests to help themselves
4. Canapés are meant to tie you over, not fill you up. If it's a canapé event, eat beforehand.

Tapas

The idea of Spanish tapas is to order one single type of dish per person and to share with friends. Typical tapas dishes consist of olives, anchovies, fried croquettes, freshly shaved Serrano ham, chorizo sausages, patatas bravas, fried calamari, grilled green peppers, marinated octopus, local cheeses and pinchos — a creative layering of different meats and cheeses, speared through the middle with a toothpick. Serve with freshly baked bread and bottles of fresh local wine.

Antipasto

Is a European term meaning before the meal and is the first course of all Italian meals. Traditional antipasto includes cured meats, olives, pepperoncinis, marinated mushrooms, anchovies, artichoke hearts, various cheeses, pickled meats, and vegetables in oil or vinegar. The food selected is seasonal and regional. Antipasto is then served on a shared platter for guests to help themselves.

Dinner

Wherever you are, this is always the big one. You could be setting up and serving anything from two to ten courses. The following is a traditional menu plan for ten courses:

1st course:	**Amuse bouche or appetizer.** The first course to amuse the mouth and invigorate the palate. Serve: savory parmesan crème brulée, steamed mussels Asian style, fresh shrimp or one anchovy fillet on fresh bread with Irish butter.
2nd course:	Soup. Served hot or cold. Consommé, bisques, coulis, broths, potage, vichyssoise or gazpacho.
3rd course:	Fish
4th course:	Roast
5th course:	Game. Rabbit, deer, duck, wild boar, kangaroo, and emu.
6th course:	Salad. Light, crisp, refreshing salad with light vinaigrette.
7th course:	Dessert
8th course:	Fresh fruit, crackers & cheese offered with coffee (Demi – tasse) The perfect cheese plate will have variety. One aged, soft, firm and blue. Serve with seasonal fruit and good quality crackers.
9th course:	Petit fours
10th course:	Nuts and raisins

* In French 3 Star Michelin restaurants there is usually a champagne sorbet served between the Fish/Roast and the game.

- Master Class: Serving Memorable Meals -
The step-by-step guide to delivering meal service to the richest people in the world

Your first and foremost job responsibility is to be the eyes and ears for the head chef and galley. The galley team needs to be informed all of all guest movements. The head chef must know when the guests are sitting or late for the meal, when they are about to finish, when you are clearing, when they're ready to go on to the next course and any feedback that you glean. The chefs want their food to come out hot, still perfectly presented and on time! It is your job to deliver the food and top up the drinks. Sounds easy right? Oh, no, the pressure!

Let the galley know the guests are sitting, and it will be 15 minutes before the 1st course is needed
Assist with seating all guests. The chief steward will begin seating guests by pulling out the choicest seats first. Chairs facing the room or point of interest are considered the best. As you are doing this, work your way around the table, take the napkins from the place settings and place it in guests' laps. Place napkin rings as they become available on the sideboard.

1. As per guest preference, offer hot and cold towels now
2. Wine is served before water. Present the chosen wine and serve. (This is very dependent on guest requests)
3. Offer still and sparkling water to each guest. On the waiter's station have sliced lemon, lime and ice ready to go
4. Serve bread with serving cutlery with fresh butter, olive oil and balsamic vinegar already on the table
5. Clear all unwanted glassware that will not be used. For example, clear the champagne glasses from the men that you know will only stick with red for the whole meal and wine glasses from the liquor drinkers.

Call the galley and let them know you are ready for the 1st course
(Usually it has already been sent up and is ready to go in the back of house. Hopefully it's a chilled dish as hot dishes waiting create panic)

1. Announce and serve 1st course. Place the starter dish on the large main plate with charger (service plate) underneath
2. Give it five minutes or until they've taken a few mouthfuls. Come back to the host and ask if everything is OK with the food. This is also an opportunity for the guests to ask for anything else they might need.

Before clearing, call the galley and let them know you are beginning to clear
1. Before starting to clear the table, top up waters and wine. To keep guests happy always ensure they have something to drink and eat in front of them
2. Clear starter and main plate underneath, leaving the charger. Remove corresponding cutlery.

Call the galley and let them know 1st course has been cleared, and you are ready for the 2nd course.
1. Announce and serve 2nd course, placing on top of the charger
2. As per guest preference, offer wine to correspond with the course being served
3. Wait five minutes and come back to the table and ask, "Is everything OK with the meal, Sir" or "How is everything with the food?"
4. Turn on kettle/coffee machine in anticipation of coffee after dessert — if it's a three-course meal.

Call the galley and let them know you are clearing 2nd course

1. Top up waters and wine (before clearing the table, again so they have something to drink while you're busy)
2. Clear main plates, chargers and main cutlery
3. Remove salt + pepper shakers and all condiments. There should be nothing left on the table except dessert cutlery, water, and wine glasses
4. De-crumb table. Take a folded serviette (about the size of your palm) and a clean bread plate. Walk around the table clockwise, sweeping crumbs onto a small plate. In top-notch restaurants, they use a small hand-held brush to do this
5. Pull down dessert cutlery so that the fork is on the left and spoon is on the right of the place setting.

Call the galley and let them know you are ready for the next course

1. Announce and serve 3rd course – dessert.
2. Serve coffee and tea, only if they prefer to have it at the same time. Have sugar and milk ready to go on the table
3. Clear the dessert course, corresponding cutlery and extra glassware off the table.

Call the galley and let them know dessert has been cleared

1. Serve petit fours (mini chocolates) and a cheese plate if requested
2. Offer tea and coffee again
3. Now is the ideal time to offer hot or cold towels for guests to freshen up
4. Keep serving wine, waters, and coffees until guests signal enough or until the head guy departs.

When all guests have departed the dining area

1. Extinguish candles and allow to cool before storing
2. Clear table, countertops and wipe down
3. Wash, dry and stow all dishes and table settings
4. Yo big mouth! Keep noise to a minimum.

Whatever the guests do, inform the galley. If a guest leaves the table, if they are slow eaters, if the children aren't eating their food, let the galley know. Clear communication is essential

✓ Never ever, ever, ever stack plates on the table. Or scrap and stack plates in full view of guests. All plates are to be taken two at a time back to the galley
✓ When a guest uses the incorrect cutlery, take it and the cutlery they were supposed to use away and replace it with the appropriate cutlery for the next course
✓ If a guest leaves the table during service, take his/her napkin and fold neatly into four. Place on the back of the chair or to the side of their setting. Attend to the place setting: clear plate, refill water, tidy up. Reposition chair
✓ Have cigars and cigar ashtray, plus corresponding paraphernalia ready to go after dinner. Never take an ashtray unless you have one to replace it.

- Back Up Lady, I'm Doing Service Tonight -
Wait staff etiquette in the caviar and champagne training program

This is how it goes. There is ONLY ONE person in charge of running the symphony of the meal. It is their job to invite people to the table, communicate to the galley of timings of each course, let the crew know the guests are seated for the meal, when they have finished dessert — after they are happy and fat, the captain may come out and discuss the follow day's itinerary with them — and when the guests have left the table.

The person in charge of running the meal service will know who eats bread, what type, who drinks still or sparkling water with ice, who drinks wine, to what level, who drinks coffee afterwards with cognac and smokes cigars. They would have studied the preference sheet or done meal service with them a few times and remembered every detail to make each meal service smooth sailing.

We know you are trying to help, but when we leave the table/service area to grab something or get a quick bite in while the guests are eating, it makes us nervous about what you might be doing. Imagine you're doing breakfast service and you duck into the pantry to make coffee. The girl scheduled on beds and heads sneaks out to the table, refills the water glasses with orange juice and offers them all pancakes, and then comes into the pantry with orders for iced double lattes!

Nothing happens at the table without first running it past the head person orchestrating the meal. If anything happens behind the lead server's back, such as calling for the next meal without her knowing, you are going to make that person in charge very uptight and stressed out. They might even send you to bed!

There needs to be communication with everyone to keep the service flowing. There should be no overlapping of orders placed or wine glasses being over filled by two servers. As a team it embarrasses us. No-one heads out to the table without prior permission from the head bitch in charge of running the service. He/she directs everything. Got it?

TABLE SETTINGS

- Setting The Perfect 7-Star Table -
Table settings are all about having the tablecloths perfectly starched, charger plates in place, glassware gleaming and an exquisite centerpiece to complement the meal, theme or location

Easy tips to begin with:

1. Begin by creating ambiance with music, lighting, and temperature. If there is too much light, pull down blinds or privacy curtains. Ensure all candles are lit before guests sit down

2. Guests are to be arranged evenly around the table with enough elbow room to move. Measure it out, so that the table is perfectly spaced

3. Charger plates are always impressive and should be mandatory for every meal. At all times there should be a plate in front of each guest – except the break before dessert

4. Set cutlery so you work your way inwards for every course. Knife blades to face inwards. All cutleries are to be precisely perpendicular to the edge of the table and minimum exactly two fingers from the edge of the table

5. Cutlery and glassware should be checked for fingerprints and dust. This will be the first imperfection people notice

6. All labels on the glassware, plate and bread plate are to face the edge of the table, towards the guest. Our guests will pick up the plate and glass wear to check who made it

7. Centerpiece table decorations should be low enough so that guests can see one another across the table. Great idea is to have an extended centerpiece of designer platforms. Serve a variety of sweet and savory canapés, cheeses, dips and fruit compôtes for guests to help themselves before and after the meal. Alternatively, create little canapés that look to be part of the table setting decoration or

even edible art pieces that are equally impressive! You gotta mix it up and get creative for everyone to talk

8. Candles are to be low and unscented

9. N.B no labels on the table. Everything is to be decanted into glass and real silver bowls or bottle

10. Glitter is a bitch to clean up. It gets everywhere. Never use outside on the deck. It'll blow, get wet and stain the teak.

DID YOU KNOW?

To bring service to another standard: Creatively place the owner's initials into anything that you're serving. Be it in their double skimmed latte in the morning, initials seared into hamburger patties or a cursive lettering on their dessert plate

- Create Mind Blowing Theme Nights On Super Yachts -
This is the WOW factor right here

Forget about everything else you've learned, this is where we're going to be judged. If you're new to the industry, start researching inspirational ideas on Pinterest and yacht stewardessing Facebook groups. This is a major opportunity to impress guests on board. To begin, choose a theme or colorway and let your creativity out to play. Use local produce, flowers and found objects. Create matching themed cocktails and shots. Get all the crew involved in dressing up to add to the excitement of your theme night. Think random, outside the box, strange and quirky. This is the fun part of our job. If it makes you get excited, do it! Check out our theme night suggestions:

Nautical
Navy and white. Or the hipster version, red and white. Create a centerpiece of shells, dried starfish, driftwood, white candles, lighthouses and little novelty boats. For the cute factor, get the crew to dress as old style sailors. White starched navy hats, white collars and nautical striped shirts. In the middle of the table make the biggest, highest arrangement of lighthouses you can find. Sprinkle small pebbles around the bases and place small souvenir boats floating along the table. To make this theme pop, dress the edge of the table with matching small triangular flags that tie back into the centerpiece.

Tropical
Think leafy greens and colorful flowers. Lay oversized leaves that contrast with the straw placemats as the table runner. Fold napkins into a bird of paradise flower. Add found coral pieces, half shelled coconuts, giant palm fronds, and tall white candles in glass vases with sand in the bottom. Source mini birds on stiff wire and tuck them in randomly around the table. Blow the budget and hang as much greenery and flowers from the ceiling as you can. Turn on the misters — water sprayers around the ceiling — with lightly perfumed jasmine for the full experience.

Oriental
Color directions: red and black, red and turquoise or pink orchids on a white background look visually appealing. Eastern designed tablecloths, napkins and heaps of orchids strategically placed on the table, help this theme along. Think contrasting Asian style soup bowls with chargers and chopsticks placed on top, napkins folded into fans, sake glasses and dipping bowls. Have the stewardesses on board dressed as Japanese Geishas with the full make-up. Alternatively choose the Chinese look of dragon-embroidered blouses and oriental flowers in the hair cascading down. For the wow factor: sit a centerpiece of multiple assorted sized pandas on top of a world-map table runner with gold coins, pearls and diamonds sitting at their feet. Finish off the scene with miniature traditionally dressed dolls peaking out from the animals or put the dolls under the animals, squishing them - make it crazy!

Old style opulence

White starched napkins folded in the tallest style you can make, gold rimmed plates, white tiger lilies, individual salt and pepper shakers next to the handwritten guest place cards, and multi-tiered, massive white candles make this setting pop! This table setting deserves to have as much personalized material as you can. Menus, place settings, plates and food with guests' names, and the name of the yacht will surely delight all. Do it all on the most expensive paper, handmade plates and food as you can source. Anything else will look tacky. Check the table decorations cupboard and stock up while in Monaco.

Pirate night

This is an easy one. Head to the nearest dollar store and pick up eye patches, hip swords, bandanas, paper pirate hats, fake coins and costume jewelry for dress-ups. Buy the most elaborate treasure box you can find and to create a wow-factor centerpiece. Group together giant skulls surrounded by miniature skull candles. Add marine netting, fairy lights, mini buoys, massive big vases filled with treasure in the bottom (candles on top) to this theme. For the show, carve everything (meats) at the table with the girls serving sides on massive silver platters. Next level: place live lobsters in the bottom of the salt water pool/Jacuzzi with their claws rubber banded together. Have the kids and adults dive for their entrée course and grill them on the BBQ as soon as they are caught.

Vegas night

Use green felt as your tablecloth and create a centerpiece with poker chips, gold coins, roulette wheel and playing cards. Provide bow ties, feather boas and costume jewelry for the guests. Get the crew looking good by dressing them as blackjack dealers (white shirts and visors) and playboy bunnies (bunny ears, loose bow ties, pom-pom tails and long white gloves.) String up the Christmas tree lights and download a winning soundtrack to complete the ambiance. Ensure the Mulata Daisy cocktail garnishes are over the top and keep them coming.

Hollywood, Cannes, Oscar night

Have treasure chests ready for your guests filled with feather boas, long strand necklaces, top hats and bow ties as guests hit the red carpet to the dining table. Decorate the multi-million-dollar yacht with the HOLLYWOOD sign, cut-out cardboard models of your favorite movie stars begged or borrowed from the local cinema and as many fairy lights as you can get your hands on. Pre-order Emmy award statues for the table and to hand out to guests. Ideas for centerpieces include: camera film, tinsel, oversized gold stars, admit one tickets, gold helium balloons, and candles (lots of them and dim the lights.) Commandeer the service trolley to convert into a roving bar, ladled with designer garnishes and mixes for bespoke cocktails. Make this an event to remember with polaroid cameras around the table to capture this star filled night! This could be part of your guests' videos you create as their departure gift when they leave the boat.

4th of July

Americans love this traditional annual family holiday. Set the scene with multi-sized red, navy and white balloons hanging from the ceiling. Alternate coverings on chairs in red, navy and white lycra. For the table: a navy and white star table runner, red and white striped placemats and white napkins. Create a centerpiece with mini American flags and tinsel/gold cutouts of fireworks. Use white candles placed in tall glass vases, topped up with layers of navy, white and red sand. Of course, no 4th of July would be complete without a specular firework display. Make it happen!

Magic/Magician night

Some of the best nights are the unexpected and what better way to surprise your guests than with a world-class magician! For this theme to work, import massive, over the top props to set the scene. Imagine an enormous top hat with bunny's ears poking out. Complete the stage with curtains, stage act signs and a smoke machine. As a warm up act for after the entertainment, get in a professional bubble blower — they're on a different level to the ones that you see on the street.

Masquerade Ball

We pull this one off every year for the Venice Masquerade Ball. We're here to delight, amaze and wonder. Be the flame and not the moth. The red carpet entrance up to the yacht is staged with naked flames from fake trees, fire blowing performers, high rose bushes in full bloom (imported) and posing women wearing nothing but skin-colored full length body suits and deliciously over the top masks with feathers. Hanging over the passer rail entrance is a grand crystal chandelier and to the left — the owner magically makes this happen every year — is a caged live lion hanging from the crane from the top deck aft. Onboard the interior of the yacht is converted to replicate the scene from Eyes Wide Shut plus some. There is a roped-off champagne fountain, infinity pool with glass sides complete with naked mermaids swimming and millions of tea light candles floating on top and black bow tie wait staff serving canapés with dry ice fumes floating from the middle of trays. That's nothing though, I love the life sized wooden artist mannequins placed around the boat in different sexual positions. Bench mark.

Mariachi bands

Oh yeah! Mexican night! Think tequila, margaritas, big sombrero hats and shakers! Fun, fun, fun! Mexicans are a happy bunch who love bright colors! Create a night to remember with cheerful blue tablecloths, woven Mexican table runners, thick handmade plates, margarita glasses and handmade crepe animals as centerpieces. You'll be surprised to learn that Mexicans dig roses. Tuck them into napkin ring holders and create pattern displays with them.

Music theme night

Folksy 60s, swinging 70s night or electric 80s … Whatever your guests grew up listening to, help them recreate the best years of their life in style by relieving them of their cash to create a night they will never forget!

Christmas Eve/Day

Boom! this is your time to pull out the big guns. Think little Christmas forests, with small single potted pine trees, nativity scenes, fake snowdrops, miniature Santa Claus, reindeers, baubles hanging from twigs and fake snow falling from the ceiling as the guests enter the dining room. Want to stand out from the rest? Have a train set weaving through the trees and Polar bears on the table with Santa Claus riding shotgun.

For these theme night and table settings succeed, it's imperative to choose a theme and stick with it. No half/half of anything or mismatching. Aim for a no budget-limit movie finish with your team.

<u>- Throwing Fabulous Unforgettable Parties That You Can Be Smug About -</u>
Girl, this is the shit right here

Throwing fabulous parties is an art form. It's a skill perfected over late-night drinking sessions, with minute-by-minute planning and terrifyingly brilliant execution! Most people hire a party planner to do the grunt work, but hello! You're on a yacht — you are the party planner!

As the perfect hostess (luxury yacht stewardess) you will be called upon to throw parties for guests, often at the last minute. It's common to walk past guests and be informed that there are seventy-five people coming for sunset cocktails and canapés tomorrow night. Sounds easy but even the simplest event on yachts requires wait staff, decorations, cocktails, garnishes, food prep, platters, ice buckets, lighting and a killer playlist ready to rock. FYI a couple of these short notice party stunts can lead to chef breakdowns.

Parties can range from small intimate anniversary dinners to walloping great elaborate challenges, complete with guests being helicoptered in with the red carpet waiting. More importantly you will be called upon to throw parties for the crew. When the crew are happy, everyone is happy! We may be working on these special days but every small effort is appreciated for Christmas, Easter, Australia Day, birthdays and farewells. Everyone loves a party and any excuse to throw one, we're there!

Planning for small cozy affairs to full-on glitzy celebrity-filled events!

1. Budget
For the most part, there is no budget on yachts. Darling, let your outrageous imagination out! These people have seen everything. Make it over the top. Ship in thousands of dollars-worth of flowers, outside catering, international DJs, high profile entertainers, animals in cages, security in Armani, sexy half-naked bar staff and crates of vintage champagne.

2. Finalize the guest list
You want an equal ratio of females to males. Remember good-looking people like hanging out with good-looking people. To make the party a real success, here's my trick: Invite one STUNNING person from either sex. I swear all the boys will be on their best behavior and the girls, a fascinating version of themselves. It does not matter if you invite funny, intelligent or smart people or not. That's what the liquor is for.

3. Decorations and settings count for a lot
It's the deal breaker for any delightful celebration. Why would you throw a fabulous affair and not have a marvelous setting for all the social media pictures? At the very, very minimum have a stand out floral arrangements as decoration.

4. Decide on a time

5. Pick a space/deck/venue
Will there be enough room? Will everyone be impressed? Is the view Instagram-worthy?

6. Send out invitations that set the scene
Never, ever skip on the quality of your invitations. Get them professionally printed. Avoid sending out rubbish ones printed on your home printer or a FB invitation. How pedestrian!

7. Food
What's a party without food? People get hungry when they drink. You must serve food. If there is no food people will leave to eat elsewhere. Have canapés ready to go. Please don't be the hostess and be in the galley/kitchen the whole time while your guests have come to see you. Delegate someone else to do that.

8. Have a fully stocked bar with a couple of choice cocktails of the day
These can be made in batches beforehand, ready to be shaken on ice or blitz in the blender.

Fabulous garnishes such as orchids tooth picked into pineapple wedges and crazy umbrellas can also be prepared in advanced and be chilled.

9. Focus on lighting

Where is the main foot traffic? Will tables be lit up? Can people still see without tripping over? Are we doing hidden mood lighting or well-placed lamps? Please note that one should never have naked flames on a yacht, it makes people panic! Same goes for sparklers as I learnt from nearly setting off the fire sprinklers.

10. Take care of logistics

How is everyone arriving? Do we have adequate parking? Do they need to be let in by security? Do we have a driver on hand to take wasted people home?

11. Brief the crew on their roles

First delegate a team leader for the party planning execution. As team leader, it is necessary for you to make everyone feel important with the roles they are playing. Be completely transparent with all information when discussing timing of guest arrival, drinks, food and pack down. Everyone has to be constantly in the loop. "VIPs are in sight. Everyone to attention."… "We have three guests arriving, can I have one girl out here with welcome drinks."… "They're slowing down on the food, let's hold off on canapés for fifteen minutes."… "The madam's best friend is getting sloshed and flashing her vajayjay. Let's slow down her champagne drinking so she can keep her respect and get laid tonight."

12. Finishing touches to make it the party of the year

Greet guests with a show stopping entrance. Organize a seven-piece string band on the top deck, boys/girls dressed in samba gear circulating the canapés, hot models lounging in the hot tube, flower arrangements that will be talked about for the next ten years, temporary water fountains installed in the pool and dry ice cocktails. If you can think it up or heard about it from the luxury hospitality fairies, make it happen.

13. Continuously be present with your guests

Mentally have something agreeable to say about them as you introduce them to one another.

14. Do not run out of glassware, plates, cutlery, napkins, food, liquor or waters

Keep everyone fed and well topped up.

15. To always be the gracious host and end the party on a top note

Start serving coffee and petit fours an hour before you plan to wrap it up. Mysteriously run out of alcohol. Gain everyone's attention by turning off the music, flickering light switches and tapping on the side of your glass. In true hostess fashion, give a heartfelt thank-you-for-coming-and-making-the-night-a-success speech.

16. If all else fails and people stick around because they found more booze

Enlist your party friends to round up the troops and head to the nearest bar with the hottest guy and shortest dress, of course! If you have been hired to facilitate the party; the celebrations are over when the person with the most money decides it's over.

- Confessions Of A Fat Girl In A Skinny Girl's Body -
Learn quickly about stew arse

Before we let you anywhere near the handmade lobster ravioli with champagne sauce, best-kept secret Alsace seared foie gras, triple cream Puglia burrata cheese, hand shaved Italian truffles and the best ice-cream in the world from FG food lab in Rotterdam, you need to know about STEW ARSE. This term refers to stews with oversized derrières. It is created unnoticed by the host, by pounding the crew buffet, scoffing extra servings not eaten by guests and consistently getting first dibs on the extra desserts. After a couple of months consistently putting everything in your pie hole, none of your clothing will fit and people will start to comment on how healthy you look. This is without doubt the hardest part of our job — not eating!

This is the truth:

1. First class meals taste better because of the organic salted butter it is cooked in. Fat cells lubricate the taste buds enhancing the flavors. This is why you cannot stop eating

2. Chefs, if they dislike you or the guests, will not hesitate to add another stick of ready-to-go, pre-melted butter on the windowsill, to their concoction. It is their form of sly revenge on ungrateful people

3. If the chefs won't eat their dessert, don't touch them either. Heed their first warning when they say, "I wouldn't eat that, it's full of fat," and "I never eat my desserts." Proceed with caution

4. You do not need to eat everything. Remind yourself that you have already tasted the canapés/cheese/dessert/chocolates. ONE BITE IS A TASTE. TWO BITES AND YOU'RE EATING

5. The golden rule if watching your weight. *Anything good does not go in my mouth.*

6. We like to stick to the Giselle skinny bitch diet. "Would Giselle, the skinny bitch eat that?" "No! I'm not either."

Note this warning very well. The guest food is tasty because of all the fats. Stick to the veggies so when the yacht pulls up to St. Maarten, you can join in with everyone else who is dancing nearly naked on the beach showing off their toned bodies.

DID YOU KNOW?
If someone looks at you and repeatedly taps their chin, it means you have something in your teeth.

8.

SOCIAL
LUBRICANT
SERVICE

Promote
What You Love
Rather Than
Bashing What
You Hate

When's a good time for?

If your out and its past ten- its liquor. For something different try it on the rocks. Atleast this way you can taste it!

7am onwards
Lets start this day off right with bloody mary's

If your still up & trying to impress; try a "proper adult beverage" anything with wiskey.

shots
The beginning of the end.

9am
any time is a good time for chamagne. Did you need an excuse?

10pm

12 am/pm

9pm
perfect for a irish coffee.....

9   3pm

6pm

10/11 onwards.
White wine goes well with lunch. Only a few though- unless your sailing on a yacht.

8pm
try a after dinner port or cognac (but only the best!)

6pm

Red wine with dinner. Please, please chill if your in the southern hemisphere or spain for the summer. Warm wine is the worst!

Ora sea breeze if your feeling a bit fancy. The garnish always makes it ☺

5pm
perfect sundowner cocktail - mojitos. Liquor before wine your in the clear - remember?!?

- Darling, Is It Time For A Drink? -

Be prepared to be dumbfounded. Wine and liquor on yachts is a whole different world. Some nights you'll be serving €2400 bottles of just-bought-at-auction red wine and other nights you'll be pouring Veuve Clicquot like it's water. Working on yachts should come with a warning label: beware of developing a taste for expensive wines!

The following section is the beginning of your career in bartending and wine tasting. We stress that with the elegance and class that these UHNW guests demand, you must understand the complexities of serving wine and liquor to provide the best hospitality. Learn as much as you can, do courses, ask, watch YouTube videos and practice.

THINK LIKE A WINO

- Demystifying Wine Notes -
The wine onboard is worth more than a deposit on a house

1. Warmth, light, normal fridges and storing wine upright destroys the complexities of the wine and dries out the cork, thus allowing air into the bottle. Ideal storing conditions are wine fridges and cellars. Anything but these cool temperatures accelerates the aging process and oxidation of the wine, which can quickly dull the taste

2. Vibration affects wine, especially the sediment. Do not store bottles near engine rooms, generators or in bilges. Ideal storage for the shed loads of wine on yachts is laid flat, under the beds in the air-conditioning

3. Keep the storage temperature of the wines consistent. 55°F/7-18°C is the optimal temperature to store red/white wines. **For every 1°C degree above you lose 1 year off the shelf life**. Humidity around 70°C is ideal

4. Wines with a crumbled cork or a cork that breaks when opening can still be OK. Sniff the cork first, and always taste the wine before serving

5. All American & Australian wines by law have sulfates, a preservative agent that has been used since Roman times. The sulfates take away from the storage life of wine. It is not mandatory for Italian & French wines to have sulfates, therefore they can lay for twenty plus years

6. At the table always pour and serve drinks from the right of the guest

7. Before pouring the wine ask the guest (with a look or very quietly) if they would like a top-up. Alternatively, hover the wine bottle ready to pour over the glass and if there is no signal of I've-had-enough, pour. Allow guests to nearly finish their glass before topping up. This lets you and the guest keep count of how much they've drunk

8. Fill wine glasses to the thickest part of the glass. Where the stem turns into the bulb and where it rounds out to the fattest part, this is the level where you stop pouring the wine. Never fill a wine glass more than 2/3 full. Give the bottle a slight twist as you finish pouring to avoid any drips. Finish the pour by wiping the mouth of the bottle with a service cloth

9. White wine is to be poured so that it splashes one side of the glass and rolls around to aerate

10. Red wine is to be poured slowly into the glass to form tiny bubbles on top of the wine. This is how the red wine aerates and begins to breathe

11. When viewing wine in the glass hold up to the light with a white background:
    - ✓ White wines will become straw like in color with age
    - ✓ New reds will be purplish in color with color extending to the edge of the wine in the glass
    - ✓ Older reds will become brick in color and start to be translucent around the edges

12. Always hold the stem of glasses or the bottoms of un-stemmed glasses to take them away. Never put your fingers in a glass.

WINE DESCRIPTIONS

- WHITE WINE -

Pinot Grigio (Pee-no gree-z-o)

Generally, the Pinot Grigios are a lot thinner and dryer in texture than the Sauvignon Blancs. These can be beautiful wines with depth of character and complexity. Best served not overly chilled to gain the full appreciation of the bouquet.

Alternative names: Pinot Gris (French version.)

Body: Ranges from light to medium bodied. Light bodied: light and crisp with ample fruit flavors. Medium bodied: fresh with more complex fruit flavors.

Flavors: Perfumed pear, apples, orange skins, honey and light sharp minerals

Characteristics: Light, crisp and clean in the medium weight extending to luxurious, extravagant and long-lived finishes

Where it's best: Venezia (Venice) and Alto Adige regions in Italy.

Food pairings: Versatile with its food alliances. Can be served with almost anything: salads, seafood and lighter fish (plus smoked salmon), white meats, curried dishes to desserts. Well suited with Thai or spicy Chinese cuisine. This grape variety is also great drunk on its own at any time of day.

Sauvignon Blanc (Saw-vee-nyohn blohn)

Sauvignon Blanc is one of the most famous grape varieties due to its pleasing personality. French in origin, this grape prefers cool climates. Serve this wine well chilled and as always, best to go for quality over quantity.

Alternative names: Pouilly-Fumé (Loire Valley, France) / Sancerre (Loire Valley, France) The same grape is used in Fumé Blanc (Loire Valley, France) wine, which is its drier version.

Body: Light to medium bodied.

Flavors: Tropical fruit flavors that can be highlighted with freshly cut grass, flinty minerals, grapefruit, melon, and figs. Other notes that can be found are sourness of green apples, pears, gooseberries, mangos, and blackcurrants.

Characteristics: Always zesty and vibrant with an herbal character. Bright aromas and a strong acid finish.

Where it's best: This grape is grown in several areas of France, California, South Africa and Australia. Lately it has seen great success in New Zealand. (Sauvignon grown in the southern hemisphere has a stronger fruitier complexity.)

Food pairings: Sushi, oysters, vegetarian, Chinese, Korean, Vietnamese, fatty cheeses, antipasto, appetizers, seafood, poultry, and salads.

Semillon (Say-mee-yaw)

Wonderful as a late harvest wine, it is the primary varietal used in the winemaking technique that is famous for how the grapes are left to rot on the vines. When they're picked and pressed, the wine has a honeyed, botrytis flavor. This thin-skinned, easy to grow grape ripens early and is found blended with Sauvignon Blanc to delimit its intense berry-like flavors.

Alternative names: Hunter Valley Riesling, Blanc Doux, Columbier, Chevrier, Wuyndruiff

Body: Thick and full-bodied.

Flavors: Lemon, apple, pear, green papaya, figs, and grass. Depending on where it is grown, it can be a palette cleansing wine, similar to a Sauvignon Blanc or a creamy lemon-flavored wine like Chardonnay.

Characteristics: Very sweet, flat acidity, oily. Viscous and chewy.

Where it's best: Major grape of the Bordeaux region in France but also grown in Chile, Argentina, Australia, California and South Africa. Mate, Australia is where it's best!

Food pairings: Can hold its own with Indian and Asian spices due to its zippy flavor. Goes well with fish, sushi and pickled ginger. A dry Semillon pairs well with clams, mussels and pasta salad. Try this wine with foie gras, rich chocolate and caramel ice cream for a take-your-panties-off surprise.

Gewurztraminer (Guh-wur-z-tra-MI-ner)

A perfumed, aromatic variety that is ideal for sipping. Gewurztraminer means spice in German. Late harvest wines of this grape are usually sweet due to the higher sugar content in the grape. This leads to tremendous fruit concentrations and is likened to drinking dessert or a floral honeyed cordial.

Body: Medium bodied.

Flavors: Very fragrant with floral aromas: slight grapefruit, ground pepper, lychees, peaches, apricots, roses and allspice.

Characteristics: Exuberant and flamboyant, intense aromas, relatively thick and oily flavors. Nutty in taste.

Where it's best: Alsace, Germany and the Loire Valley (Savennières, Vouvray). This grape is also seeing success in Italy, California, Canada and Australia.

Food pairings: Spicy and non-spicy Asian cuisines, pork and grilled sausages. Pop a bottle into the picnic basket to get your date quietly drunk while finishing off the dessert course.

Riesling (Rees-ling)

Rieslings should taste fresh and express themselves differently, depending on the region and style of wine making. Germany's top notch Rieslings are usually blended slightly sweet. Rieslings from Alsace (France) and the Eastern US are consistently made in a different style, equally aromatic but typically drier (not sweet). California's Rieslings are much less successful, usually too sweet without sufficient acidity for balance.

Alternative names and similar grapes: Albarino (a Spanish white varietal).

Body: Wine can range from heavy, sometimes slightly sweet to full-bodied, dry late harvest versions. They have great acidity to balance out any residual sweetness.

Flavors: Citrus, grapefruit, fresh apples, limes, tropical fruits, pear and quince.

Characteristics: Can be described as silky, sleek, fresh and delicate with floral aromas and fruit blossoms.

Where it's best: Riesling is widely planted but is well known for its success in Germany. Also, well-noted is Alsace in France, Australia (Clare Valley) and Austria.

Food pairings: Best paired with fruit, cheeses and desserts. Also works well with root vegetables, raw vegetables, delicate fish, shellfish, oysters, shrimp and most Asian cuisines. Dry versions go well with fish, chicken and pork dishes.

Chardonnay (Shar-do-nay)

Today there are thirty-four different clones of Chardonnay. This grape grew in popularity in the 1990s due to wine critics waxing lyrical about it. The classics come from Burgundy in France but it is now widely planted around the world. This grape is easy to grow and tends to give good yields which appeals to wine makers. Chardonnays are often more complex and structured in the body with a velvety, voluptuous thickness compared with other types of dry whites. Chardonnays, when aiming for perfection, have a rich, graceful style that lends themselves well to being oaky, floral, lean and silky.

Alternative names: Chablis (a cool vineyard area in northern France), White Burgundy, Pinot Blanc and Pinot Chardonnay.

Body: Light to full-bodied.

Flavors: Many of the aromas and flavors are due to oak-aging and not the grape variety. Butter, vanilla, spice, and toast are the common descriptive words with top notes of apples, lemons, pears, white peaches, tropical fruits, tangerines, pineapples and honeysuckle.

Characteristics: Full-bodied versions of this wine are capable of immense complexity and finesse.

Where it's best: Burgundy, California, Australia and the Champagne region.

Food pairings: A good choice for fish and chicken dishes. Oysters and shellfish: the richness of Chardonnay plays well with lobster, crab and other fatty dishes. Hard and soft cheeses are also exceptional.

- RED WINE -

Viognier (Vye-own-YAY)

This classic French grape can be adapted easily to different styles of wine making. It's a fresher, aromatic and fuller drinkable version of a Chardonnay. It's on the rise and if you're into trends, this is the one.

Alternate names: Bergeron, Barbin, Rebolot, Greffou, Picotin Blanc, Vionnier, Petiti Vionnier, Viogne, Galopine and Vugava.

Body: Medium to full bodied.

Flavors: Violets, peach, apricot, apple, minerals, nutty with undertones of spice.

Characteristics: Fragrant, low in acid, dry with loads of fruit flavors.

Where it's best: France, northern Rhone and there are the notable wines coming out of Washington state, California and Australia.

Food pairings: Moroccan tagines, mild Indian curries, Caribbean dishes and Thai cuisines. Goes well with soft and semi-soft cheeses.

Pinot Noir (PEE-no nwahr)

A classic grape variety that is widely planted around the world. Arguably a grape with an extreme range of complexity, it is capable of the greatest heights. In the mouth (when purchasing a stella bottle) expect a velvety texture with lush and heady aromatics. Prized for its difficulty to grow and complex bouquet, it is rarely blended because it has no roughness.

Body: Light to medium, occasionally full.

Flavors: Cherries, red currents, cranberries, strawberries, blackberries, chocolate, forest floor, fresh mushrooms and herbs.

Characteristics: The structure can be delicate and fresh, crisp and lightly spicy. Tannins are very soft to make it seem well-rounded.

Where it's best: Wines of New Zealand have won many awards for this grape lately. Good examples can also be found out of California, Australia, South Africa and Burgundy.

Food pairings: Salmon, tuna, roast chicken, lamb, veal, Peking duck, smoky BBQ, Mediterranean and Vietnamese dishes.

Bordeaux (bor-DOE)

Not a grape but an area in France. The regional blend here is predominantly Cabernet Sauvignon, Merlot and Cabernet franc.

Merlot (Mair-LOE)

Easy to drink, it has a softness to it which makes it a good jumping board for new red wine drinkers. Smooth tannins and soft finishes are the characteristics of Merlot wine, which make it well suited to lighter foods. This is your go-to wine that can be easily adjusted to suit your environment. It's smoother than any of your boyfriends and can be enjoyed all night long with no talking back or complaining.

Alternative names: Petit Merle, Vitraille, Crabutet Noir and Bigney.

Body: Medium.

Flavors: Red berries, strawberries, blackberries, black cherries, plums and herbal flavor. Hints of cedar, tobacco, chocolate, toffee and fruitcake are well-noted flavors.

Characteristics: Spicy fruitcake, Christmas cake and chocolate characteristics often give Merlot away.

Where it's best: California is producing some of the best Merlots outside of Bordeaux.

Food pairings: French, Italian and Spanish foods. Roasts, hamburgers and other grilled meats.

Grenache (Gruh-NASH)

Alternative names: Garnacha (Spain).

Body: Medium to full.

Flavors: Raspberries, licorice, pepper, herbs and lavender flavors can be highlighted with a spicy finish.

Characteristics: Silky and voluptuous. Can be recognized by its weak colors, soft tannins, and high alcohol content.

Where it's best: Rhone Valley (France) and Spain.

Food pairings: All poultry, roasted meats, vegetarian, pizza, casseroles, stews and mac & cheese.

Cabernet Sauvignon (Ka-bur-nay So-vee-nyo(n)

This grape has traveled well from its spiritual home in Bordeaux to become a natural choice for the new winemakers of the world. Now cultivated in Australia, South Africa, North America and South America, Cabernet Sauvignon wines tend to have a high alcohol content and strong tannins which make it perfect to age in cellars for many decades.

Alternative names: Petit Cabernet, Sauvignon Rouge, Bouche, Bouchet and Vidure.

Body: Medium to heavy bodied with hard tannins.

Flavors: Vanilla, blackcurrants, blackberry, black pepper and green pepper. Top notes can develop into cedar, cigar boxes, violets, peppers, dark cherry, dried blackberries, and dried ginger with chocolate notes on the finish.

Characteristics: Young wines start off fruity with the more complex aromas developing with age. With age, they can be crisp and spicy, well-rounded on the palette and firmly structured with brooding intensity.

Where it's best: Bordeaux, Tuscany, Napa Valley, Sonoma Country and Australia.

Food pairings: Best with simply prepared red meat. Cream and butter sauces also work well too.

Shiraz / Syrah (Shi-raz or Sah-ra)

Born in the Rhone Valley, this is a late-ripening grape that thrives well in hotter climates such as Australia, South Africa, Chile and California.

Alternative names: Hermitage, Antourenein Noir, Candive, Entournerein, Hignin Noir and Marsanne Noir.

Body: Medium to full.

Flavors: This varietal produces wines with a broad range of flavor notes including blackberries, cassis, pepper, tar and coffee. Toffee notes, if present, come from the wine having rested in oak barrels. These are hearty, spicy reds.

Characteristics: This thick-skinned grape produces potentially tannic and long-lived wines. They are fleshy, powerfully flavored, hearty, full-bodied and sometimes spicy.

Where it's best: Northern Rhone Valley, South Australia (Barossa Valley, McLaren Vale, and Clare Valley) and California.

Food pairings: Grilled meats, pates, smoked foods, wild game, stews, charcuterie, Kobe/Wagyu beef. Shiraz excels with hard cheeses.

Sangiovese (san-joh-VAY-zeh)

The principal grape variety is used in Chianti, a wine blend of Tuscany, Italy. In a pure varietal form it has a floral, herbal and cherry aroma. This wine is typically aged in oak barrels and is often blended with other red wines to add body and color. Sangiovese wine is known for its high acidity, smooth texture and medium to high tannins.

To appreciate this wine entirely, best let it breathe by decanting.

Alternative names: Brunello, Sangioveto, Sangiovese Grosso, Sangiovese Piccolo

Body: Medium.

Flavors: Velvet undertones of strawberries, raspberries, spice, herbs, fresh mushrooms, meats and smoke. Known to be oaky and nutty. It has texture on the palette.

Characters: Strong acidy with medium to strong tannins.

Where it's best: Southern Italy and is very popular in California.

Food pairings: Roast turkey, hamburgers and Italian cuisine. If you want to impress your friends — fast food. A Sangiovese wine will cut through the greasiness.

- CHAMPAGNE -

The favorite quaffs of princesses, yacht owners and multi-estate owners the world over. No delightful event or occasion would be complete without a few pallets of this excellent stuff kicking around. Elegant and poised, please serve well chilled. Champagne loves sitting on ice to bring it to the right temperature and not stuck last minute in the freezer. This golden drop is one of the few wines that can be enjoyed any time of day and night and is impossible to drink without a smile on your face.

Champagne is not an actual grape but a style of wine making and is produced from a blend of grapes varietals grown in the Champagne region in northern France. The most successful combination is of Chardonnay, Pinot Noir and Pinot Meunier grapes.

The term champagne is a derivation of a French term for chalky soils, which makes up most of the terrain found in both champagne and cognac. To call it Champagne it needs to follow rules that demand secondary fermentation of the wine in the bottle to create carbonation (either by adding yeast or saturating the liquid with carbon dioxide.)

To pour champagne correctly:

1. Avoid shaking and tapping the bottle. This will excite the gas inside and make it difficult to open the bottle. Take the foil wrapper off and undo the metal cage keeping the cork in place. It will help grip the cork better. Ease the cork off by holding it and twisting the bottom of the bottle. The proper way to open the bottle is with a quiet shhh... not a loud pop!
2. Pour ¾ inch into each glass to prime it. Wait till the bubbling subsides and fill the glass to halfway. Champagne is to be savored and sipped unhurriedly, then regularly refilled. When refilling one's glass, pour champagne slowly and if possible tilt the glass and let the liquid slide in without the bottle touching the glass.

The size and behavior of the bubbles in the champagne glass is indicative of how the champagne got its fizz and therefore, also a good indicator of the quality of the wine. The finer and more consistent the bubbles are, the better quality. The bubbles in better quality champagnes tend to form a trail from the bottom of the glass to the surface. Lesser quality champagne bubbles tend to stick to the side of the glass. To gain a proper appreciation of the champagne bouquet, use Riedel Veritas champagne glasses. The larger bulb will enhance normal $50 champagnes to a taste in the $3000 mark.

Body: Firm with well-cut acidity, taut, dense, full and elegant. It's like a beautiful blond with a perfect bum. You can't stop yourself from going back for more.

Flavors: Fresh citrusy notes, green apples, pear, black currant, toasted almonds, honey, smoky minerals with top notes of white peach.

Characters: It's hard to describe a whole region of the finest champagnes. Some are delicate, crisp and tight. Others are complex, creamy and rich, well-rounded, pleasing on the pallet and still very drinkable when warm.

Where it's best: From the Champagne region in Northern France.

Food pairings: Caviar, poached eggs, smoked salmon, oysters, seasonal fruits and sorbets.

- ROSE WINE -

All rosés have this much in common: They start out as red grapes. The pigment in the skins is what gives red wines and rosé their complex colors. When making red wine, the skins are left to soak in contact with the grape juice for days or weeks, until the suitable color is achieved. If a winemaker wants to make a rosé, he has to separate the juice from the skins within a matter of hours.

Rosés from around the world:

Combining the light lively freshness of white wine with the fruit and depth of reds, a good rosé pairs well with a remarkable range of foods. It plays well with others and is very food friendly. It would not be too much to call this wine the tomato sauce of the wine world. When purchasing rosé, it's best to ask for a dry version. With rosé, the newest vintage is the freshest wine and most sought after. Best consumed as soon as you've parted with your cash so don't get any ideas about hoarding this wine in your cabin.

Body: Light.

Flavors: Grapefruit, strawberry, tart cherry, raspberry, wild strawberry, red bell pepper, blackberry and berry jam.

Characteristics: Fresh on the palate, slightly tart, with little or no oak to big fruity extracted gems.

Where it's best: South of France is your typical go-to place for the best of the best. Wines from here can be drunk all day, in the sun, in the pool till you go to bed, and you won't fall over drunk!

Food pairings: Begin drinking when you fire up the BBQ or stepping onto the yacht on a mildly hot day. It doesn't need food to be enjoyed.

DID YOU KNOW?
Rosé champagne is the only rosé created by adding red wine to white wine.

- DESSERT WINE -

Also referred to as pudding wines, these are sweet wines usually served with the dessert course. Presented in a feminine une verre dessert wines are meant to be sipped slowly, and treasured like a fine-aged scotch. Slow down and enjoy the texture and sensual pleasure in your mouth. Dessert wine is created by sweet wine grapes or grapes that have been left on the vine to shrivel, rot or freeze. In order to make this wine sweet, the fermentation is stopped before the yeast turns all the natural grape sugar into alcohol.

There are 5 types of desert wine:

1. Sparkling dessert wine (Moscato d'Asti, Asti Spumente, Sparkling Gewurztraminer)
2. Lightly sweet dessert wine (Gewurztraminer, Riesling)
3. Richly sweet dessert wine (Constantia, Muscat-based dessert wines, ice wine)
4. Sweet red wine (late harvest reds)
5. Fortified wine (PX, Rutherglen Muscut, Tawny Port, Fino Sherry).

Body: Heavy and full bodied. It's a real mouthful.
Flavors: Floral and aromatic. Honeysuckle, sweet sun-ripened berries and tropical fruits.
Characteristics: Plush, luscious and full bodied in the mouth. When drinking, it is impossible not to slow down and savor it like the last moments of a good holiday.
Where it's best: Germany, French and Hungary.
Food pairings: Desserts, bakery delights, fresh fruit and soft creamy new cheeses.

DID YOU KNOW

The difference between a proper wine connoisseurs and a phony?

A proper wine connoisseur will simply place the glass to their nose, smell it and nod yes or no. They will not taste the wine after it has been poured for tasting at the table. Instead he will wait for his date to be poured a glass as well and then drink.

This is because:

✓ You are not smelling the wine to see if you like it. You are smelling the wine to see if it's off/corked
✓ You have already CHOSEN the bottle and therefore cannot return it if you do not like it.

- Make Your Mouth Sing By Paring The Best Wines & Food -

Paring wine with food is an art & should be a pleasurable experience that can blow out to interesting full-length discussions

FOOD PARING RULES

1. Serve wine that is sweeter than the food
2. Serve local wines with local foods. They match
3. Soft wines are pared well with light palette foods
4. Generally heavy foods will need a more robust wine
5. If your guests love drinking chardonnay, chances are they prefer it with everything. Just give it to them!
6. Serve better wines before lesser ones after two to three glasses, your pallet's gone and will no longer taste the wine.

- Teach Yourself Wine Terminology Ten Minutes -

These are the proper terms used in the finest restaurants around the world. Learn the lingo and apply them to impress the crew, guests and your hot date in the Hamptons

Aerate: Exposing the wine to oxygen either through decanting or allowing the wine to breathe after removing the cork. It allows the off odors to blow away in older wines and to soften the aromas in younger ones.

Aperitif: A drink served before the meal, to get the digestive juices following. Examples are: Champagne, G&T's, Campari cocktails and martinis. Usually, only one or two of these drinks are consumed.

Balance: The different components in wine — alcohol, residual sugar, acid and tannins to make a well-finished wine. A well-balanced wine is a good indication of quality.

Barrel aged: Wine that is fermented in steel barrels and aged in oak barrels.

Barrel fermented: Wine that is fermented and aged in oak barrels to impose a deeper, richer impression.

Blend: Different grape varieties or the same grapes from different areas are blended together to form a unique wine.

Body: The impression that wine has in your mouth as you sip it. Wines are categorized into light, medium or full-bodied.

Bouquet: The distinctive aromas that one can smell and taste in wine. The more developed and complex aromas are said to be in mature and older wines.

Brut: A champagne or sparkling wine style that is very dry, as there little or no residual sugar.

Champagne: Only sparkling wines made in Champagne, France and are verified using the Méthode Champenoise winemaking process can be labeled Champagne.

Chateau: A wine produced from individual vineyards in the Bordeaux region in France.

Complex: The opposite of simple. A wine or aged spirit that makes your heart sing with happiness.

Corked: When the wine is off. The bottles have been left in the sun, are too old or have not been turned over. Wine that is corked smells like dirty socks, old mildew like your yucky ex-boyfriend's bedroom.

Crisp: Wine that is fresh, a little tart with the initial tasting. No aftertaste on the palette.

Decant: To transfer the wine from the bottle to a wine decanter. Decanters are glass, with a big base and a smaller neck opening. Decant old, fragile wines twenty-five minutes before serving. Younger, more robust wines may require up to two hours decanting before consuming. To err on the side of caution, forty minutes before serving is safe.

Estate: A property that grows grapes and makes wine from its own vineyards.

Fermentation: The process where yeasts converts sugars to alcohol.

Grand Cru: The best growths or specific vineyards in the region are recognized and labeled Grand Cru. It takes years to reach this status symbol, and one cannot give oneself that reputation.

Legs: After gently swirling the wine in the wine glass, look at the way the wine clings and falls on the inside of the glass. The slower the wine falls down, gelling to the side of the glass, creating a curtain effect and thicker legs, indicates a higher amount of alcohol in the wine.

Length: The sustained impression that wine creates when rolled across the tongue.

Oxidized: Having been spoilt by exposure to too much air. Wine left uncorked overnight will have this effect. The taste will be sharp on the minerals and feel tired across the pallet.

Premier Cru: A first growth picked for the season from the highest quality vineyard.

Proof: The measure of alcoholic content. 100 proof is fifty percent pure alcohol by volume.

Reserve: Apparently a higher quality than the vineyard's standard version of the wine.

Rosé: Is produced from red wine grapes.

Sommelier: A professional wine steward.

Sparkling wine: Refers to all other wines with bubbles that are not produced in the Champagne region in France.

Sulfur: Used in winemaking to restrain wild yeast and bacteria. Sulfur can be blamed for the worst hangovers.

Sweetness: Level of dryness.

Tannin: A substance that is found in the stems, skins and seeds of grape vines. Oak barrels can also impart tannins to give the wine definition. It helps with the structure, texture and age-ability of red wines.

Terroir: Is the environmental photograph that captures all the elements that mold the unique characteristic of a wine. Factors are taken into account (but are not limited to) such as: soil, climate, sunlight, latitude and longitude.

Vintage: The year in which the grapes were harvested.

Yeast: One-celled organisms responsible for turning fermented fruit into wine.

juice/ standard water

whiskey

brandy

shot

martini

cocktail

wine - varies in 'bowl' volume.

champagne

Lip

bowl

flute

stem

foot

- It's About Time. Making Trouser Dropping Cocktails -
Remember the rule:
Liquor before wine, you're in the clear. Wine before liquor and you're feeling queer

Etiquette is to ask guests if they prefer a particular brand of dark or white spirits. Hopefully their liquor choice will be listed on the preferences sheets so you can stockpile before the big trip. Always use a standard pour for consistency, unless they request otherwise.

STANDARD SHOT IS 30 mL or 1 US oz

Bellini
Fill ⅓ of a champagne glass with chilled peach puree or juice.
Fill to ½ inch from the top with your choice of champagne or sparkling wine.

Lazy Days (A personal favorite — it fixes all problems)
4 chunks watermelon
1 shot of peach schnapps
½ shot of lime juice
½ shot Monin coconut
Dash of egg white
- ✓ Crush watermelon with muddler in a metal shaker. Add ice and pour liquids over the top.
  Shake, strain and serve in a martini glass.
  Garnish with a thick slice of dragon fruit cut into a star shape using a cookie cutter.
  Alternatively, use a wedge of watermelon with an orchid tucked discreetly into it using a toothpick.
- ✓ Have the egg white ready to go in a clear, sterile kitchen-sauce squeeze bottle.

Bloody Mary
* Makes four. In a blender mix the following ingredients:
1 shot dry sherry
1 shot olive brine
1 shot pickle brine
3 tablespoons lemon or lime juice
3 teaspoon Worcestershire sauce
8 drops of hot sauce
3 teaspoon prepared horseradish
½ teaspoon pepper
½ teaspoon celery salt
¼ teaspoon old bay seasoning
2 to 3 stalks of celery without the leaves.
- ✓ Blend until pulpy. You want a nice thick consistency. (Mixture can be pre-made and will last a couple of days.)
- ✓ Add to blender:
4 shots of vodka
2 cups of chilled tomato juice.
Give it all a quick blitz to mix it in.
- ✓ Pour over ice in cocktail glasses and top up with tomato juice. Garnish each glass with a celery stalk with leaves on the end, crispy bacon slices, shrimps and a toothpick with olives lying across the glass. Add two straws and enjoy.

Bourbon Sour (traditional)
1 shot of bourbon
½ shot of lemon juice
Generous splash of simple sugar syrup

1 egg white

Bitters to garnish

- ✓ Fill a cocktail shaker halfway with ice. Add bourbon, egg white, lemon juice and simple syrup and shake vigorously for 10 to 15 seconds. Pour into a cocktail glass, float 3 drops of Bitters on the surface and serve.
- ✓ You could improve this cocktail by reducing your own sugar syrup flavored with vanilla beans, whole cloves, a cinnamon stick, 3 star anises and a hunky piece of fresh ginger.

Cosmopolitan

1 ½ shots of vodka

½ shot of Cointreau or orange liquor

1 shot of cranberry juice

Dash of lime juice

- ✓ Pour everything into a shaker filled with ice. Shake and strain into a chilled martini glass. To finish add burnt orange skin to the cocktail surface. See directions below.

Classic Gin Martini

2 ½ shots of gin (ask, some prefer vodka)

½ shot dry vermouth

1 or 3 olives or lemon twist for garnish

Orange or Angostura bitters (optional)

- ✓ Pour all ingredients into a mixing glass filled with ice cubes.
  Stir for 30 seconds
  Strain into a chilled cocktail glass
  Add a dash of orange or Angostura bitters, if desired.
  Garnish with the olives or lemon twist

Variations: Chill a martini glass by putting ice in, then tossing. Coat the inside of the glass with dry vermouth, swirl and flick out the excess liquor. Fill a shaker half way with ice, add 2 ½ shots of gin. Shake. Strain into the glass coated with dry vermouth. Garnish with olives on a toothpick.

- ✓ Dirty martinis are made by adding olive brine.
- ✓ A hip garnish is to take a long thin strip of lemon. Wrap it around a straw and hold in place with a toothpick in either end. Place in ice to make it hold its shape. Take toothpick and straws out, drop into glass to complete the cocktail.

Caipirinha

3 brown sugar cubes

1 lime cut into 6 wedges

2 shots of Cachaca white rum

Juice of half a lime or lemon

- ✓ Muddle limes and sugar together. Add 2 shots of Cachaca, lemon juice and ice cubes. Shake hard. Pour the whole blend into cocktail glass. Add a fresh lime wheel as garnish.

Dark and Stormy (A Bermuda and Caribbean favorite.)

- ✓ Pour dark rum over ice and top up with good quality ginger beer.

Espresso Martini

1 shot of vodka

½ shot Kahlua

Shot of espresso

- ✓ Pour all liquids over ice in the shaker. Cap and shake aggressively to create a satisfying foamy crème. Strain into chilled cocktail glass and garnish with 3 espresso beans.

Happy Days
⅓ shot of Monin apple
1 ½ shots of vodka
⅓ shot Cointreau
Generous splash of lime juice
2 shots cranberry juice
✓ Shake and serve in a chilled martini glass.
  Garnish with a fresh orchid or a short straw stuck to the outside
  of the glass (use soda water)

Adios MOF (The perfect way to drink up the leftover charter guest alcohol)
1 shot Aperol (or whatever you have most of on hand)
½ shot Pama pomegranate liquor
1 shot blood orange juice
1 shot lemon juice
½ shot sugar syrup
Dash of egg white
✓ Shake and strain into a chilled martini glass
✓ If you're in for a party, top the glass up with Champagne.

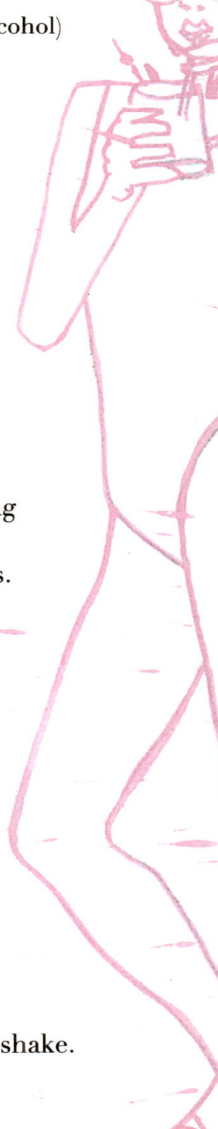

Panty Dropper (one for the ladies)
½ shot Midori melon
½ shot coconut rum
Pineapple juice
✓ Pour all ingredients into a cocktail glass topped with ice.
  Float coconut milk on top using the back of a spoon touching
  the inside of the glass.
  Garnish with a pineapple wedge, pineapple leaf and cherries.

Kir Royal
Pour a splash of Crème de cassis into the bottom of a
champagne glass.
Tilt the glass and fill it with champagne or sparkling wine
Drop in a maraschino cherry for decoration.

I Lost My Bikinis on M/Y Bad Girl
1 scoop mango sorbet
1 shot Pama pomegranate liqueur
1 shot Havana club rum
1 shot coconut flavored rum
1 shot pineapple juice
3 drop peach bitters
✓ Muddle all ingredients in shaker. Add ice and give it a good shake.
  Pour into a chilled martini glass.

Layover in Singapore
1 shot of vodka
½ shot St. Germain
1 large slice of fresh pear
2 lemon wedges
2 pieces of fresh jackfruit
Splash of simple sugar syrup
✓ Muddle and shake with ice.
  Garnish with a piece of jackfruit and a pineapple leaf on a designer skewer.

Long Island Iced Tea

(An easy way to remember; it's 5 white spirits)

1 shot of each of the following; vodka, gin, white rum, tequila and triple sec

1 shot of sweet and sour mix (if not on hand add more coke and lime juice)

✓ In a shaker full of ice add all the above liquids. Shake until you feel the ice cubes slightly melt. Strain into a tall highball glass filled with fresh ice. Top with coke. Garnish with an orange and lime wheel or fresh orchids.

Margarita

Run a slice of lime around the rim of your margarita glass.

Dip rim of margarita glass in salt.

In a cocktail shaker add ice then pour the following on top:

1 ½ shots of tequila

½ shot triple sec

½ shot of lime or lemon juice

Add sugar syrup to taste

✓ Shake and stain into glass

Variation: In a cocktail shaker add ice,

1 ½ shots of tequila

1 ½ shots of sour mix

✓ Shake and strain into glass

*Sour Mix

3 cups of water

3 cups of sugar

2 cups fresh lemon juice

2 cups fresh lime juice

✓ Combine water and sugar in a large saucepan. Stir over medium heat until sugar dissolves. Bring to the boil, cool syrup. Mix syrup, lemon and lime juice in a pitcher. Chill until cold. Will keep for one week.

Mimosa

Half fill a glass with chilled orange juice and fill to the top with Champagne or sparkling wine of your choice.

Man Mosa

Champagne

Orange juice

Mandarin vodka

✓ Pour according to the severity of hangover. Mix with a delicate hand.

Mint Julep

3 shots of bourbon

1 white sugar cube

A hand full of mint leaves (6-10 leaves)

4 drops of bitters

Splash of club soda

✓ Muddle the mint and sugar in the shaker, then add bourbon and bitters. Fill to the top with ice cubes and shake hard.

Strain into a new glass filled with new ice. Top up the drink with club soda.
Garnish with a sprig of fresh mint.

Mojito

1 ½ shots of white rum

½ club soda (or try tonic for a refreshing alternative)

✓ In the bottom of the cocktail shaker add:

10 fresh mint leaves

½ lime, cut into 4 wedges lengthwise

2 tablespoons of white sugar or to taste

✓ Use a muddler to crush mint and lime, releasing the aromas. Add ice and pour rum over the top. Shake and pour into a glass (not straining) and top up with club soda
Garnish with lime wheel and cocktail straw.

Variation: Monday Morning Mojito

1 ½ shot spiced rum

⅔ shot of vanilla and cinnamon syrup

1 handful of mint – slightly crushed in the bottom of the shaker.

1 shot of lime juice

1 shot ginger beer

✓ Make the same way as a normal mojito and top up with ginger beer instead of the soda water.

Negroni

½ shot of gin

½ shot of sweet vermouth

½ shot Campari

✓ Pour liquors over ice in an old fashioned glass. Stir with a cocktail spoon until drink has chilled. Top with fresh ice if necessary. Mist with burnt orange peel over the surface of the cocktail.

Next Level

1 ½ shot of Rum

¾ of a shot of St. Germain liqueur

½ shot of pineapple juice

½ shot of lime juice

Crème de Violette to float

✓ Place all liquids in the shaker except Crème de Violette. Give it a good shake and strain into a chilled martini glass. Float Crème de Violette and garnish with an orchid.

Piña Colada

1 ½ shots of coconut cream such a Coco Lopez

2 shots pineapple juice

1 shot of rum – white, dark or coconut rum.

Splash of sugar syrup

1 cup of ice

✓ Blend all ingredients in the blender to form a nice slushy consistency. Pour into the most lavish cocktail glass you can find.
Grate nutmeg on top
Slice a pineapple wedge, tooth pick an orchid in it and slit into the rim of the glass
Drop a maraschino cherry with stem next to it
Add two straws, one slightly bent and serve on a crisp starched white napkin.

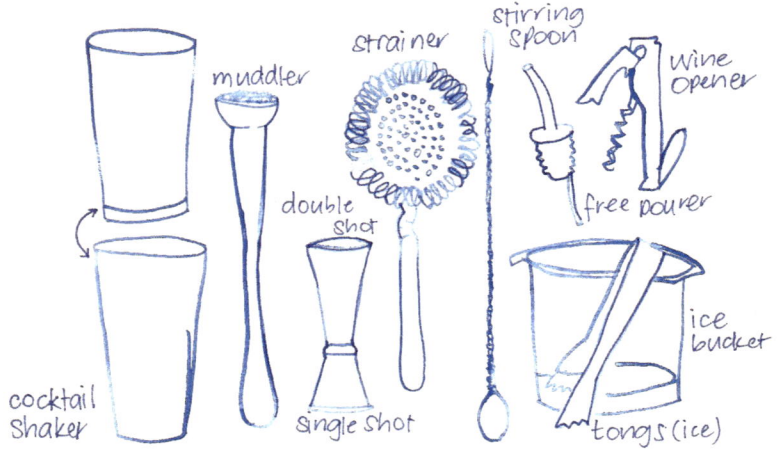

muddler
strainer
stirring spoon
wine opener
double shot
free pourer
cocktail shaker
single shot
ice bucket
tongs (ice)

Player with a Passport

1 shot vanilla vodka
½ shot Kahlua
½ shot Mozart Black
1 shot espresso
⅓ shot of White Chocolate Monin
✓ Shake and serve into a chilled martini glass.

Sea Breeze

2 shots of vodka poured over ice
✓ Top the glass up half way with cranberry juice
Fill the remainder of the glass with grapefruit juice
Garnish with a lime ring and cherry.

Screw Driver

2 shots of vodka poured over ice. Topped up with orange juice.

Variations: add a cream floater and grated nutmeg.

Sex on the Beach

1 shot of vodka
½ shot of peach schnapps
1 shot of orange juice
1 shot of cranberry juice
¼ shot of Chambord or Crème De Cassis (optional)
✓ Add all ingredients to a shaker filled with ice. Shake and strain into a highball glass filled
with fresh ice. Garnish with an orange wheel.

Sundowner

Handful of mint leaves
1 shot rum
⅔ shot sour rhubarb liqueur
2 shots of guava juice
Splash of vanilla and cinnamon sugar syrup
✓ Clap mint to release aromas and place into a shaker. Add ice to shaker and all liquids
Shake hard until the ice cubes lose their crispness.
Strain into a short fat whiskey/cocktail glass filled with ice
Garnish with 1 maraschino cherry.

- Cocktail Garnishes Education 101 -

Citrus Fruit

Burnt zest: by far the easiest way to take a drink to the next level. Peel a slice off about the size of your thumb. Place zest over drinks and squeeze in half, so that the oils spritz all over your drink. At the same time, light the oils on fire with a lighter. Rub peel on glass rim before dropping into the cocktail.

Grated zest: lime zest is fabulous for the aroma on top of Caribbean cocktails. In the spring/autumn, grate orange peel on top of chocolate-based drinks.

Lemon & Lime wheels: slice eight mm wheels thick, slit in and place on the rim of the glass. Spruce up this garnish by tooth-picking orchids; pineapple leaves and tiny figurines on the wheel.

Lemon wedges: are outdated on the rim of the glass. Only really cheap cafeterias do this. Avoid. When using wedges in beverages, remove the white pith and seeds.

Spirals: Use a peeler with round holes to take off the skin, not touching the pith. Place in the glass before adding ice.

Fruits

Strawberries: slice in half, put a slit in the half and place on the rim of glasses when serving cocktails, pink fruity drinks and sangrias.

Blueberries: smash blueberries in the bottom of glasses for decoration when doing fruity cocktails.

Maraschino cherries: yes, they've been around for ages but who doesn't like eating them? They instantly say holiday! Drop on the top of whip cream cocktails and in the bottom of whiskey based drinks.

Star fruit: slice into wheels and then dip into white chocolate. After they have cooled, put a slit in it and put on the rim of the glass.

Pineapple: cut pineapple into wedges, leaving the skin on. Decoratively place on the rim of the glass. Pineapple wedges are a good base for tooth-picking other fruits onto and then balancing on the glass rim.

From the panty cupboard

Cinnamon & Nutmeg: sprinkle onto to creamy based drinks but for something different try it on fruity iced teas.

Olives: the good old favorite. Use the brine for bloody Marys, dirty martinis and just a touch in aperitifs. Spear olives three apiece on a toothpick when dropping in a cocktail.

Jupiter berries, star anise and pink peppercorns: amazeballs for taking white-based spirits to another level.

From the chef's fridge

Sprigs of Lavender: peel the flowers off the stem, leaving only an inch of flowers on the end. Pop into G&Ts, vodka, white chocolate-based drinks, iced teas…everything. Lavender is pretty and classed as an antipsychotic. Perfect for uptight guests.

Basil leaves: One, two leaves are perfect for garnish in the bottom of fruity drinks.

Cucumber: we're no longer doing wheels. Slice horizontally with a peeler, so the slice is not thicker than three mm. Curve around a massive red wine glass, adding ice afterwards. Float a few star anise and pink peppercorns on top to make it killer.

Mint leaves: Smack the leaves in-between your palms beforehand to release the aromas. Mint plays well with sugary white-spirit based drinks.

Celery: a must for bloody Marys. It's a bit strange in anything else.

We're different!

- ✓ Fresh orchids and miniature edible flowers frozen in designer ice-cube makers
- ✓ Dried rose buds & cucumber long slivers in G&Ts
- ✓ Strawberry quarters & basil leaves in aromatic cocktails
- ✓ Sprigs of thyme & lemon wheels in vodka based drinks.

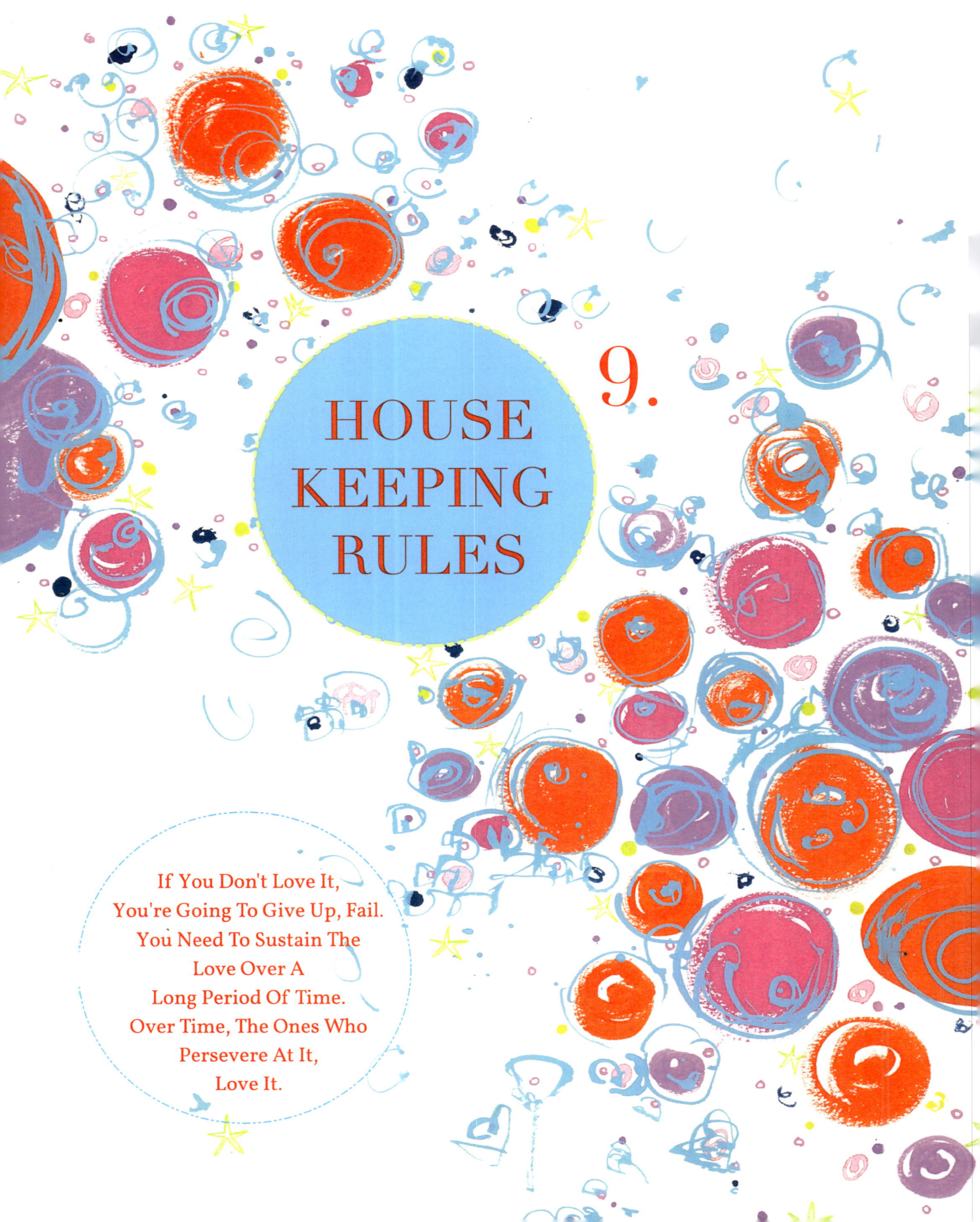

9.

HOUSE KEEPING RULES

If You Don't Love It,
You're Going To Give Up, Fail.
You Need To Sustain The
Love Over A
Long Period Of Time.
Over Time, The Ones Who
Persevere At It,
Love It.

Every Object
Has A Place On
The Yacht

- How To Reach Eternal Perfection In Cleanliness -

The secret to the domestic science of detailing yachts and estates to showroom perfection is ensuring all surfaces are fairy tale shiny and clean. Every single item, soft furnishing, floor covering and finish must look like it's brand new, just unwrapped and seriously expensive. You'll know the feeling when you back out of the room and your soul is basking in the glory of perfection. It'll take your breath away with the brilliance of it all! The goalposts in this job are to leave no surface, crack or light fitting untouched.

It is expected that you'll have a solution for every housekeeping crisis or have people on speed dial who can solve it for you. There is now no water damage, children playing unsupervised or drunken escapade that you cannot fix. Get ready for it: M&Ms smashed into ancient priceless tapestries, fried chicken handprints on the Dolce & Gabbana light blue suede chairs, trailing blood stains on the newly-installed three-inch thick, white wool carpets and the, "what is that? Is that cum stains on the ceiling?" My gosh darling, you're going to see and smell it all.

At the beginning of your career, it is smart to develop a systematic procedure for completing jobs. At the end of the season the methodical habit of continuous handling luxurious finishes will see you fit to handle any end-of-the-world crisis that will arise. This is a results-driven industry dealing with obsessive billionaires. The quicker they see results, the quicker we all have time for a well-earned cup of tea.

- Professional Cleaning Caddies -
Your carryall for all the cleaning products your heart desires

At the start of every new cleaning quest pack your cleaning caddy station with everything you could ever desire:

- ✓ Microfiber clothes
- ✓ Clean white rags (old T-shirts are perfect)
- ✓ Vinegar and water — 3:1 in a clean spray bottle
- ✓ Rubbing alcohol in a spray bottle — for the windows and glass
- ✓ Disinfectant spray (or antibacterial wipes)
- ✓ Ivory soap and water in a spray bottle — not just any soap will do. Normal soap leaves an oily residue
- ✓ Wood cleaner/polish
- ✓ Disposable gloves
- ✓ Handheld swiffer pads
- ✓ Cotton buds
- ✓ Toothbrush
- ✓ Toothpicks
- ✓ Mini speakers to get into the groove.

Set up your station by placing a drop cloth (piece of cloth, old tea towel, etc.) under the cleaning caddy at all times. This is to protect the surface on which you're placing your caddy from any spillage and leaks. Stains caused by cleaning products are a nightmare to fix, as they're either oil or acid based. Don't worry if you get lazy doing this and can't be bothered. One tiny spill of a product on a reactive surface equals massive panic, and could cost you $20,000 to fix. After one spill, you will be bothered.

- Detailing A Yacht That Has Just Come Out Of The Shipyard/Owners Trip/Storage -
It's your first day working and the captain expects miracles

1. Start with the master cabin, following onto the VIPs and other cabins. Getting the cabins done first shows the captain/HOD what you are capable of accomplishing in set time periods.
    Once each cabin is brought up to immaculate show room finish, close the door and don't go in there again except to give it a dust/vac. Other areas such as the saloon and bridge will still have heavy foot traffic and are most likely being used as storage areas. Do these last to avoid cleaning it over and over again

2. We always work from the ceiling to floor down

3. Wipe down all surfaces beginning with the ceiling. Do this first, so you are not stepping on the bed or touching the walls afterwards

4. After the ceiling, wipe all surfaces — walls, tables, chairs, everything — in a clockwise direction. Be consistent — do not jump from one area to another

5. Pull everything out of cupboards, dust and clean all objects. Open everything up, wipe and re-arrange in a methodical manner. Replace all objects in cabinets in the most anal, OCD way you can imagine. Color code all objects and line up all corners

6. Check the state of the owner's clothing. Wash/iron/steam all clothing as needed. Hang all garments in color order. Do the same for their shoes

7. Make the bed the same day as detailing the room. It's a good thing to show your superiors that the room has been completed and there is no need to go back. Yes! The linen can sit on the bed for up to a month before it needs to be changed or freshened up

8. Complete a SMUDGE TEST. Walk around the room and look at the surfaces from different angles of a guest perspective, sun angles and lighting. Wipe off

9. Complete each room by wiping floors in ensuite bathroom and detailing all corners with ear buds

10. After guest cabins move on to the salon, main dining room, the bar, the sundecks, guest hallways and elevators. Then, behind the scenes: main pantry, accommodation deck pantry, galley and pantry. Dry store and crew mess. Then, crew corridors need a good detailing, then laundry and storage areas. When you've finished this, start from the beginning again!

- I Want to Sleep In That Bed -

1.   All bed linens should be perfectly pressed and starched. Fold sheets minimally to avoid unnecessary creases

2.   Begin making the bed. Start with a fitted sheet, pulling the sheet as tight as you can around the bed. Spray lightly with water or iron to remove wrinkles

3.   Iron pillowcases now on the flat sheet to remove creases. Hang on the back of a chair

4.   Place top sheet on, evenly on both sides of the bed. Either bring the top of the sheet to be in line with the top of mattress or bring it past the top of the bed with an excess thirty - forty cm, to be folded over the duvet, once the duvet is in place. Again, spray lightly with water or iron to remove wrinkles

5.   On top of the top sheet, put the woolen blanket on, to the equal height as the top sheet. Tuck both the top sheet and the woolen blanket in (leaving the top section of the bed), underneath the bed with sharp hospital corners and no creases. You do this before the duvet, to avoid the sides under the mattress becoming too chunky. If there are any creases here, they will show through the duvet.

6.   Put the duvet evenly on the bed, forty - fifty cm from the top of the mattress. Fold over the top sheet and wool blanket over the top of the duvet, if you left excess. Tuck it in with razor sharp corners. Again mist with water/iron to remove wrinkles

7.   Put pillows in the well-starched pillowcases. Make sure the corners of the pillows go into the corners of the pillowcases and seams of the pillow and cases both line up. Smooth out creases in pillows towards the edges, so they are not visible through the pillowcase. Place pillows on the bed - upright for daytime use - with colorful cushions and white guest pillows towards the back of the pile. Straighten up any floppy corners

8.   Check your work, specifically wrinkles. Smooth them out by pushing the fabric towards the edges of the bed. Make sure the pillows and cushions line up with the middle of the headboard. All the duvet piping must be even as well

9.   Put fur/feather/cashmere throw on the bed in a creative design

   ✓ Avoid roses or any flowers as decoration on the bed. Yes, the intoxicated lovers you are making the bed for will immediately take the fresh flowers on the bed as an explicit invitation to make love. Squishing and staining the petals into the custom-made Italian sheets.

- Exceptional Turn-downs For High Profile Celebrities -

Guest cabin evening protocol

Turndowns is a hospitality term that refers to the practice of readying a guest's room for sleeping. The vacated cabin is cleaned and refreshed, blinds are pulled down, late night snacks and water is presented and the bed is prepared for sleeping. Let's begin!

1. Clean cabins as per morning routine
2. Replace linens and towels as needed. If there is a stain, it's wet or looks used, send it down to laundry
3. Strip bed neatly of daybed cover, decorative cushions and throws
4. Turn down one corner of top sheet & duvet to form a triangle on the bed. Iron down for a perfect crisp and neat fold line. Tuck excess flap of the fold under the mattress
5. Pull tight the duvet and sheets. Spray and iron wrinkles out if need be. Position the four sleeping pillows, so they are lying flat. Line up the center ends of the pillows with the center of the bed head
6. Position turndown cards and chocolates in the middle of the triangle fold down on the bed or on the bedside tables. If your current charter guests are the sloppy trust-fund babies kind that can't be trusted, do not leave chocolates in the cabin. Place turndown chocolates in a bowl, at the base of the stairs where guests can help themselves on the way to bed
7. The turndown tray, which is placed on the bedside table or desktop, is to have a filled water jug and water glasses, with doilies underneath
8. Put covers on portholes or close blinds and curtains. Shut out all the sunlight
9. Check cabin fridge and replace what is needed
10. Lightly spray pillows with Nighty Night or an alternative aromatherapy mist that induces sleep
11. Finish by dimming lights or turning on nightstand lights.

- Do You Really Know How To Give Good Head? -

This is a minor, yet thankless part of the job. Listen, no one grew up thinking they would be doing this for a living. Let's get in there and be quick smart.

1. Plastic gloves on first. Protect your dignity. Just because you are well to do, does not mean you have good toilet etiquette
2. Check toilet – lift up the lid, seat and stuff. Wipe down all surfaces with a disinfected wet cloth
3. Give the inside of the toilet bowl a quick scrub with a biodegradable cleaner because we prefer not to kill the wildlife with our chemicals
4. Check toilet seat hinges — on top and underneath — for grime buildup. Give it a quick go around with ear buds
5. Replace toilet paper if more than two-thirds have been used. Do a decorative fold in the toilet paper to let the whole world know you serviced this toilet
6. Wipe down the sink and surrounding surface with disinfectant spray. Move all toiletries and clean underneath
7. Wipe down the outside of all toiletries. Put all toiletry products back where you found them with all labels facing out. All pump bottles should be facing the same way too
8. Check the inside of all cupboards and drawers. Make sure that everything is neat, tidy and lined up
9. Wipe down mirrors with alcohol
10. Wipe down all walls, checking for fingerprints and smudges
11. Replace hand towels if needed or top up paper hand towels

12. Empty bin
13. Wipe down the floor as you are backing out the door
14. Bask in the glow of your achievement in such a short period.

THE SCIENCE OF YACHT FINISHES

- Make That Wood Shine -
Wood, it's everywhere and not so easy to please

No matter how much taste the owner has, all yachts will be finished in a type of wood. Varnished, lacquered, hot pressed, bare or fake, there's a whole spectrum of timber finishes out there. To begin cleaning wood, avoid any products with abrasive grit or solids containing beeswax. You'll end up spending days buffing this mistake out.

Options for cleaning wood

1. Always begin with hot water and soap. Use water as hot as you can stand, wearing thick plastic kitchen gloves. Add 2 – 3 drops of Ivory soap. Normal dishwashing soap is too harsh, and baby soap does not cut through the grime. Using a white cloth — colored cloths will bleed in hot water - dip, wring and wipe over surface. If the water is not hot enough, it will not evaporate and will leave smudges
2. Murphy's soap. Follow directions on the bottle. Do not let this product sit and dry. Buff out as soon as you spray it on
3. Pledge multi-surface. Use this stuff on everything from wood, marble and glass for a streak free finish. Quick, easy, with no residue that needs buffing
4. Vinegar and water — ratio 1:20. Spray on and buff out with a microfiber cloth.

How to remove white marks from a varnished surface

Placing hot plates and cups on varnished surface creates white ring marks, which look like the end of your career. It is not uncommon to freak out as a re-varnishing job for three square meters, can cost upwards of $10,000 bucks.
To save your career and banish these white marks from your life:

1. Fold a clean white cotton napkin (serviette) into four — you want several layers between the varnish and the iron — and moisten down with fresh, clean, water over the white mark
2. Run the steam iron over the white mark and cotton napkin on a medium heat setting
3. Hold for approximately fifteen seconds and keep checking to see if the mark has lifted
4. Resist the urge to turn up heat up higher on the iron
5. Repeat until the white stain disappears.

How to remove permanent marker from stained wood

1. Apply a dab of non-gel toothpaste to the permanent marker stain
2. Scrub it hard with Dude-I-hate-my-life-can-I-marry-for-money-already elbow grease and microfiber cloth.

Clean wooden kitchen doors with a buildup of grime

Mix 1 part vegetable oil & 2 parts baking soda

1. Place towels below the working surface to catch any spills
2. Apply paste with a toothbrush and work in
3. Keep re-applying paste till surface comes up clean
4. Wipe down with warm water
5. Apply your chosen wood polish.

How to remove scratches out of wood

Option 1

Take one shelled walnut and rub it on the scratch. Keep going until the scratch disappears. Make sure you only stay on the scratch as the walnut is quite oily and it will show up if you get messy.

Option 2

½ cup of olive oil

½ cup of white vinegar

Mix two ingredients together and apply to scratched-up surface with a white cotton cloth. Rub until the whole surface is uniform.

- Cleaning And Polishing Metals -

The professional product and cleaning guide for handling fine metals

If you're new, you must ask! Metal on boats and luxury estates is very fine, temperamental and highly reactive to random chemicals. There is no room for trial and error. DO NOT use ANY deck/exterior products on the interior — they WILL scratch the surface, and it will be impossible to bring it back to the original finish without consulting experts. Before using any products, first establish if the metal is plated or solid metal. Plated metals easily rub off, revealing the base metal underneath. This can only be rectified by re-plating again by a well-known expert who is always hard to find in a different city, and very expensive!

Silver cutlery & antiques

To tell the difference between silver-plated and solid silver look for markings stamped into the item. Silver-plated items will not have any markings to be found and will be light in weight. They usually have a mark saying EP (electroplated) or ESPN (electroplated nickel silver.) Solid sterling silver will be substantially heavier and will show a minimum of three stamps/marks on the bottom or inside of the object.

Silver is the first metal to tarnish, easily turning black. It is always recommended to polish by hand and not dip silver in silver cleaning solutions. The solution eats away at the silver and you have no control of how the metal will react. Over time this will eat into your metal object, thereby reducing its quality and value.

Standard markings on silver

925 — The object is sterling silver which means it has 92.5 of silver metal in it.

Makers Mark — Tiny stamp that indicates who made it.

Assay Mark — Stamp of the country of origin with the amount of silver in the object.

Plat or Platinum — which means the piece is not to be confused with silver, it is platinum. This metal is worth more than gold.

Even if you have handled silver and fine metals before, you must do a spot test in an inconspicuous area with your chosen polishing product. Before beginning:

1. Cover the whole surface on which you are working with towels
2. Always wear plastic gloves when polishing. The harsh chemicals you are using are meant to strip metal, ruin manicures and eat away at the skin on your hands
3. To begin polishing cutlery and antiques, keep the silver organized all the way through. Handle each

object one by one. Grabbing and dumping fine metals together will finely scratch the surface, which you then have to polish out as well

4. Polish the silver hard, to warm up the metal and remove the fine scratches
5. Use old clothes, soft jewelry brushes, toothpicks, and ear buds for hard to reach nooks
6. After polishing, always handle silver with white gloves. The chemical and sweat on your hands excites the metal to begin tarnishing again
7. Recommended products: Red Brasso first to remove large scratches. This solution works like very fine sand paper
8. Finish with Blue Silvo, it has a finer degree of grit and will give your silver the greatest shine
9. To do the last buff on the metal use soft flannel cloths.

For badly tarnished silver cutlery (Thanks to Mr. Peter Vogel from IYS for this! He is AMAZING)
The best way to remove tarnish from in-between silver fork sprogs:

1. Line a large baking dish/pan with aluminum foil, shiny side down
2. Place a layer of salt (approx. one kg to one liter of water) and the juice of one lemon
3. Place cutlery (not touching each other) on top of the salt
4. Add boiling water to the salt and cutlery. Put a lid on the pan, to keep the steam in
5. Steam bath your cutlery for approximately thirty seconds to see results.

Handling silver cutlery during meal service
1. Take each piece of cutlery, one by one, out of its custom made velvet slot, using white cotton gloves
2. Sit cutlery on a tray lined with a white service cloth
3. Do not bunch the cutlery together — avoid them touching each other
4. Once finished with each course, take the cutlery away on a plate
5. Once in the pantry, place the silver cutlery all together in a container (lunch box containers are perfect). At all costs avoid the cutlery sitting in ANY water. Sitting silver cutlery in hot soapy water speeds up the tarnishing process
6. At the end of service pick up each piece of cutlery one by one. Clean using a soft sponge dipped in hot soapy water and then rinse off
7. Dry immediately using flannelette cotton cloths
8. With your white cotton gloves on, place cutlery back in the drawer.
✓ **Never ever put silver cutlery in the dishwasher!!**

How to treat interior stainless steel with a shiny or matt finish
✓ These products are easy to use and do not leave smudges or streaks
✓ Pledge multi-surface (my go-to short-cut shit)
✓ Cinch multi-surface cleaner (harder to find and expensive but man it's good)
✓ Half vinegar, half window cleaner solution — Windex is magic for a streak free finish
✓ Pure rubbing alcohol
✓ Vinegar and water in ratio 1:3 for hard to remove surface tarnishing. Soak a cloth in the solution and sit it on the metal for ten minutes. Buff it out afterwards
✓ Flitz will remove any tarnishing that the above products cannot remove. Use only as your last resort. This is a abrasive paste and you need to apply a silicon coat — such as insulator wax — afterwards. This stops the metal from being porous and tarnishing again.

Method:
Mist product onto cloth, wipe onto surface and buff out with a microfiber cloth. If product does not work, change cleaning products and trail application with paper towels.

Dealing with gold-plated fixtures and gel coat gold metal

No matter how badly tarnished the gold may have become NEVER USE ANY PRODUCTS ON GOLD PLATE. Chemicals will strip away the gold finish, stripping it back to the bare metal underneath. The only way to treat gold work is to wipe it with a wet chamois and then buff out the watermarks with a soft dry cloth. If you're desperate to get the accumulated green tarnishing out of gold plated fixtures, try this:

1. Mix 1:3 parts water to vinegar in a clean container
2. Apply solution to fixture using a soft cloth soaked in the mixture
3. Leave it sitting in or draped over gold fixture for fifteen minutes
4. Gently wipe around fixture to remove tarnish, no scrubbing!
5. Rinse with clean water and repeat if necessary.

If it has become obviously terrible, call in professionals to re-plate the gold.

Brass

Determine whether the item is solid brass, brass plated steel, zinc or cast iron. Plated brass fixtures are to be cleaned with hot soapy water. Anything stronger than soap and water with aggressive polishing will remove the brass finish.

These products have been tried and tested on <u>solid brass fixtures</u>:

1. Tomato Sauce (Ketchup)
2. Brasso
3. Never Dull
4. Flitz

Method

Strictly follow manufacturer's directions. Test in an inconspicuous spot first. If soft cloths are not working, try giving it a scrub with a very soft toothbrush. Do not rub too hard, as brass is very soft and you will start lifting up layers. You just want to remove the accumulated tarnish.

<u>- Caring For Bouchy Finishes On Yachts -</u>
Stupidesses turning tricks!

* Bouchy – when something is really filthy or obscene.

Suede ceilings & walls

At one stage in the interior decorating world, suede was a benchmark in luxury yachting standards. Designers and owners were eager participants, putting the stuff everywhere, much to the dismay of anyone having to clean it. If your yacht has not seen a major refit in a while, suede starts to age and looks dated with watermarks, discoloring and the dirt it attracts, much like a hooker who never gave up men, drinking or cigarettes. Your job is to tighten it up, make it over and bring it back to life with our following tricks.

First trick

Take a paper towel roll and run the whole roll (still intact) across the ceiling. The paper towel roll should rid the surface of fingerprints and pick up excess dirt. Repeat, running the roll in one direction, in line with the ceiling edge and panels. Failure to be consistent in running the roll across the ceiling in a straight line will make the suede ceiling look even worse than it was.

For fingerprints, dirt and watermarks that cannot be removed with the paper towel roll technique, try this:

Fill a bucket with water as hot as you can stand it. Add 2-3 drops of Ivory dishwashing soap — too much and you have to lift the soap out of the material.

1. Put on heavy-duty kitchen gloves to protect those delicate hands
2. Use a clean WHITE cloth dipped into water and squeeze out the excess
3. Roll up the cloth and wipe over the suede walls in one direction
4. Because you've added moisture to the suede, it may seem a little loose/saggy. As it dries, the suede will tighten up and rid itself of the sagginess. Let the suede dry overnight in a room with all moisture removed from the air
5. This trick also works well for removing salt stains in the material that have appeared from leaky overheads.

The humidity causes this synthetic fabric to sag. All moisture from the air needs to be removed for the material to tighten up again. Place the dehumidifier machine in the room and keep it running all night. Be sure to empty the water catchment container regularly as dehumidifiers turn off when full.

If the fabric keeps on sagging the only option then is to replace the ancient suede with faux leather, stretched and glued over thin board and stapled into place to prevent it sagging again.

Cleaning micro-fiber couches & walls

1. Spray couch/walls with pure alcohol from a clean spray bottle
2. Using a clean white sponge rub the area till the white sponge comes up dirty
3. Rinse the sponge out in clean, fresh water
4. Repeat until the stain is removed
5. When dry, use a clean white kitchen brush, lightly brushing against the couch surface to soften the micro-fibre bristles.

How to clean uber glamorous white walls

1. Use a magic eraser dipped in water to remove scuffmarks, dirty fingerprints and stains
2. Wipe the wall down afterwards with the hottest water you can stand with 2-3 drops of Ivory dishwashing soap
3. Wipe the whole surface in one direction using a clean white nappy cloth
4. Wait until the surface dries to check for streaks. If they appear, re-wipe again with hot water and soap and buff out straight away with a clean, soft cloth
√ Alternatively use vinegar and water. Spray onto a cloth, wipe on and buff off straight away with a microfiber cloth. If the wall is dirty, best go with the hot water method.

How to treat gold foil/leaf walls

If it is real gold leaf, the surface will be coated with a thin clear varnish. Use little to no cleaning techniques on this surface. Should the gold foil come off from rubbing with a cloth or an abrasive cleaner, then the whole wall or coated finish needs to be sanded back and replaced. Treat this surface like baby skin and only let a soft Swiffer duster touch it. If a major accident arises, such as old horny, charter guests coated in suntan lotion banging hookers naked against the wall, you'll need to think of alternatives instead of calling in expert cleaners, as this will eat into the APA money, greatly reducing your tip. Clean the surface with the mildest, organic baby soap and water. Refrain from spraying vinegar and water onto this surface. Vinegar is an acid and will eat away at the gold.

How to remove scuffmarks and accidents from colored walls

Start with less abrasive solutions and work your way up to harder ones:

1. Always try water and a white microfiber cloth first
2. Rub the marks with a rubber eraser. This works well on paint and varnish finishes

3. Tooth paste on a toothbrush — use a non-gel variety, it's the baking soda mineral working
4. Magic eraser
5. 'Goo Off' when nothing else is working and then use a magic eraser to get the oil residue out.

How to remove blood from textile finishes

Surprise! Betcha didn't see this one coming! The easiest way to remove blood from textiles — if it's a material and it moves, it's a textile — is hydrogen peroxide, a highly diluted form of bleach. Purchase the 3% solution that is sold as a mild antiseptic from any drug store, general merchandise or paint store. Buy in bulk. Medical grade hydrogen peroxide is safe to use on synthetic, protein and plant-based fibers.

To use:

(As with any product that you are using for the first time, do a patch test in an inconspicuous area.) Apply the liquid to the bloodstain and lightly scrub the surface with a toothbrush to loosen the fibers. Let the hydrogen peroxide sit on the stain and bubble up. If the bloodstain is fresh, the blood will disappear. If not, repeat until the stain disappears and wipe out the hydrogen peroxide with cold fresh water afterwards.

EXPENSIVE SURFACES

- The Quickest Way To Take Care Of Marble and Granite Surfaces -

Marble is a porous material even when coated, and one needs to be careful leaving liquids sitting on the surface. When handling marble, be wary of:

✓ Acids: coke, lemon juice and sodas spilt on your marble bar top
✓ Salad dressings and even fruits on your marble cheese board
✓ Toothpaste and bleach in acne beauty products are disastrous for marble bathrooms
✓ Placing hot pans on top of marble can cause it to crack.

Liquids that sit on the surface will eat at the marble and will result in the whole surface needing to be re-sanded. Place drinks on coasters at the bar, cosmetics on a tray in the bathroom and don't let water collect in marble showers.

To clean:

Use a mixture of baby soap, or castile soap and water mixed in a spray bottle. Apply to surface and wipe off with a microfiber cloth. Never use anything harder than this, especially your dishwashing detergents. Vinegar and water will eat the surface.

To remove stains left in the marble — read: nightmare!

1. Mix a thick paste of baking soda and water
2. Apply paste to stain. Cover with plastic wrap and tape down, not letting any moisture in. Leave the mixture in the plastic bubble for at least twenty-four hours. The idea is for the paste is to absorb the stain
3. Buff out paste with water and let dry.

Use extra protection on marble

To seal the surface and stop it absorbing liquids, apply a layer of Gel Gloss, Cleaner & Polish. This product can also be used on glass and metal for a shiny finish that only needs a buff with a micro-fiber cloth to remove water spots. Resist the urge to apply Gel Gloss to marble floors as it makes them dangerously slippery when wearing socks. Rachael A., this means you — anything to stop doing more work! To have Gel Gloss working to maximum effect, re-apply at least once a month. For the time it takes to re-apply Gel Gloss, it will save you three thousand times that amount of time polishing on charter.

- Holy Shit! White Carpets -

First and foremost, you must know if the carpet is synthetic, natural or protein-based, then breathe

Synthetic

A manmade fiber that consists of a plant cellulose base mixed with a solvent to form a solution. It is then passed through an extractor to make fine hairs then cut at intervals to form the fibers. Because the fiber is now a form of plastic, liquids do not adhere easily. All stains — except for other enamel plastics, such as red lipstick and nail polish — can be washed out with water and fabric detergent with a light scrub of a toothbrush.

Natural

Plant-based, such as bamboo and sisal (linen). Treat this fiber with care as any harsh chemicals you use can leave a residue mark and damage the fiber. Start off lightly brushing the stain with water and fabric detergent, then work your way up to hydrogen peroxide and baking soda.
*Cotton is never used in flooring; it is not hard wearing enough.

Protein

Can be categorized as any fiber that is derived from an animal. Silk and wool are the two most common protein fibers used in carpets. Great care must be taken with protein fabrics and carpets. To make each thread, each fiber is overlapped and spun. The longer the hairs used, the better quality the thread and therefore the carpet. Harsh scrubbing and heavy foot traffic, will force the fibers to come undone, resulting in a hairy finished carpet that looks terribly messy. To remove stains from protein-based carpets, especially white ones, use a fabric stain remover — spot tested first in an inconspicuous location — and lightly brush with a toothbrush. Do not let the stain remover dry, keep the carpet slightly moist, always blotting the stain out with water and paper towels.

NEVER, EVER, use bleach on protein-based materials, it will burn the fibers and turn the material dirty yellow. The burn mark from the bleach can never be removed and the whole carpet will have to be replaced.

- Let Me Tell You About Leather and Animals, So You Don't Fuck Up –

Telling the difference between real & fake leather

How can one tell the difference between real and fake leather? Smell it! Have you ever noticed the old ladies sniffing handbags in stores? Real leather smells of a tannery. Plastic does not have a scent. The best way to tell the difference though is to hold a naked flame to the leather. Plastic will melt but real leather doesn't burn. (It has been used as a fire protectant for centuries). The other way to know if it's real leather or not — you will visually see creases and small pores in the leather hinds. Animal hides are not uniform and will differentiate across the skin. Leather hinds are thicker across the spine of the animal and the hair decreases in thickness towards the stomach.

Cleaning & maintaining leather

Use good quality leather cleaner and protector — two separate products — is sufficient. Spot test first and follow directions. For any nasty marks that don't come out try:
1. A magic eraser
2. John Deer hand wash — see procedure for cleaning white leather couches & walls.

When using the leather protector, it has the tendency to dry with oily smudges across the surface. Leather is a porous material and the skin has a different absorbency rate across the hind. To avoid stains and keep the leather looking uniform, apply a few coats of the leather protector, letting it dry between coats to saturate the leather to a supple finish. A coat a day for a couple of days may have to be done to get the perfect finish.

Cleaning white leather couches & walls

Think of leather as human skin. It is to be cleaned and moisturized to prevent it drying out and cracking. Too much moisture before cleaning will saturate the skin, thus making the cleaning more difficult.

Game Plan!

Use John Deer hand wash. It smells like oranges and has lots of grit in it. It works better than any detergent, shampoo or clothing detergent as it is specifically designed to clean skins. It can be easily purchased from hardware stores. This trick also works well on light-cultured leather and spot stain removal on faux leather walls. Once you start cleaning leather with this product, be prepared to do the whole surface as it cleans so well!

1. Place towels/floor protection down — it's going to get messy
2. Dampen surface with warm water
3. With a sponge apply John Deer hand wash. Work small sections at a time, making the hand wash foam up. Wipe away dirt that comes up and reapply soap. Do not scrub too hard, as the color may lift off from the leather. You'll know how far to go. Do not mistake the dirt caked in the creases of the leather with wear and tear. If it's a bit tight getting into the creases, use a toothbrush
4. Wipe off all residual soap with water
5. Apply a leather conditioner.

Cleaning leather is a time-consuming project. Pick your time wisely. Two days out from an owner's trip is not a good time. This trick is worth thousands of dollars as owners will replace the object had you not come along and saved them a ton of money. When using this tip, be sure to cut some deal along the way, as the cost of replacing the object or getting professionals in, is more than your yearly salary.

Cleaning & maintaining FAUX leather interiors

We recommend using Amor Leather Protectant on fake leather. It absorbs into the material and leaves a superior finish that only needs maintaining once a month.

How to treat metallic leathers

To maintain and add shine to metallic leather, regularly buff with leather cream liquid. Do not use wax or silicon products on metallic leather. They don't allow the leather to breathe and tend to show scuffs marks more quickly. To maintain metallic leather, polish and buff once a month.

- Cleaning Dead Animals -

It was not so long ago that divorce was uncommon and men only had a few options to prove their masculinity, such as shooting animals and collecting medals, instead of taking another trophy wife. The social acceptance of these practices is now waning due to our extinct wildlife and social-media shaming. However, there is still a minute class of people in this world who possess illegal dead animals. Don't take this job if you have seen all the dead animals onboard and your animal cruelty morals make you want to burn the boat down. Whatever your moral stand on this matter is, your owner is not paying you to pass judgement. As professional yacht crew, it is now your responsibility to keep these artifacts well maintained. Negligence and ignorance in the proper care techniques can result in termination, as these objets d'art are considered priceless.

Before attacking the deceased, decipher what the animal was and how old the antique is. You'll find the animals and hinds are so dry from the air-conditioning, sunlight and guests use, that one must work slowly and carefully to avoid the creature disintegrating in your hands. Drama!

You may have never seen it in a museum but it'll be in a billionaire's private collection

- ✓ Whale foreskin bar stools with whale's teeth as foot holders and carved whale bones as arm rests on the bar
- ✓ Plaques on the bar wall with miniature chairs upholstered with python and anaconda skins with matching snakeheads
- ✓ Priceless whale bones/teeth/spleen carved into decorative objects and grouped together on pearl inlaid coffee tables
- ✓ Rhino heads mounted as trophies. There's one kicking around on a yacht, where the head

comes away on hinges from the back panel to reveal a drinks cabinet behind

- ✓ Elephant hinds on the floor upholstered into seats, tusks mounted on the wall and elephant feet used as umbrella holders
- ✓ Carved ivory statues/objets d'art
- ✓ A collection of extinct animals onboard a fifty-meter yacht to replicate Noah's Ark. We're talking stuffed adult lions, tigers, jaguars, polar bears, zebras, elephants, birds and snakes — just in the guest areas! Each private cabin is decorated with an extinct animal theme. The tiger room has a white Serbian tiger head stuffed in an attacking facial expression on a plaque above the bed. A white Siberian tiger floor mat, matching wallpaper and black, silk, tapestry daybed cover with contrasting white piping. Matching cushions and massive black tassels on the corners of the bed and pillows. The pull-down window blinds are white and the whole room and boat, is accented with gold fittings and gemstones set in designs behind glass cabinets. The other cabins are finished with the same crazy, out-of-this-world show of wealth, following the similar design themes in soon-to-be-extinct polar bear, zebra, lion, American black bear and grey mink
- ✓ Fur throws and rugs made of Colobus monkey, mink, blue fox, coyote, Mongolian sheep, rabbit and beaver
- ✓ Hides of lions, jaguars, tigers, zebras and leopards — mostly with their heads still attached
- ✓ Taxidermy prize fish as plaques on the wall
- ✓ Stuffed trophies in the cigar room. If it's extinct, foreign and hard to get, it's here to enjoy while drinking your cognac and smoking your cigar
- ✓ Maps of the world made out of mother of pearl and highlighted with precious stones
- ✓ Extinct monkeys displayed as art. They can be found wearing diamond chokers and drinking from miniature martini glasses
- ✓ A family of armadillos, trekking their way across the main saloon coffee table
- ✓ Taxidermy birds – owls, parrots, penguins, turkeys, and peacocks. You'll find them placed on shelves, above walkways and in glass domes
- ✓ Rare and extinct insects pinned in glass cabinets
- ✓ Trinket boxes made of python, stingray, toad and fish skin, finished with a massive, precious crystal formation on top as the handle. There's a store killing it in St Barts that specializes in just this and nothing else.

To clean

Fur and Feathers

Always begin with the softest utensils you have, increasing the amount of abrasion as required. Start with Swiffer pads and progress to children's hairbrushes with the softest bristles if need be. Avoid brushing out the hair on the animal, your aim is to remove the dust. Refrain from using a vacuum cleaner. These dead animals are too delicate for that.

Skins

Avoiding washing these artifacts, no matter how dirty they are because when they dry this can result in the skin cracking. If there is an oily mark, remove the stain by gently wiping it using a large car sponge dipped in warm water and baby soap. Always follow the grain to avoid the sponge getting caught and damaging this delicate skin. #asseenonmyaqualuna

Protect the skin from drying out by adding a delicate leather conditioner specifically made for that skin. Avoid using traditional leather polish and saddle polish. These heavy products will not sit well, and you will have to buff very hard to get the product out again, resulting in a cleaning job that you will have to hide.

To care for snakeskin walls

1. Never apply an adhesive sticky tape or blue painters tape on snakeskin walls. The leather is too delicate and will easily rip apart from the base leather that the snakeskin is glued onto

2. Keep snakeskin out of direct sunlight. When the boat is not in use, have the blinds down, keeping as much sunlight out of the room as you can

3. During a shipyard period, cover as much of the snakeskin wall as possible to keep it dust and dirt free. You will also be glad that you covered it after you see the many workmen walk past and run their grubby hands down along the entire wall to feel the texture. Use rolls of blue plastic and blue painters tape to cover the wall, always overlapping to the other walls, so as to never touch the snakeskin itself. Alternatively, string a pole from two removable hooks in the ceiling and hang a sheet over that.

- How To Remove Bodily Fluids From Fur and Luxury Finishes -

First and foremost, you must know if the carpet is synthetic, natural or protein-based, then breathe

Please tell me that isn't semen in the fur rug! Did that spoilt dog just pee on the bear rug? FML

1. You need to remove all bodily fluids off the surface a.s.a.p. The acid eats at finishes leaving the surface acid-etched

2. Take a dust mask with a few drops of calming essential oils inside

3. Gloves! Unless it's your child or best friend, no one is paid enough money in the world to clean up someone else's excrement. Use latex gloves to get rid of any chunky material. Besides we're too pretty for that shit

4. Clean all the vomit up using the heavy-duty exterior vacuum cleaner, the one that does not have a vacuum cleaner bag inside and can be washed out. Alternatively use lots of paper towels and a garbage bag

5. Wipe down the surface with a concoction of water, baking soda — to clean and remove the smell — and shampoo — to mask the smell — blot out all water with paper towels. Water can leave watermarks on fabrics that can only be dry cleaned out.

    a. Fur skins: gently work the solution into the hair. Then lay the fur out flat on a towel and roll up inside to soak up all excess liquid

6. If the smell of excrement has set in, apply a paste of baking soda and water. Leave it for an hour and wipe off with water. Afterwards, spray with Febreze

7. Always dry in the shade. Drying in the sun or over a heater will dry out the leather, causing the hair to fall out. Same with using dry cleaning agents.

If none of the above works, send it out to be dry-cleaned or replaced.

Caring for dead animals with no guests on

Animals and furs do not need to be maintained with conditioning agents as they are already mummified. As soon as guests depart, cover all animals with a light cotton cloth to keep the dust from collecting on top. Pull down all the blinds, keeping the room in as much darkness as you can.

- Why Flower Arrangements Are The Deal Breaker -
Without love and flowers, there's no reason to live

Nothing in this world screams opulence more than a heady, fragrant display of costly flowers. Only the very well-to-do can afford to spend money on something that is already dead when picked. Yachts and estates have an allocated flower budget that can run into thousands of dollars every couple of weeks. Flowers are the full stop in luxury, the finishing touch when setting the scene to impress.

When purchasing flowers for the yacht always refer to the guest preference sheets and profiles of the charter guests. Madams — owners — can be quite picky with the height, volume, type of flowers, foliage and arrangements chosen. Crosscheck with madam's PA for her current preference and take notes when she make comments on your bouquets.

Most mega yachts and estates will have a large walk-in fridge, dedicated to keeping cut flowers, which are picked fresh and flown in weekly. As soon as you receive confirmation of guest arrival, place your order with your florist a.s.a.p. Flowers are grown and shipped from the Netherlands, Columbia, and Eastern Block Europe. The minimum transit time from the moment the flowers are picked to being delivered to the estate is two weeks. Leave your flower order too late and there will be minimal stock to choose from, and the flowers will already be on the wilt. Once you get your flowers on board, you have to make them last!

If you are a cut flower, you do not like:

1. Stewardesses who do not smother you with love every day
2. Sunlight
3. Dirty water
4. Wind, draughts and hot air
5. Changes in temperature
6. To be moved around
7. Moisture or rain on your petals.

✓ All yacht flowers prefer pure drinking water. No water from the dock or unpurified from the tanks please

✓ Unpurified water is too salty and will kill your plants.
The rule is: if you wouldn't drink it, don't give to your plants

✓ Always use a flower preserver. Failing that, add an aspirin and a penny to the water. The aspirin makes the water acidic, and the penny acts as a fungicide. You can also use Listerine.
Add 2 capfuls per a gallon. The Listerine contains sucrose — food — and a bactericide

✓ Change the flower water every day

✓ No leaves in the water, it will quickly sour it.

To care for flowers
Before placing stems in the chosen vase, cut the bottom of the flower stem on an angle with sharp scissors, just above the knuckle.

Green stemmed flowers
Dip the stems into boiling water for thirty seconds after cutting. The hot water kills the bacteria and opens up the stem to allow the flowers to take water up more easily

Woody stemmed flowers
Hammer the last two cm of the stem to take up water. Use a bar muddler for this.

Hollow-stemmed flowers
Turn the flower upside down and fill the stem with cold water. Plug it with cotton wool

Lilies

The anther at the end of the stem should be removed from flowers. If the pollen drops or rubs, use mineral oil to the remove pollen stain

Orchids

Are temperamental. They prefer to live somewhere with a view but never in direct sunlight. Once you give orchids a home, leave them. Moving can result in dying. The rule is: if you can keep your orchids alive for more than a year, you're ready for children.

1. If the leaves are deep green, they need more sunlight. If they are starting to yellow, the roots are too moist

2. If the roots are in chunky loose matter, the original home of this orchid is high in the treetops of the rainforest. To care for this type of orchid, mist flowers and leaves with bottled drinking water at night. They'll be fresh in the morning

3. If your orchids are growing in moss, do not mist the flowers and leaves. Every two to three days, place a couple of ice cubes next to the stem

4. If the orchid flowers start to wither, the roots do not have enough water

5. Every couple of months, treat your orchids to specific food for them. It will help them grow back.

ALL EXCEPTIONAL YACHTS HAVE GOOD STATIONERY

- The 180 Million Spent On The Yacht Means Nothing If The Stationary Is Cheap -

All classy yachts have exceptional quality pens and paper

Beautiful quality stationary is a representation of the yacht, the owners and the crew. Creative, intelligent, visual branding of the yacht is a clear reflection of how seriously one takes one's job and the level of pride the ship owner has. Ordering and organizing outstanding stationary separates great stewardesses from the mediocre. As money is no object we find Smithson (London) and Dempsey & Carroll (New York) to be the best. When in doubt, ask for paper with embossing — raised lettering with gold leaf — samples to be sent. Everything should complement each other, whether through type, color schemes, yacht logo or using the blueprint of the boat. You want the yacht's hand pressed, embossed letterheads, envelopes and matching business cards to scream old money. Computer printed thank-you cards, and cheap business cards will just not do.

To finalize your order:

1. Order business cards with the yacht logo — a packet each for the captain, engineer, first officer and chief stewardess

2. Calling cards with envelopes that can double as thankyou cards

3. Headed paper for letters

4. Matching envelopes

When in doubt of the quality to order for your yacht, check into the nearest 5-Star hotel. Your stationary should be equivalent to this. After all, a yacht is an asset, a holiday destination and a status symbol.

10.

LAUNDRY

Watch Where
Your Thoughts Go
In The Laundry Room.
There Are Only Three Things
You Should Be Focusing On.
Your Health, Your Wealth
& Your Career.

- With Every Drop Of Water You Drink, Every Breath We Take, We're Connected To The Sea, No Matter Where We Live On Earth -

Never forget that we have one home and once it's ruined beyond repair, we all die. As of 2017 it is wide-spread knowledge that the world has fifteen years left of fossil fuels. Our world is already becoming dangerously sick. Our oceans are polluted, our food sources are spoiling and there is a limited supply of natural, non-government-tainted drinking water available. We must be conscious of everything that we put into the water as the ocean provides seventy percent of the oxygen we breathe. Every careless action we take when maintaining our yachts creates a rise in global temperature and global warming, which results in our world dying. We have the option to buy detergents, chemicals, and products that are biodegradable, fragrance-free, sulfate free and organic. Use it.

- Making Laundry Magic Happen On A Professional Level -
The professional's guide to perfecting the art of handling multimillion-dollar wardrobes and eighty-four loads of laundry a week

Laundry on yachts is a whole different ball game. One person — usually green — is expected to pump out laundry to the same level as a 5-Star hotel. Now is not the time to make assumptions. The laundry department is the biggest deal on a yacht mainly because you are working unsupervised and are entrusted with multi-million dollar wardrobes, thousands of dollars-worth of linens and crew clothing.

Whatever you do, please:

1. Keep your laundry area clean
2. Refrain from using from bleach — Bleach is the cause of most accidents
3. Do not apply bleach on white silk fabric or carpets, it will turn the fabric burnt yellow and cannot be removed
4. No heat/or hot water on wool and unidentifiable fabrics, they will shrink
5. Apply laundry ethics to every load
6. Check every washing label before washing.

- The Difference Between Guest and Crew Laundry-

✓ Wash ALL guest clothing in mesh bags as a minimum. Hand washing guest clothing is recommended, but mesh bags are the cheat's way. It prevents the garment from being smashed, torn and pulled in the wash cycles. Please use your judgement, anything with beading or that looks stupidly expensive — send it out to be dry-cleaned

✓ Place a safety pin with a colored bead — a color assigned to each guest room — onto each individual piece of guest clothing to distinguish guest laundry and its corresponding cabin. Less time-consuming than writing each piece of clothing down and ensures the right clothes go back to the correct cabin

✓ Do the same with used damp guest towels to be dried instead of continuously washing them

✓ Never dry guest clothing in dryers. They may shrink and the wear and tear of dryers will fade clothing. They're usually expensive fabrics. Hang to dry

✓ No guest laundry is to be done on the day of guest departure. Yes, even though our guests are grown-ups, they get very upset if their favorite jeans are in the wash when they're dressing for departure. Oh! The drama!

✓ Always iron guest laundry and place it back in their rooms the same day

✓ If crew laundry cannot go into the washing machine, don't wash it. The crewmember has to wash it themselves in their free time.

✔ Crew laundry is only done on the assigned day for that crewmember

✔ Crew personal laundry is not ironed. An exception is made for the captain. For all other crewmembers, it's upon request with bribery — designer candy or drinks at the bar will do.

- The Expert Chief Stewardess's Guide To Washing -

✔ Turn everything inside out. This includes dark colored work pants and work shirts. The washing and dryer damages clothing and fades colors faster .

✔ Check all pockets for treasures before placing in the washing machine. Yes, this is your job

✔ Zip all zippers to the top and button. Avoid the nightmare of this getting caught on anything .

✔ Unbutton all shirts. Buttons pulling on holes adds stress to the fabric.

✔ Warm and dark colors: Cool water.

✔ Whites: Hot water .

✔ NEVER MIX WHITES AND DARKS. Mix these two and see how crazy your chief stew gets. Potentially you can get out of laundry duties for a while, or get fired!.

✔ To hold dye in fabrics that tend to run, soak them for a few minutes in half distilled white vinegar and half water before washing. This works well for clothing that has an intense color and white trim .

✔ Too much fabric softener used continuously will stop towels from being absorbent. Follow directions. The formula is concentrated. Use only 1/3 of a cap. Think of the environment and wean yourself off that fabric softener smell. It's so ghetto!

✔ Do not soak any silks or delicately printed fabrics in Oxi Clean. This product will strip color from the garment. #truestory.

✔ Color catches are where it's at. They are square pieces of absorbent tissue that catch run off dye in the washing cycle. When in doubt — which will never happen because you're a professional — throw in a few of these sheets in and cross your fingers. If you have to use more than one, you shouldn't be doing that load!.

✔ Laundry pods (single load detergent encased in a dissolvable squishy pouch) are the way to go. Less mess. They also stop front loaders from smelling moldy.

✔ Apply laundry ethics to every load. Tea towels stay together and away from guest clothing. Resist the urge to chuck lingerie bags in to top up a load of napkins. Laundry karma will come and get you!.

✔ Wash all galley tea towels and chef aprons together. Separate from other clothing as it will make the whole load smell funny. Also add a ½ cap of laundry disinfectant to every load.

How to hand wash like a professional yacht stewardess

1. Check garment over for stains. Stain remove if needed
2. Fill a tub with cool water and add an appropriate amount of delicate laundry detergent, hand wash soap or baby shampoo — it's the least abrasive. Add a tad of fabric softener for the smell. Yes, fabric softener can go in with the laundry soap and still work
3. Soak garment for ten minutes beforehand washing
4. Lightly rub the fabric together, squeeze and release, pushing clothing around in water
5. Gently wring out detergent water

6. Fill the tub with clear fresh water and rinse out garment
7. Gently wring out fresh water
8. Lay garment flat on a dry towel and roll the towel up with the clothing inside to remove all excess water
9. Hang to dry or place knitwear on a fresh dry towel to dry to avoid distorting the knitted structure.

Washing business shirts
1. Stain remove collar and cuff if need be. If they are awful, use the same trick for removing armpit stains (as per the haute couture stain removal guide
2. Unbutton shirt. Washing adds stress to buttonholes and buttons
3. Place in the laundry bag and wash with similar colors
4. Alternatively, hand wash and wring out extra moisture
5. Place on a hanger to dry. Avoid the dryer, it accelerates color fading and will quickly damage delicate fabrics.

How to wash jeans and dark colors
1. After checking all pockets for treasures, turn garment inside out
2. Wash in cold water with laundry detergent made for dark clothing and wash only jeans with jeans. Towels will smash the jean fabric, and jeans will damage finer fabrics
3. Hang inside out, out of direct sunlight. Sunlight will fade colors quick smart
4. Iron inside out.

How to wash T-shirts
1. Wash all T-shirts in mesh laundry bags. This will stop the knit from being distorted and pulled out of shape
2. Dry T-shirts on a hanger. The dryer will shrink knits.

How to wash evening fabrics with delicate beading
1. Get Mr. Google online and find the closest dry cleaners with the quickest turnaround time! Failing that and you've been called upon to wave your stewardess wand …
2. Follow hand-washing instructions
3. Roll in a towel to remove excess water
4. Allow garment to drip dry on a hanger
5. To press: lightly steam on a hanger to remove all wrinkles.

How to properly wash swimwear, lycra leggings and gym wear
1. Soak swim wear in a proper swimwear laundry detergent that can be purchased from any good homeware store or provisioning establishment
2. Wring out and rinse in fresh water
3. Place in mesh laundry bag and chuck in washing machine for a quick spin cycle
4. Hang on hangers and let drip dry.

*Note: Never wash Lycra in washing machines or dryer. This is the quickest way to disintegrate the garment.

How to remove that musty smell from clothing
You know that musty smell that you can never get rid of? This trick eliminates the smell from:

A: Clothing/towels that have sat in the washing machine for too long

B: The smell from sweaty boys' clothing that has sat in their cabin for weeks on end turning sour

C: To remove the mildew smell from wet clothing that has traveled long haul (many days flying)

1. Place clothing in the washing machine and add two cups of vinegar to wash cycle. It does not need detergent
2. Wash on the hottest water setting the garments can stand
3. Repeat if necessary. Two cycles will definitely get rid of the smell.

DID YOU KNOW?

The difference between a knit and weave structure? In a knit structure the vertical thread is looped under and over the previous and next vertical thread. That is why when a thread breaks, it creates a run. Anything that pulls in multiple directions is a knit. Examples are T-shirts, workout apparel and hoodies.
The threads in a weave structure are cross hatched — like individual little 't' — to form its bond. Examples are cotton trousers, tea towels and sheeting. Woven fabric will not pull horizontally or vertically, only pulling on the diagonal, which gives it its strength.

- Dry Cleaning -

Fingers crossed that all guest laundry is sent out for dry-cleaning. The nightmare is finding dry cleaners when you're anchored off rocks in some remote location. Get the purser onto it.

Dry-cleaning is a process where garments are washed in chemicals and never touch water. It's the best for fabrics that can disintegrate in water and delicate fabrics that cannot withstand being beaten up in washing machines. After the clothing has been washed in the chemicals and dried, it is then ironed.

- Ironing Luxurious Fabrics-

1. Starch the wrong side — inside — of business shirts, napkins and tablemats. If you starch the surface you are ironing, the hot iron will pick up the starch solution, burning, and will quickly turn your iron brown. If this happens, let the iron cool and clean it with non-gel toothpaste.
2. Do not iron in fold lines in garments. You'll find in perfect tailoring, ironing seams in is the sign of an amateur. Use a ham — tailoring term for a long sausage filled with foam — placed inside to remove creases. T-shirts and napkins with ironed-in fold lines have to be removed before using. Stop it, you lot!

=Note: Always start with a warm iron and work your way upwards in temperature if in doubt.

The proper technique to ironing business shirts

1. Starch the inside of the shirt and the outside of the collar
2. Iron sleeves first so they can hang while doing the rest of the shirt. If you do them last, you'll notice the rest of the shirt becomes crinkly. Line up underarm seam so the top sleeve edge is even and press
3. Hook the right front shoulder panel over the round edge of the ironing board. Begin ironing the right front shirt panel
4. Hook the back shoulder panel — under the back collar — over round edge of the ironing board and begin pressing the back of the shirt. Move fabric across ironing board to iron the whole back shirt panel
5. Repeat for last front shirt panel
6. Iron inside of collar.

- Steaming Avant-Garde And Bespoke Dresses -

Believe me, it is very stressful deciding how to get the wrinkles out of the £6000 Ellie Saab, delicate, lighter than silk dress with hand-made embroidery details. Everyone wants their laundry now and all the guests have sent down their garments for tonight's Met Gala ball. Let's begin with steaming first as it doesn't burn the fibers like a hot iron does.

Professional steaming

1. Hang the garment
2. Fill the steamer container with water. Let the machine heat up and when it's hot, hold the head of the steamer directly onto the fabric
3. Use it on everything. It's quick and doesn't leave creases. Well worth the investment.

What to do when the professional steamer has kicked it

1. Use your iron and turn it up to the hottest heat. You can't damage fabrics with hot steam unless it's wool. Wool will tangle with heat. To remove wrinkles, iron on low heat with a hankie in-between the iron and wool
2. Hang the garment so it isn't touching the floor, start steaming from the bottom up, holding the hem of the garment towards you and pull the fabric so that when you steam it, it gives the wrinkles room to fall out
3. Hold the iron approximately fifteen to twenty centimeters away from the fabric. You do not want your hot iron to ever touch the fabric in case it burns
4. Hold down the steam button continuously and move the iron quickly over the surface, not letting it sit in one place for too long
5. When you're satisfied that all the wrinkles have been removed, hang the garment in plenty of space to ensure it does not get wrinkled again.

✓ Achieve the same effect as steaming when you're in a rush with your party dresses by hanging them in a steamy bathroom.

- Successfully Caring For Hand-Made Suits -

Wool is a natural fiber and will shrink and matt when in contact with heat. Heat and hot water shrink wool. Under no circumstances are you to spray wool with water and apply heat. This is the same as putting a wool/cashmere jumper into the washing machine on a hot cycle.

The proper way to care for woolen suits is to steam the fabric — not applying water — and then brush it in a downward direction with a large soft-bristled natural hairbrush. Woolen suits, when taken care of and properly aired, are only meant to be dry cleaned a maximum of four times a year. When dry cleaning suits, please ensure that the matching top and bottom stays together to avoid one-piece fading quicker than the other.

✓ Suit jackets should never be immersed in water, only dry-cleaned. The cheaper suits — anything bought off the rack — are constructed with glued on interfacing* to give the jacket structure, and to make the garment mold to the body. This lowers costs instead of the traditional method of hand stitching the interface structure in. Hand washing suits will cause the glued on the interfacing to come apart, making the shoulders and front panels of the suit jacket bubble and sag.

* Interfacing is what gives the suit shoulders, collar and front panels structure. It's a different weight material than wool, usually heavy cotton and it is attached to the inside of the jacket via the shoulder seam and side seams. A sown-in interfaced jacket will look like it has been molded to the body. It will keep its structure even when hanging from the chair. A glued in interface will be a thinner jacket, lacking in a structured body-molded shell. Lately, to cut corners and bring the prices down, manufacturers have been using thick synthetic webbing with glue on the front. It is pressed onto the front panel of the jacket. The price will also be a dead giveaway as to how the jacket was made.

- Servicing Machines -
The lint filter will catch on fire

It is part of our job to maintain all machinery. You can't find the experts when you're out at sea and the engineers sometimes have no clue. Always seek the advice of the chief stewardess or engineer before attempting to service machines for the first time.

Servicing washing machines

1. Once a week wipe out the barrel of washing machine with vinegar and water
2. Once a month run a hygienic cycle — use the hottest cycle of your washing machine with one cup of vinegar or Simple Green — this has the same effect as a fat kid eating ice-cream. It cleans it right up!
3. Drain washing machine at the 'off' water point. This fitting is found on the front panel of Miele washing machines. In the right-hand corner, you'll find a hatch. This can be pried open by slipping a butter knife in the top and gently prizing it open. Have a container ready to catch water. Unscrew the plug gently to release water. Empty out all water and unscrew. Here you'll find lost treasure — monies!
4. Once a month pull out the draw where you place laundry detergent and clean out the soap buildup
5. To polish silver on the front of washing machines use Sheila Shine for the quickest results.

Servicing dryers

1. After every load clean out dryer filters. The engineers freak when they see you have not cleaned it
2. Once a week, wipe out the barrel with vinegar and water
3. At the same time hit that dryer with a Swiffer pad and vacuum cleaner. Detail under filters to get as much lint out as you can. This keeps your machine running smoothly and prevents fires
4. Once a month, pull out condensers. Rinse them out under a fully open running tap but do not soak.

Servicing irons

1. Use only filtered, non-mineral water to avoid calcium buildup and brown ooze from coming out of the steamer holes
2. Clean scum build-up from the silver metal plate so it doesn't iron starch and acrylic prints on T-shirts. Apply a mixture of whitening toothpaste and bi-carbonate soda with a toothbrush
3. Let the mixture sit for as long as you can and scrub off using the same toothbrush
4. Turn on iron and steam on a white towel to remove all residue.

- 3 Tips For Stain Removal Like A Pro -

1. Most stains can be removed with water, a dab of washing detergent (and/or dish washing detergent) and a light scrub with a toothbrush. You don't want to lift up the fibers. Just enough to loosen the stain
2. Failing that, spray with pre-wash or stain remover. Give it another light brush with the toothbrush
3. If it's heavily soiled, such as grease or dark stains on white, saturate with a stain remover and let the solution sit on the stain for ten minutes. Using the toothbrush, give it a brush. Test for colorfast first, soak in Oxy Clean or Napisan for ½ an hour. Never soak anything overnight. Stains should come out within an hour.

The Haute Couture Stain Removal Guide -

Can't choose your battles here

Arm Pit Stains	1. Mix 1 tsp. Dawn dishwashing detergent, 3 to 4 tablespoons of hydrogen peroxide, 3 to 4 tablespoons of baking soda. Scrub with a toothbrush or rub the fabric together. Let dry, brush off solution and wash as normal.
	2. Rub half a lemon on the stain. Let dry and wash out.
	3. 'Carbona' stain devil Rust & perspiration.'
Ball Point Pen	1. Place fabric between paper towels and blot out with alcohol. Apply pre-wash and launder.
	2. Apply hand sanitizer to magic eraser and gently rub on stain.
	3. 'Carbona' stain devil – Ink & crayon.'
Ball Point Pen In Leather	Spray either cologne, perfume or nail polish onto an ear bud. Gently work at the ball point pen stain. Buff out product afterward.
Beverages (coffee, tea, soft drinks, wine, alcoholic beverages)	Sponge or soak fabric in cold water. If stain does not come out: blot dry, apply pre-wash stain remover (or liquid washing detergent or paste of laundry powder) work in into fabric with toothbrush and launder as usual.
Blood	Apply hydrogen peroxide as soon as possible. Let it soak in, bubble up and brush lightly with a toothbrush to loosen the fibers. Stain should disappear before your eyes.
Butter / Margarine	1. Spray on a kitchen degreaser that can also be used on fabrics.
	2. Saturate stain with laundry detergent. Allow fabric to soak in hottest water possible. Wash. (Warm water for darks, hottest water for whites. Always check for color fastness)
	3. Spray stain with K2R. Let it sit until K2R dries and has time to absorb stain. Launder as usual.
	4. Apply baking soda to the stain. Hand wash in hottest water garment can handle.
Candle Wax	1. Scrap off excess wax. Place fabric between sheets of paper towels. Rub hot iron on top of paper towels till all the candle wax has been melted and absorbed.
	2. Apply "Goo Gone" and follow directions.
Carpet Stains (& anything off a mattress as well)	1. Make a quick mix of hydrogen peroxide and "Blue Dawn" dish soap. Apply and work gently with white toweling cloth.
	2. 'Resolve' carpet stain remover is one of the best on the market. Always pre-test, though.
Chewing Gum	1. Apply "Goo Gone" and follow directions.
	2. Place garment in freezer to harden gum. Peel off.
Chocolate	Brush excess chocolate off garment. Rinse in cold water to dilute stain. Apply pre-wash stain remover and wash.
Coffee	Baking soda
Collar / Cuff Stain	1. Make a paste from powdered washing detergent and apply. Brush gently into stain for the fibers to release stain. If possible soak and wash in hottest water possible.
	2. 'Resolve' stain remover. Apply and brush in with a toothbrush.
	3. Make a paste out of "Oxi- clean" powder and water. Apply to stain and launder as usual. Test first for color fastness. This product with strip color from garments.
Cooking Oil / Olive Oil	1. Spray on a kitchen degreaser that can also be used on fabrics.
	2. Cover oil stain with baking powder and let sit. Shake; apply clothing stain removal spray and wash.
	3. K2R Spray on let dry and wash as usual.
Crayon	1. Scrap off excess crayon wax. Place fabric between sheets of paper towels. Rub hot iron on top of paper towels till the entire crayon has been melted and absorbed.
	2. Apply "Goo Gone" and follow directions. Apply pre-wash stain remover if needed and launder in hottest water possible. "Goo Gone" can be known to leave an oily residue as well.
Dairy Products	Apply pre-wash, work in and let sit. Soak for as long as the garment will let you.
Deodorant (white stains on darker clothes)	Lightly rub with 'distilled white vinegar' and launder.

Glue	Apply "Goo Gone" and follow directions.
Grass	Vinegar
Grease/Engine Oil Grease	1. Use a pre-wash stain remover. Select the pre-wash cycle and add 'Oxi-clean'. Choose the hottest water cycle possible and wash with like garments.
	2. "Jamaica houseboy's way" Apply 'Cif', 'Crème cleanser' or 'Ajax' to the stain and rub the fabric together to loosen stain. Let sit for 10 minutes and wash on cotton setting.
	3. Apply K2R - Spray on, let dry and wash as usual.
	4. Apply "Goo Gone" and follow directions.
	* If the stains are heavy you might need to do this a few times. *Remember to wipe out washing machine barrel afterward with vinegar and water.
Ink	Milk
Lipstick (To remove lipstick stains from napkins)	1. Place the napkin on top of a couple of layers of paper towels. Dampen another towel with rubbing alcohol and apply by dabbing. Repeat until stain is gone.
	2. Prewash stain remover on both sides of the fabric. Let dry, rinse. Repeat if necessary.
	3. 'Carbona' stain devil – 'Make-up.'
	4. Try baby wipes as well.
Make-up	Apply shaving cream and let sit for 5 minutes. Lightly brush with a toothbrush.
Mascara	Apply pre-wash stain remover. Brush lightly with a toothbrush. Lauder as usual.
Mildew	This is a secret – if it's white, apply a crème cleanser cleaner. Rub into the stain with a toothbrush, let dry and wash. If this is a dark garment; it's beyond repair.
Museum Gel	1. Apply 'Goo Gone' with a microfiber cloth, and then rub lightly with a toothbrush to get in-between fibers. Avoid soaking material.
	2. Use a magic eraser pad, rub lightly onto the fabric.
Red wine	1. The easiest way- "wine away" spray that can be purchased from most western supermarkets.
	2. Spots caused by wine can be removed from 100% cotton, cotton polyester, and permanent press fabrics if done so if done in 24 hours. Sponge 'distilled white vinegar' (the stuff we buy by the gallon) directly onto the stain and rub away the spots.
	3. Pour club soda over the stain, letting it bubble up (if its fresh)
	4. If the stain is still wet - blot out excess. Pour as much milk onto the stain as you can or blot with a paper towel. Let it soak in. The stain should be gone in an hour or less.
	5. Blot out the stain with white wine.
Paint	1. Water based – rinse out with water and apply pre-wash treatment before washing.
	2. Oil based – saturate then blot paint stain with paint thinner. Repeat till stain disappears. Apply pre-treatment and wash.
Rust	Apply 'Carbona' stain devils, rust & perspiration. Follow directions and pre-test.
Stickers / Labels	Apply "Goo Gone" and follow directions.
Tobacco	Dampen stain and rub with bar soap and rinse. Pre- treat fabric again and launder.
Tomato Sauce	If it has dried, dab hydrogen peroxide or white vinegar on the stain, till it comes out.
Tree Sap	Apply "Goo Gone" and follow directions.
Bodily Fluids	Apply pre-wash stain remover
White Out / Type Writer Correction Fluid	Let stain dry thoroughly and brush off excess. Send out to professional dry-cleaners and let them know what it is.

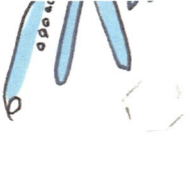

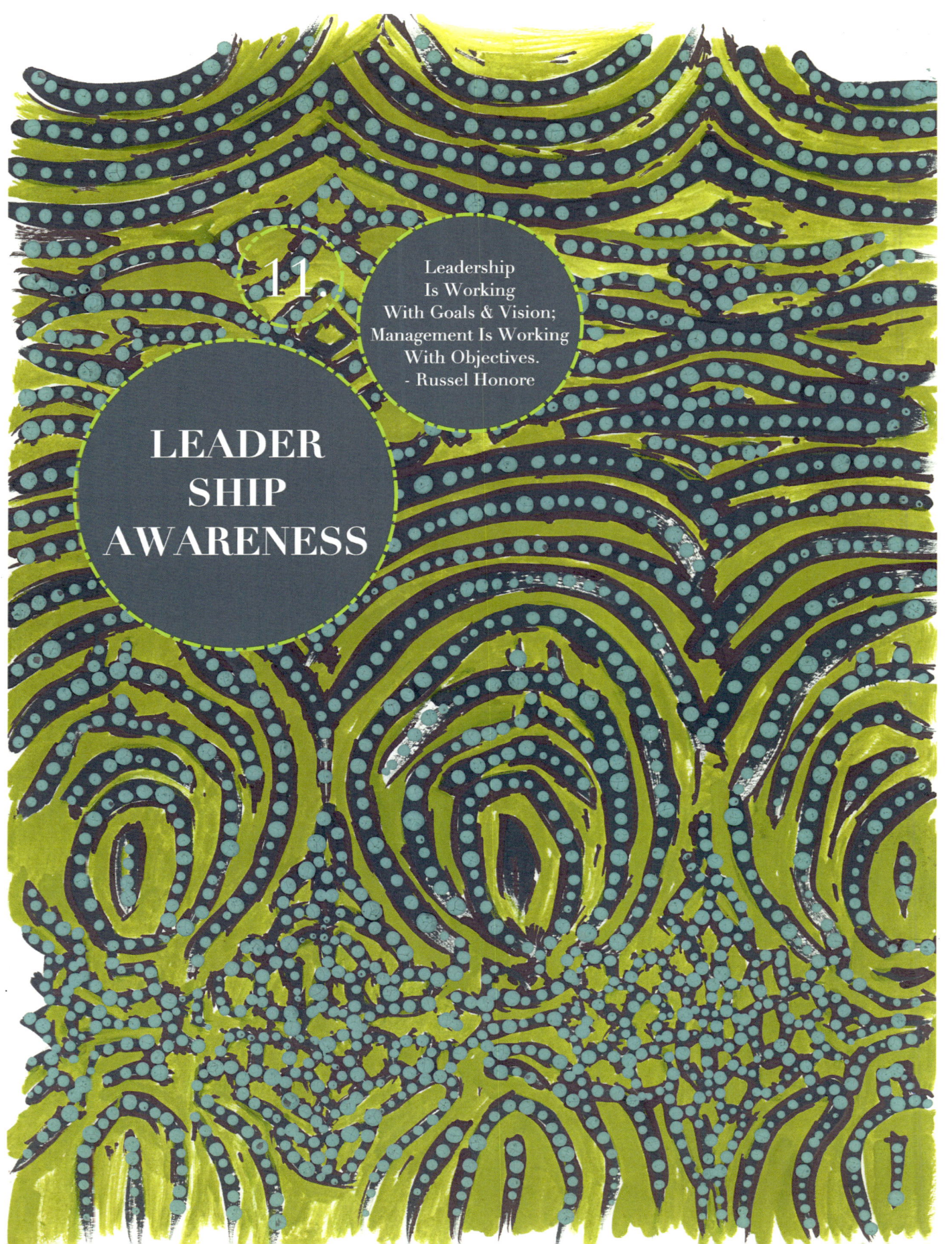

11.

LEADER SHIP AWARENESS

Leadership
Is Working
With Goals & Vision;
Management Is Working
With Objectives.
- Russel Honore

- Lobster Training Program -
Creating leaders that kick goals on a multi-million-dollar scale

Leaders are like lobsters. Lobsters only grow when they are uncomfortable in their skin. Growing is a vulnerable time for lobsters as they are forced to shed their skin and open themselves up to predators. The same goes for leaders. They need to feel desperately uncomfortable and out of their depth to make leadership awareness changes. This period of change is necessary for world-class leaders to acquire the relevant tools in their leadership toolbox. To lead and manage people is the hardest thing to do in the world; it must be practiced continuously.

What's in it for me to build a dream team?

Reputation = trust = value

To create a personal reputation

To create an industry reputation

Your working environment becomes less effort.

Great leaders create blueprints which define their teams

1. **Vision** (goals and department objectives)
   These gives the team a shared vision and a clear understanding of what they are striving for.
   As a team, together our goal is: ….
   It is this core vision that keeps the team together
2. **Brand** (values and identity)
   In this case, branding can be the reputation of the yacht and the services it provides
3. **Mission** (tasks and responsibilities)
   Breakdown of who and how are we going to accomplish our goals
4. **Method** (systems and procedures)
   Systematic outline of how we are going to do this
5. **Success** (measurement criteria)
   Defining clear goal posts of what a successful job looks like.

Your goal as a leader is to

1. Set goals and clear expectations
2. Stay connected by regularly monitoring the work. Don't leave people to do the work and freak out at the end when the results are not as expected
3. Give feedback. Preferably in the constructive shit sandwich. Start with positive feedback regarding all the hard work this person has done and what a great job they are doing. In the middle of the two pieces of conversational bread, be specific about the shit that went wrong. What and/or how certain skills and behaviors require improving. Suggest how they can improve these skills to add value to the team, their repertoire of personal skills and/or increased monetary value. Finish the shit sandwich off by pointing out what great things this team member is doing with positive examples. Always end with cutting the shit sandwich by expressing your gratitude for their hard work.

To be respected leader is all about self-awareness and possessing certain character traits.

Management tips

✓ Give clear expectations

✓ Don't look for your team's approval; they're always going to talk behind your back

✓ Justify and explain your choices

✓ Listen and repeat back what they are saying

✓ Understand the company's direction. Explain your goals. If they aren't clear, your team will be disappointed. People need to know where they are going

✓ Keep the lines of communication open by being completely transparent and available
✓ Give people value. Are you giving people what they need so that they are committed?

There are four reasons people will do things for you. Look for what makes team members tick
1. **They like you** (Character)
2. **The want something from you.** Knowledge, qualifications or association (Competence)
3. **Money value** (Swapping their time for money)
4. **They have to.** (Rank)

- Essential Key Points For Conducting Meetings & Briefings -
Facilitating meetings that meet the requirements of all team members

Holding smart daily meetings

A meeting should always be outcome focused with a clear purpose that is understood by all attendees. All items listed on the agenda should have a required action with a time/date by which the nominated person should achieve the task. Begin the meeting by checking off the following points:

1. **Initial preparation.** Inform team members of the time and place, and the agenda to be discussed. This enables crew to be forewarned so they can chew over ideas and consider opinions on the topics to be discussed

2. **Open the meeting with topics to be discussed** in order and give an expected finishing time. Control the meeting in a relaxed, informal manner
   - ✓ Always start meetings with information about next trip/charter/owners' locations
   - ✓ What the boat is doing and where it will be going
   - ✓ Goals that the team are working towards. Standards, time limits, time management or project completion
   - ✓ **Be clear about your objectives.** What are you hoping to achieve?

3. Ensure that each person is valued by listening to them. Even if the leader/head stew has planned her intended action, a clever leader will gather the thoughts of her staff. This creates team member collaboration on ideas, the project, the event and the tasks involved. Gathering and listening to ideas ensures the team feels valued, which is a far better idea than to propose the action and then ask for the crew's opinions. There is no group contribution in that

4. **Clarify**, when necessary, without sounding condescending or patronizing. If you do not know the answer to a question, acknowledge the question by replying, "*This is a very good question. Unfortunately, I do not have all the information at hand and would like to come back to you at the next meeting with a definite answer. I am also open to suggestions.*"

5. If the discussion escalates, offer to talk to the person involved on a one-on-one basis after the meeting

Points to cover during weekly meetings

1. I appreciate all the hard work that you've done for this team
2. Special mentions of exceptional work completed (Recognition)
3. Foreseeable projects and events on the horizon
4. Take short hand notes of topics covered during the meeting. Compile and email them to the team to reiterate and confirm the points discussed
5. Recap on the team's mission statement.

Points to cover during one-on-one meetings

1. What do you need from me to for you to become a better team member and how can I lead you better?

2. I require our standards to be clearly understood and attained by all team members
3. Let's agree that we keep the same policies and procedures. Provide a hardcopy outline of "must dos" and "should dos" to clarify the black and white of the issue. There are to be no grey areas
4. Develop and stick with the coaching and training plan.

Briefing for missions that require execution

SMEACS provides a clear structure to follow when briefing teams of all sizes and scenarios. If you follow the format consistently it will make you look good and organised with all details.

- ✓ Situation
  What is the event/scenario?
- ✓ Mission
  What is required of the crew members?
  What are we trying to achieve as a team to provide a 7-Star dining experience?
- ✓ Execution
  How will we do it? What equipment will be need? Where will it be held?
- ✓ Administration
  From the yacht/beach? Following which paperwork?
- ✓ Command / Communication
  Ear pieces/radios/mobile phones/hand signals?
- ✓ Safety
  Hazards

- Smart Tools To Conduct Skill Training -
Setting your team up so everybody wins

Briefing for skill training

The four-step method is the best way to breakdown skill training.

- ✓ Introduction
  Explain the skill and why it is important.
- ✓ Demonstrate
  Demonstrate the skill correctly from start to finish.
- ✓ Practice
  Have one person, a team or all crew copy what you have done
  Crew practice repeatedly to ensure correct performance of the skill.
- ✓ Conclude
  Performance is reviewed and further instructions are issued.

Diagnostic questions for skill training

To determine the level of competency and engagement of crew that you are training, ask the following diagnostic questions. The example of ironing an expensive business shirt has been used here, swap it as necessary with your preferred skill.

1. Can you iron a business shirt?
2. Have you ever ironed an expensive shirt before?
3. Have you ever done this at a professional level?
4. Have you ever done anything similar to this before and can you explain?
5. Can you explain to me step by step how you've done it?
6. Would you like to learn the proper technique?
7. Is this something that would interest you?
8. Would you be confident to go ahead after you've been shown?

Now repeat back to me, using one or several of the following phases

1. What is it that you have to do?
2. Can you explain to me what your task is?
3. Can you tell me in your own words what you think the task is?
4. How do you feel about this task?
5. How confident do you feel about completing this task?

Considerations

✓ The training should be as realistic as possible
✓ If training in a scenario, it should include the skill you want to develop
✓ The skill should be challenging yet achievable
✓ The skill should not be overcomplicated or too big.

- The Intelligent Chief Stewardess's Guide to Managing Behaviors -
Why are they acting this way and how can I help?

Urg, there is always one on the team who is difficult. Consider the following underlying causes:

✓ Fatigue
✓ Discomfort: Working conditions too hot/cold
✓ Vision/hearing problems
✓ Language/literacy/numeracy difficulties
✓ Maturity level
✓ Attention seeking: a learned response … is the person isolated/lonely?
✓ Re-directed aggression. Small unrelated event triggers an disproportionate response
✓ Conduct norms. If expressed behavioural norms are not enforced students have little investment in adherence
✓ Cultural differences. Varied backgrounds, environments and experiences
✓ Task challenges. Conscious incompetence
✓ Stimulation. Too much/not enough
✓ The person really hates their job and wants to bring everyone down to their level of bitchy-ness. The usual.

Ask yourself the following questions to assist evaluation

1. What is the behaviour? What is the situation? Be objective: describe the action
2. Instead of stating he/she is rude, observe her/him and the "x" number of times they have interrupted the briefings
3. When does it happen? Is there a time pattern: i.e. at the end of sessions, after they have eaten carbs? Before their sugar and coffee fix?
4. What is going on before, during and after the behaviour? Reflect your communication, fairness, consistency with all team members
5. Who is involved or affected? Who is bothered?
6. Is the behaviour harmful? To the other team members, you or others?
7. How do you feel about the behaviour? Threatened, anger resulting in emotionally reacting
8. What changes would make the behaviour or situation acceptable?

Managing negative behaviour

- ✔ Set the example with your language and behaviour
- ✔ Naughty team members will observe you and their fellow crew. They will imitate behaviour that generates acceptable responses
- ✔ Reward desirable behaviour. *This could be as simple as praise*
- ✔ Do not ignore unacceptable behaviour. Peers can observe this as consent. Consequences for uncivil behaviour should be immediate to avoid others seeing them as role models
- ✔ Address the crew member away from the group. Never negatively talk of anyone, especially in-front of team members
- ✔ Identify what the undesirable behaviour is. State what is observed
- ✔ You may/choose to give rationale for unacceptance. This could gain understanding/compliance. Be wary, this also provides an opportunity for the student to disagree and debate
- ✔ Ask: is the crew member aware? What else is going on? Determine the cause
- ✔ State the required change by expressing desirable behaviours
- ✔ Remind the crew member that attitude is assessed and is reflected by the actions and behaviours demonstrated.

- Above The Belt Ways To Deal With Conflict -
Strategic planning to avoiding conflicting personality traits

Given the tight quarters and international personality traits, it's only natural for there to be conflicts. It is not only the team leader's responsibility but also all those in the team to resolve issues and keep good working relationships. The quicker conflicts get resolved in a positive way, the quicker the team can move forward in kicking goals. To add further value, if the team is caught fighting by the captain, he has no issue letting people go. It pays to play nice in the sandpit!

The action plan to dealing with conflict

1. Analyze team members to anticipate and avoid/predict conflict
2. Hold many short conversations to avoid conflicts and more problems in the future
3. Agree how you are going to work together. "This is how we are going to behave so that you become a self-reliant worker"
4. Create a checklist system where everyone is on the same page; familiarization of new crew, crew mess etiquette, laundry, pantries, service and turndown procedures, the list goes on…
5. Actively have each team member create his or her own job description. Fun!

Focus on the following points to resolve the issue. The only way forward is to listen!

- ✔ How will you open the conversation?
- ✔ What will you say? Be clear
- ✔ What will you agree to?
- ✔ What does he/she need?
- ✔ What do you need/want?
- ✔ What is our mutual goal? To provide high standards?

Stay on track during the conversation. Don't bring up issues from the past. Only bring solutions that you can both agree on to move forward.

12.

REALITY CHECK

LIFE ON CHARTER

Emotional Pain
Only Lasts 10-20 Minutes.
Anything Longer Is
Actually Self- Inflicted By
Over Thinking & Over
Analyzing.
Which Makes
Things Worse.

- How To Act In The Coolest VIP Club -

Pretending to be a billionaire when you get invited on as a guest

Any Dick, Harry or Sarah can create an impression with a $120,000 Hermes matte crocodile Birkin Bag as seen in Vogue, or splurge on a $10,000 bottle of rare wine at Le Louis XV, Alain Ducasse à l'Hotel de Paris in Monaco, but yachting is the domain of those with the uppermost echelon of wealth. Our world is obsessed with getting onto one of these floating palaces as guests. This is the last frontier of luxury, the unattainable elite club on the horizon glowing with the most fashionable lights that only mega money can buy.

If you are one of the lucky few or part of the most beautiful people in the world club, and have managed to make it into this select echelon as a guest, congratulations! You're doing something right that the rest of us are missing out on, or that's lacking in our circles of friends. To look like you belong in the Yacht VIP club and avoid bitchy comments made by those who pretend to be rich, read on:

What to wear

Anything that says, "Darling, I'm fabulous, look at me. I'm somebody! I belong here." Aim to style yourself on the most tasteful, coolest-kid-on-the-block outfit that money can buy. Choose a winning outfit that draws attention when boarding or debarking on the passer rail. You can only dress like a bummed rock star if you're a supermodel trying to shake the paparazzi. This 'statement outfit' should never be created with more is better. Dress appropriately for the sun and weather. Bring a 100% cashmere sweater or a large oversized knit in the season's latest colors, just in case it gets a little chilly on the water. Matching earrings and necklaces are a given. Tropical-fruit-sized real jewels will quickly establish you as the pack leader. And yes, all the ladies and crew will google the setting of your jewels, check the label on your shoes and matching handbags. Scuffmarks and vinyl is unforgivable. It's a fashion competition on these yachts. Even small children are rocking this season's Marc Jacobs and Lana Marks' clutches.

Hats look better if they are authentic Fedora in any shade other than white, or extra-large brimmed. No lace, fake flowers or feathers. Attempts at recycling race/derby/polo hats will not be tolerated, unless you have just come from a funeral. Over the top looks can only be pulled off by fashion designers, mother of the yacht owners and complete extroverts. Think like an Italian woman, one that shops at Celine and holidays in St Barts.

Where you should be

Wherever your host has placed you. Stick with the group. No peaking in offices, guest cabins or the bridge, unless invited. You're not supposed to be surrounded by the priceless artifacts on your own! Crew areas are by invitation only, and you need to respect their privacy. No, we do not like it when you come down to shoot the breeze, or invite yourself into the galley to fix yourself a sandwich. It's our job and you're not helping! Go back to getting drunk and being indolent on the sundeck, for goodness sake!

How you should act

Whatever anyone tells you, do not make yourself at home. Don't touch, don't touch! Keep your hands to yourself. Everything has been polished to a 7-Star showroom standard, and it takes a team to maintain the yacht's finish.

There is an over-abundance of free-flowing socially lubricating choices. Know your drinking limit. Standard practice is to keep pace with your hosts to avoid the she-drinks-too-much glances. Keep your shit together. Try not to stumble and throw up over the side. This kind of behavior will not help you snag a boyfriend no matter how drop-dead gorgeous you are.

Always remember, money doesn't buy you good taste, good looks or good manners. Be charming to everyone, get the hell off Instagram and bring a few choice conversation topics to the table that everyone can join in with. Don't compare which college you went to, argue about the rich and poor of this world, or politics. Just put your sunscreen on, drink the expensive imported Pavan cocktails and play nice with the other kids on the sundeck. Surely you can keep yourselves entertained while you wait for your other friends to arrive by private helicopter from the other yacht.

What to say

Yacht owners love it when you gush about how impressive their yacht is. Choose words such as:

"Wow, your boat is so big!"

"Your yacht is the best-looking one here."

"Amazing, look at the wood finish."

"Your interior decorator did a splendid job."

"You have the best taste I've ever seen."

It's an ego thing. Everyone wants the biggest and best yacht in the harbor. Even better when the dock space is too small. It makes the yacht look bigger and better.

How to treat crew

Be charming. The same people that clean your toilets are the ones who serve your food and drinks. That means please and thank-you all the way. Snide jokes about how good-looking the crew are and why they're waiting on you, don't go down too well. Mate, we're all trying to survive. If you're a male guest, don't try and bed the beautiful South African stewardesses. The wives hate it and their little jealousy demons go berserk. The stewardesses are the ones who suffer by losing their jobs, while you go back to your multi-million houses on three continents and screwing your multiple speed-dial mistresses.

Please do not

- ✓ Smoke in undesignated areas. Politely ask for an ashtray
- ✓ Refrain from having sex in or on the boat's public areas, unless you own or chartered the yacht
- ✓ No swimming without letting a crew member know. The current is vicious outside St Bart's, especially in the Hamptons and the beaches of Ibiza.

- They'll Never Confuse You With Royalty -
How to tell if someone comes from money

We're getting a global influx of new millionaires, which makes it harder to read if someone comes from old (had it for a long, long time) or new (only just got it but loving it) money. With all the credit our banks are handing out, it's too easy to purchase a Hublot Black Caviar Bang watch, Ferrari 250 LM, Brioni bespoke suit and Swaine Adeney Brigg luggage, but how does one tell it they are faking it or not? You know if they came from moneyed backgound if they possess the following traits:

1. You'll notice they have no idea how much things cost in the real world. When they talk money, they speak in millions and never complain how much something costs

2. They have expensive hobbies that only the well-to-do can afford. Keeping and racing thoroughbred horses, competing in sailing competitions for fun, flying, racing cars and traveling around the world riding motorbikes. These are the kids who were forced to take up ice-skating, rowing and ballet as children

3. When you ask them what they do for fun, they have past times that you would never think of. "Want to come game fishing in my helicopter over the Great Barrier Reef?" "My Father just bought a new Wally sailing boat. Care to join me sailing around Jamaica?" "Let's fly to London this weekend for a drink. My mate's just opened up his fourth private members club." "A bunch of us are going to Tuscany to so-and-so's castle. It's going to be terribly dull, but if you come with me, I'll cope."

4. Rich people ask you, "Where did you summer?" In return, listen for these key phases:
"My friends and I stayed at my father's house on the French Riviera."
"Yes, I love it there, my mother has a house in St Barts."
"We rented a house for the summer in Italy and the Hamptons."
"We just spent a week on so-and-so's yacht."
"We stayed at the Fairmont/Hotel President Wilson/The Connaught/The Shangri-La."

5. They have, or their parents have membership to member's only clubs such as The Meadow Club, Shinnecock Hills and the Maidstone Club in the Hamptons, Annabel's in London's Yacht Club de Monaco and the Capital Club in Dubai. To be a member your membership has to have been passed down by deceased parents, and you must be able to pay the $80,000 joining fee, and/or be recommended by a minimum of three people. It's a small satisfaction that they have to wait years before being accepted

6. People that come from money have different conversation topics. They talk about backing two sides of a political campaign, building schools in Haiti, purchasing artwork for their collection in Paris, funding charity events and being on the board of international non-profits

7. Clothing labels. It's pretty hard to fake being rich when your casual wardrobe is made up of Emilio Zegna and Gieves & Hawks for the men and Chanel and Givenchy for the women.
Their casual outfits are something that you would save up for and wear only on special occasions. Take note: if you see their name embroidered in their clothing, they're very, very wealthy

8. People with money always have well-kept accessories. Their handbags, shoes, underwear, and socks will be brand new. You will not find them with scuffed worn goods or anything with holes, unless they're designer holes

9. Food preferences. This is obvious if the children ask for top-shelf foods like caviar with Irish buttered crackers for a snack

10. Their straight posture, mannerisms and body language are refined. From a young age, they have been hounded by their parents and a constant supply of nannies to keep their backs straight, never rest hands or elbows on the table, no feet on the table and to sit neatly in chairs

11. Table manners. The men will always hold out chairs and invite the women to help themselves first. There is never a mad dash to the table to pick at the food with their hands. Moneyed people always use cutlery, plates and serviettes. The way they use cutlery is a huge telltale. Forks are used prongs down, with the curve facing you, never to be used as a shovel

12. They never cover their meal with their serviette when they've finished. The well-mannered fold their serviettes neatly, place them next to the plate, put their cutlery at an angle and leave the uneaten food in a neat pile in the middle or to one side. Same formal etiquette applies during canapé service. They do not put their used toothpicks, cutlery or uneaten food back on the tray that is still being passed around. They will keep their scraps in a napkin and politely ask you to take it away

13. Not once will well-to-do people help themselves. They will ask you for whatever they need. They will never reach over the table to get something, pick something off the floor, or leave the table to help themselves

14. As fifty-year-olds they still call their mothers, Mummy and fathers, Daddy.

IN THE MONEY GAME

- What To Do With The €5000 Tip -
Entirely possible

You hear of the fabled €5000 tip! It usually happens with minimum two-week charter trips and super happy guests. You've polished their sunglasses, served a thousand Aperol spritzers and listened to sob stories from the Madam complaining that she is not at the Paris fashion shows. Hell, you even turned over the master cabin when she was out shopping and her horny husband discreetly had back door prostitutes tendered in. Read carefully. SAVE THE MONEY. Do not pay off bills, credit cards or student loans. That is what your wage is used for. Pay yourself and put the money into your retirement fund. Be clever and use it as a down payment on a house. Do not blow it on clothing, toys, a Ducati motorbike or this season's must-have Chanel handbag. You'll only regret it like the rest of us.

- Boss Ladies Be Making Money -
MAKING MILLIONS

With luck you're surrounded by some classy boss ladies that make you understand that you cannot rely on any man for your financial freedom. You are now in the position that whatever you make is yours to keep. We're not going to talk about taxes here. You're going to have to pay taxes somewhere and explain where all this money has come from. Save it for your tax accountant back at home.

The reason we do this job is for money and travel. It has been said that women have a time limit in the yachting industry. When I first heard this I disagreed and was highly offended. But, the reality is that one day you're going to get sick of not having a back yard and living out of a suitcase with random bunch of strangers. You may even start thinking of the future, hooking up with your soul mate, planting an herb garden and cooking dinner in a real house. Do you really want to be fifty-years-old, sleeping on a bunk bed and sharing a bathroom? Nope? Neither do I.

The money in yachting becomes additive. Just one more season, just $X0,000 more, then I'll stop! To get the most out of yachting and set you up for the rest of your life, let's set some financial goals. Money is a skill that one can learn and practice. Think about it, you see these multi-millionaire kids trading the stock market at eleven years old - they learnt it from their daddies.

- How To Use Yachting To Make Your First Million -

Start this habit as soon as you receive your first paycheck. You don't want to finish seven years of yachting and have nothing to show for it.

1. Stop senseless spending. Snuff out those expensive habits. The only bill you have to pay is your phone bill

2. Spend half, save half. As you get better and see that bank account filling up, you'll want to save more

3. Clear your debts as soon as possible. The credit card is the first one. Stop using it! It's fifteen to twenty-two percent interest. If you're repaying the minimal balance, it will take you YEARS to pay off. Repay the whole loan at the end of the month to avoid charges

4. Work out what your monthly spend is. Then take it out of your bank account. Do not dip into your credit card or savings account. This will keep your spending in check and stop all those nasty transaction bills. If you're overseas, this can run into the hundreds

5. Work out where the rest of that money is going:
    a. 1000 savings
    b. 1000 credit card
    c. 500 student loan >> to begin with

6. Set financial goals. How much do you want to have saved in six months? One year? What are you saving for? A house? How much do you need to save per month to get there?

7. Set up automatic withdrawals from your bank account. Start with ten percent of your pay being transferred to an untouchable account for a deposit on a house. Once you have the deposit and then some, begin depositing money for your retirement fund. Darling, we are too fabulous to be struggling at the age sixty

8. Collect everything that can be a tax write-off. Flights, personal wet weather gear, sunscreen and sunglasses. Not much to claim when the boat takes cares of everything but try your best

9. Avoid new luxury wheels, motorbikes, bicycles and skateboards. Who knows when you might have to get rid of it

10. Don't ever sell yourself short. Build on your strengths. Know your worth when you have experience under your belt. Own it and ask for it

11. Don't rely on luck. If you don't know what you want, nothing is what you'll get

12. Check your bank account weekly. Open a overseas bank account a.s.a.p.

13. Stop eating and drinking out. Eat food that is provided by the boat. There is no need for you to drink the most expensive cocktails in the most expensive bar

14. Find a way to make a passive income

Yachting is the prime career to save money, as there are minimum expenses on your part. Your rent, food, laundry and toiletries are all taken care of. Do not waste this opportunity — bank as much as you can. Money in the bank = less worries for when shit hits the fan. Anything can happen in this world.

What should you be doing with all this money? Where should your paycheck be going?
    ¼ property
    ¼ emergency fund
    ¼ investment stocks
    ¼ retirement fund

Get cracking on this, there is nothing more wonderful than having your bank account humming when you're sleeping.

NEVER ENDING SUMMERS

- 8 Killer Tips To Deal With Fatigue When The Inside Of Your Bones Are Tired -
And you're only four days into a back-to-back season

You know you're in trouble when four days into a back-to-back Med season, you're dreaming of sipping strawberry tequila margaritas on a sun lounger in the most exclusive resort on a remote Philippine island. You want to be far, far away from this boat but your bank balance tells you, "NO! Girl, you need to work."

I swear on the next hot guy that I date, being a yacht stewardess is the toughest job you'll ever do. Are you ready for it? Prepare to push through 100+ hour working weeks. Our days are taken up with guest services and all the seemingly insignificant little details which are essential in completing the big picture for running a mega yacht. Life on charter is hectic, with lack of sleep, no privacy and social deprivation. All the positive good vibes that you once had have been sucked up by the constant rotation of charter guests who keep complaining the beers are not cold enough, the sun is too bright and the internet is too slow. You have never felt so utterly exhausted in your life and, with no contact with the outside world, this boat feels like prison. It is now normal to hit that point of utter exhaustion and cry yourself to sleep.

The constant tiredness is not your only concern. Your hardest lesson in yachting is that nothing is personal. The rest of the crew are as cranky and tired as you are. All they want to do is finish the trip and get the fuck off the boat. Now is not the time to push other people's buttons. One wrong comment, when someone is feeling exhausted will result in a hate fest against you. Crew, like tribes, are malicious and ruthless. They will turn on you, and lack of sleep will make you dead meat. These scenarios have actually happened: a captain who was stabbed to death in St. Marteen by a chef who'd had enough, the Serbian stew shouting death threats to the chief stew because she couldn't find her radio and the junior engineer slowly killing the chief engineer with butter & bacon sandwiches off the Greek Islands — all lack of sleep.

You must keep your energy high and consistent to avoid being stabbed!
Here are a few of our tried and trusted tricks to get us through balls-to-the-walls trips:

1. Focus on making a whopping great big tip happen. Every time you serve one of these wealthy Forbes-listed human beings, make their beds or clean their toilets, look them in the eye or mentally project it into their minds — $3000 tip. Repeat and repeat. Don't worry, these people have unlimited money and wouldn't hesitate to drop that on a fancy dinner or a new handbag. Even the richest people plead poor but will still drop a $100,000 on a private membership for an outdated golf club, $80 000 a year for one child's tuition and $8000 for dinner in Ibiza. I think they can afford your tip. Their poor and your poor are two very different things! Please be grateful when

you receive any tip. I once received three wooden bead bracelets as a parting gift and the hissy fit that followed was disgusting to watch

2. Smile. Somehow, pretending to be happy makes one happy. For this to work, wear your largest smile with un-gritted teeth. High five yourself in the mirror every morning and say, "Yes, today is going to be awesome."

3. Count your blessings. Give thanks for all that's happening in your life. It may be hard to achieve when you're knackered, have PMS and/or blind hate. Start with the small stuff: I am grateful for breathing, I am grateful for having busy hands, I am grateful for this experience, for whenever I'm out of my comfort zone and feeling pain, I am growing

4. Consume large amounts of caffeine and all the uppers you can get your obsessively washed hands on. Don't discriminate. Consume your preferred drug/s in huge quantities. Trial pre-workout powder and energy tablets to diminish the just-got-to-get-through-the-morning feelings

5. Wake up early and press your own green juice. The energy from this will work wonders. You can feel your cells singing when you drink this

6. Learn to meditate. Download apps and iTunes podcasts

7. Make friends with everyone on board, no matter what it takes. Life is better when you're laughing together. Don't get sucked into the misery-loves-company team. You've got time to figure out what makes these people tick. Assess who is the biggest, meanest person on board and get them on your side

8. Keep your energy levels up. Take vitamins. Focus on feeding your mind good things.
Stop complaining. If you concentrate on your problems, you'll get more of them. The people who survive and are still friends at the end of the season are the ones who are polite and never forget their manners. Everyone remembers and they'll want to buy you drinks at the end of the charter. Instead of badmouthing you and trying to run you off the wharf at the end of the night. This charter nightmare will end, I promise, then you'll get the fuck off the boat. Now that's how you deal with fatigue.

- The Ugly Truth About Dealing With Annoying People -
Not everyone is as easy to get along with as you

Let's get real here! Even though you might be a devastatingly friendly person, you have been hired to work and live in an environment where these people are neither your family nor friends. You don't know these new crewmates from a bar of soap. It's no different from choosing random people off the street or deciding to live with the guy you picked up last night after eight margaritas and a bite of one taco (28/02/2017 Racco's Tacos & Tequila bar, Fort Lauderdale)
You have, however, signed up for a career in yachting, and this is part of the job. Say hello to people's idiosyncrasies and smelly feet.

Being easy to live with is all about what you put out there:

1. When you think everyone around you is a wanker. It's not them — it's you

2. Practice not saying anything. Smiley poker face. Complete ALL tasks as requested as soon as possible

3. Don't start thinking about how inferior these people are to you. This style of thinking will get you nowhere

4. Being on a yacht is all about keeping the lines of communication open. No ignoring people, talking back or rolling your eyes when spoken to. Understand that other people communicate differently. They may come off blunt but they could be shy. Recognize that you're all trying to achieve the same goals but have different ways of doing it:

- ✓ You'll find people from the Eastern Block are very blunt, ready to knife you as soon as you turn your back
- ✓ South Africans believe they're superior to everyone els
- ✓ Australians use way too many swear words and love to color outside the lines
- ✓ Italians believe they know it all

5. Just say yes and agree. Does it REALLY matter that much? Come on, do you think that when you remember it five years from now it will have mattered how the towels were rolled? No, so just let it go. The rule is: if it does not matter in five years, do not spend more than five minutes thinking about it.

6. If you think you're wrong — even a little bit — be a big person, say so and apologize. If not, you run the risk of the other person harboring ill feelings towards you and that will make your life hell

7. Try this on for size, "I'll do my best"

8. This one's a charmer, "Sure no trouble." Then do whatever is requested of you. Remember you're here to work, and keep your job

9. Think differently about the person you love to hate. Try to project a sense of love around them. Only love can kill hate. Change how you think about them, and the way they treat you will change too

10. Some people are just plain dickheads. Just because you're in yachting and have been doing it for years does not make you a good human being. This is not something you can change

11. Catch that first negative thought. If it starts, it's all over. It will only snowball with all the long crossings, stressful situations and fiddly little requests

12. Never complain or bitch about this person to the other crew. If you put it out there, they will know.

Sounds harder than practicing Bikram yoga with a hammering hangover, but it can be done. You make your life as hard as you want it. The onboard relationships with your fellow crewmembers can make or break your time in the yachting industry. Arguing, screaming, snide comments or hissy fits are not tolerated on any boat. A one-moment disagreement and with a small but held-onto grudge could lead to long-term conflict and potentially getting fired. The objective is for the whole crew to maintain a happy, healthy environment without you being the bad apple.

- Using Life Saving Mantras To Improve Your Bank Balance -

Our lives are the stories we tell ourselves

Cut, copy and paste these on the laundry room wall and use them instead of swearing underneath your breath. Think of all the money that the universe has waiting for you, if you just chill out and let it come.

1. Don't drop the ball. Repeat and repeat
2. Thank-you universe for my life is filled with abundance. There is nothing that I need or want
3. Everything is always working out for me
4. I'm doing really well, I am right exactly where I am suppose to be, in order to experience the most of this life. I am never in the wrong place. Sometimes I am in the right place looking at things the wrong way
5. Positive thoughts attract more positive thoughts. What makes me feel good?
6. Next boat is going to be bigger and I'm going to have more help
7. Gold Rolex. Gold Rolex. Gold Rolex. Gold Rolex
8. Calm down. Fuck, does …………….. (insert your name here) really care? No
9. €7000 tip. Look guests in the eyes when thinking this and when making their bed. Put it out there for collective conscience. This works
10. On your eighth week of back-to-back charters and you cannot see straight, repeat, "I'm making money. Suck it up"
11. My personal favorite after four months straight is 'smile.' "Don't worry ……. (Insert your name here) they're paying you to be here"
12. Stop crying. Only babies cry
13. My bank balance needs topping up/doubling. A.S.A.P

RELATIONSHIPS

- Bringing Boys Back To The Yacht And Getting Away With It -

It's hard to say no to a man begging to see your yacht

Darling, it's time for us to chat. Bringing friends/guests back without prior permission is a fireable offence. Don't get confused about your living situation. Just because you live here, this is not your home. You are still an employee. We understand the situation though, we've all been tempted. He pressured you into seeing the yacht, and he was way too cute to say no.

See what you can get away with:

1. Before boarding with your friend be aware of where the yacht's cameras are. Who is awake? Who is watching the monitors in the crew mess? Are the cameras trained on the passer rail? If they are, you've got no hope. Go somewhere else
2. Do not leave your friend's shoes on the dock or the crew entrance. It's a dead giveaway. Keep all your stuff together and take it down to your cabin
3. Sneak on. No giggling or talking loudly. This is serious stuff. You must act like a criminal — you don't want to get caught before the fun begins, do you?
4. Choose the least used and best hidden cabin
5. Lock the door
6. Preferably don't even touch the bed, but if you can't resist it, crash on top of the day cover. Throw all guest pillows on the floor. No bed making here
7. At four to five am, get up, get dressed and get ready to bolt. YOU HAVE TO BE OUT OF THERE BEFORE EVERYONE GETS UP. Wake up your guest. Sober up! Do not loll around in bed watching TV

8. Make the bed up to showroom standard. Do not strip the bed

9. Collect all used water bottles, rubbish and evidence of your stay

10. Check all surfaces for fingerprints and smudges. Make them disappear with your T-shirt or sock

11. Spray the room with air freshener

12. On your way out check the carpet. Telltale signs to look for are oversized footprints, too many footprints and the carpet looks messy. To cover your tracks, roll up a towel and pull it across the floor in one direction

13. Get that boy out of there. Fingers crossed it's still dark. No kissing next to the passer rail or walking him out. Don't be seen with him. Just get him away from the boat a.s.a.p. Make him disappear. Are you getting the point?

14. Get back on board. RUN quietly through the crew areas on your tiptoes

15. Shower

16. Stay out of the guest areas. It's a dead giveaway. You don't want to be caught in that same cabin getting rid of the evidence

17. Try to remain calm and keep your big mouth shut!

You might get away with it once. But don't bring the same boy back the following night, and then sleep in thinking that no-one is going to notice because it's Sunday morning. The yacht's cameras may be off, but captain can ask the shipyard security to view the CCTV footage. If you get caught red handed, you can kiss your job goodbye. You're fired! #truestory

- The Biggest Question I Always Get Asked. DO I OR DON'T I? -
Dealing with relationships in tight quarters
OH! NO YOU DIDN'T!!

You had to do the crew, didn't you? You just couldn't help it, could you? Cue — severe headshake. I see where you're coming from. You've spent weeks at sea with this hottie and both of you are on your best behavior trying to impress each other. On your first night back on dry land, you're close to each other in the bar and ooh swoon, he smells so good! A few drinks later you're walking back to the boat and BANG! His lips are on yours and you're kissing!

No!

Want to try it another way?

The OMG-I-didn't-know-men-like-that-existed Chief Officer who takes his shirt off every Friday for Budgie-smuggler-end-of-the-week wash downs is just too scrumptious for words! We all saw it coming. How you dash to the crew mess to make him cups of tea, asking him what his favorite color is on our lunch break, and making sure his shirt is always ironed for Saturday night drinks. He is amazing. We know. After months of: "Do you think he likes me?" "Tsk, I don't know." Then, he finally asks you out. BANG! Here's your chance. You go in for the kill.

NO! no! NO! no! STOP IT.

For the most part, when you've been at sea for weeks, all the deckhands are handsome. Trust me, you're not the first one to notice that these very delicious deckhands should have signed up with FORD models, instead of polishing boats. There are gorgeous men on every boat, in every port. Do us all a favor and choose one that you're **not** living with.

Here's why we think it's a terrible idea: screwing the crew is always the worst idea.

First off, we have to hear about how wonderful he is — he seems to be the only thing that you think about. Puke, and puke again! Then, we have to hear all about your first moment. Jeez, what are you — thirteen? Then, it's the sneaking around, pretending nothing's happening in front of the crew and leading a double life on and off the yacht. It's too much! Your whole sordid little life is being lived inside a one-bedroom apartment that you share with nine other crew. Something has to give sooner or later.

Twenty-four-seven with the same person is a tough ask. Are you genuinely surprised when one half of this dynamic duo feels suffocated and claustrophobic? When you have your first fight, the world is falling apart, your life is over! (*Cue eye roll*) And we, the girls you work with have to deal with it. Not going to happen, sunshine! It'll end with two crew members fired — not good!

- How To Keep Your Sanity When Your Boyfriend Is On The Other Side Of The World -

Sucked in! The long distance relationship

I always shudder when a new stew tells me she has a boyfriend at home. Why would you want to do that? Haven't you noticed all the gorgeous blokes around that are ripe for the picking?

You know the maritime industry is intended for the toughest of the tough. You'll go for months without seeing your loved ones. So when you do meet the one, you're going to have to work hard on it to keep it going. We understand. We also know it's completely normal in yachting to fall head over heels in love with the one, and the next week your billionaire owner will be sending you off to the other side of the world. You honestly cannot plan one day ahead.

Tried and tested methods to doing long distance:

1. Call your boyfriend every day crying and complaining about not being able to have sex
2. Call your fiancé and if you catch a whiff of fun on the other end, chuck the biggest hissy fit. Make his life hell. Constantly call, pick another fight and hang up
3. Stalk him and other ex-boyfriends on FB. Hours and oodles of entertainment on watch. Keep hitting that refresh button
4. Demand to know who all the women in his life are. Use his FB friend list as ammunition
5. Make him Skype you for hours on end at random times
6. Go through every single detail of your relationship in your head. Over and over again. Pick out all his faults and remind him of them when he calls
7. Cry every day because you miss him. Give him the ultimatum. Make him quit his job
8. Or you could just break up with him. That solves all problems
9. When in doubt. Purchase one of those big electric things. A fast and quiet one that travels well.

God save your soul if you think boys are the answer to anything. I can promise you when you make this person your whole world, your life will crumble. You're depending on him too much, to be your boyfriend, lover, best friend, confidant, mother, father, sister. We all know it's hard being on a boat doing menial work, eight hours a day. Learn to control your thoughts and keep your mind in check. Meditation helps — find five or ten minutes to just breathe and let it all go, it will help clear all the repetitive thoughts. Anxiety is defined as turning the same thoughts over and over in your head and expecting a different outcome. As soon as you start thinking about him, stop! Picture something else. There are three main thoughts that you should be concentrating on. Your money, your career and your health. Focus!

- Warning. Living With Couples -

Man, this is a tough one. Imagine being in a relationship with someone who is NOT actually the one. Add to this, the mind fuck of living in tight quarters with multiple personalities. It's comparable to never leaving your office, ever. Whether you like it or not, your relationship is under scrutiny all the time. Living in small spaces with limited stimulation — what else have people got to talk about?

If you're in a relationship on board DO NOT make your problems the crew's problems. Keep them to yourself and never bad mouth your partner with other team members.

Having said that there are some awesome couples out there. Fun, professional and successful at keeping their relationship private. You never hear them trash talking each other and they genuinely love being together. These people make you want to sing and fall in love — they are such a positive reinforcement of what a good relationship is all about.

Hiring crew as couples

Word on the street — captains are not fond of this idea because if one part of the couple doesn't work out, you lose two crew. Respected leaders in the industry are rewarded for crew longevity. They hire individuals who are going to stick around.

Saying that, there are couples' jobs out there. They do exist. If you're in love and know he/she is the one, be patient, because those the dream-couple jobs do come around. When they do, it's the best. Finally!

SEXUAL HARASSMENT

- What To Do When The Owner or a Guest Takes A Shine To You -

Are you hitting on me? You can't buy me

But a fat tip or a gift of a new designer handbag may help me stick around

Gorgeous ladies, we've all been there with unwanted attentions from employers. It always starts with over the top smiles, sly comments, a pat on the bum and an invitation for drink. These good-for-nothing, ill-mannered sailors, make a game out of harassing women.

To be honest the scenario where guests hit on crew is not to be taken too seriously. The richest, most eligible men in the world have unlimited choices when it comes to the opposite sex. They see more pussy than a toilet seat. The places our millionaire charter guests frequent and the people they mix with, are the richest of the rich. Your average millionaire yacht owner is not bothered whether he gets the girl who cleans his toilets, serves his meals and waits on him day and night, into his bed for a cuddle.

Smile and keep it professional at all times. Take it as a compliment. With your biggest fake sincere smile say, "Thank you, sir, maybe in a different environment, that move would be considered seductive, not creepy, like now." IN YOUR HEAD! Should the sexual advances escalate to the point where it's really uncomfortable, report it the person above you. That's why they're paid the big bucks.

If you are a stewardess like me, who is tired of doing laundry, being a slave to rich people and you've seen the greener grass, then our story is different. Do it, give it a shot with the lonely billionaire! Then let us all know how you did it, how you figured it out so you could have the all-expenses-paid life and endless summer holidays.

- Yuck. The Sleezy Captain Advances -

Sexual harassment

Welcome to the casting couch where sleazy captains think they're God and interview stewardesses as potential girlfriends. It's no secret in the yachting industry that captains have developed a reputation for being lonesome sex-deprived sea dogs. Being at the top and making the big bucks comes at a price.

The process of hiring live aboard potential girlfriends goes like this:

A girl dreaming of a fabulous life at sea and new to yachting is desperate to get a foot in the door. The job interview with the hiring captain has been extended to a dinner invitation. "So we can get to know each other better," he says. You want the job and feel pressured to say yes. Over dinner, the captain will be charming, funny and laugh at your jokes. Warning bells should go off when he enters your personal space and touches your hand. On the way out of the restaurant, after a few too many drinks the captain makes another advance. How it plays out will be reflected in your job security. I love this line, "Good thing I'm too drunk to notice you hitting on me and get all freaked out."

We've been in this scenario:

Mr. Overweight — been eating too many carbs and has a wife and three kids at home, comes to check on you during the graveyard shift. While unloading the dishwasher in your best skort, the pantry door squeaks opens to expose the captain wearing his bathrobe undone to the waist and tied very loosely. Don't look for his pecker! "Evening Christina, how is everything?" His midnight greeting is followed by an obvious once-over ogle. "Would you like to join me afterwards for a night cap?" Best to use this line: "Oh, thank you, captain but I have this nasty little rash and I need to put some special cream on it. Maybe I can call you later to help me?"

You'll hear stories of married captains with newborns at home, accidently opening doors while stews are showering or changing. I've had girlfriends that have been cock-blocked in bars by their captains, and have been fired later for not coming home with them. Men are a possessive bunch, whether you are dating them or not.

Here's how to deal with it when you get that funny feeling from the captain when moving on board. At the appropriate time, tell all the crew that your ex-boyfriend is a professional Mauy Thai fighter for Australia. He was awesome and trained you to fight. You don't know if you could find another man who could live up to those ideals.

If that doesn't work, cut straight to the chase as soon as an unwanted advance is made. Ask him if he's looking for a girlfriend or a stewardess? "Are we having a professional working relationship, or one that has advantages?" Nip it in the bud there and then. If he thinks this is unnecessary or too aggressive at least he knows where you both stand. Life is too short.

If your captain is professional, loves his job and wants to have a happy crew on board, this type of shenanigans will never happen. On the other hand, if the captain looks like your dream man, straight out of a GANT model shoot and some of them do! — what a catch, Babe! make it happen. These single men are hard to find.

DRINKING & DRUGS

- Dealing With Professional Drinkers On Yachts -
Drinking always comes at a price

Well, you've made it this far. The crew is great and you love the social aspect of the job. Actually you've been cut four times already this week and it's only Wednesday. You're thinking that everyone is doing it and no-one has said anything, it must be ok. Time to put partying and yachting into context. Have the mentality that the people you're living with are your reference and your potential next job. Be aware of how easy it is to get a bad reputation. If you're a party animal, that's what they're going to say about you! You're supposed to be working here and saving money!

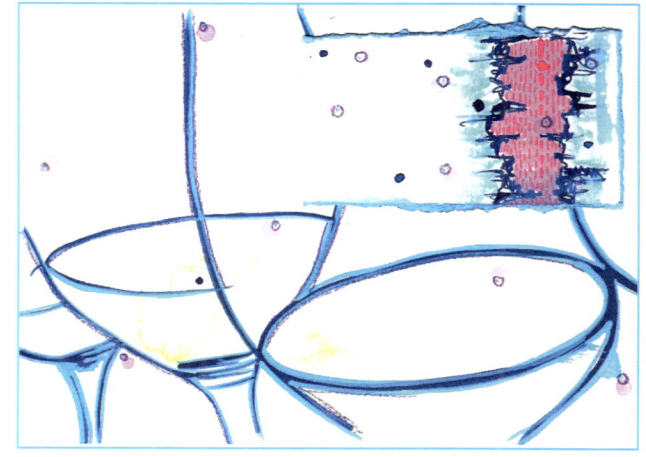

Reality check: Here we go! You've arrived in St Maarten. Captains fear this place and refer to it as destination high crew turnover. The drinks are stupidly cheap: one dollar at the Soggy dollar bar, and every bar that you walk into has several drug dealers out the front ready to cater to your every need. After the largest week night party you've ever had in your life, maybe you can get away with sleeping in or being sick — once. If it happens again, your job is on the line. There go your references, pay packet and living space! Keep it in check. Have a few quiet ones here and there.

Remember, you live in your workspace and could be called upon to work at any time.

The rule is:

You can have a few drinks with the limit being <u>three on a school night.</u>

Do not go out and drink with the guests or with guests on board. When you've got a hangover and are non-functioning, everyone else has to pick up your slack. That's just what the team needs, more work! On your first owner/charter trip – DO NOT go out with the deck crew and chef for a couple and put the bar tab on the boat swipy swipy at Atlantis Casino nightclub. Then go back to some random Mexican's yacht to drink tequila till six am. Do not fight or fuck the crew in the bushes on the way home. Do not sleep in your epaulets covered in dirt with twigs in your hair, you will get woken up by your chief stew half an hour after your shift starts. #truestory

Golden weekday drinking rule

You can drink as much as you can. Tequila shots, bottles of champagne and espresso martinis but you have to be in bed by 20:00. No later or else this trick won't work.

Hangover prevention and cure for a big drinking night

One painkiller before drinking, one painkiller while drinking and one before bed. Drink as much water as you can handle. Complete this process with more painkillers when you wake. Pray for the best.

If you're really hungover

Read carefully! GET UP! No matter how drunk you still are. No one knows except you. Wake up, put on that uniform and that big SMILE of yours, and start the day. Eat heavy carbs. Hit the Gatorade, Berocca, coffee, juices and anything else you can get your hands on to get yourself throughout the day.

Remember, you're an alcoholic if you crave it every day.

- 4 Tips To Successfully Do The Walk Of Shame Properly -
And cover your tracks after a big night out

We're a social bunch and sometimes it's hard for us to say no to any fun that is going on! Now it's time to sneak back on board without the whole marina knowing. The following advice is appropriate to use after serving irritatingly ungrateful people for five months straight on end, breaking up with the love of your life because you're too transient, or just because your best friend egged you on. These are our best-kept secrets. Please don't tell ANY captain.

1. Before heading out for a big one, stash your crummiest exercise outfit in the bushes down the street. Chuck in a water bottle and hat to look authentic. Don't forget chewing gum and a spray can of deodorant! After your big night, on the way back to the boat, take your hidden workout gear and change in the nearest bathroom, not on the street. Someone will catch you. Hide your party outfit up in the public toilets to be retrieved later. Return to the yacht dressed in your gym gear. If anyone asks, you were out running. Get dressed in your crew uniform as quick as you can and count down the hours till lunch. It takes organization, but you can do it

2. Better yet. Say you're heading out for a run in the afternoon. Have drinks, crash at a mate's place and run back in the morning

3. Sneak back onto the boat before anyone wakes. Dress in your crew uniform and nap in the crew mess until everyone surfaces for breakfast. For all they know you got up early and crashed out again. For this to be believable you have to look and smell the part. Use eye drops, cover the smell of alcohol and slather yourself in Clarins beauty flash balm. Do not lag during the day. Have a red bull for breakfast. This method only works if you nap on the crew couches, not under the table

4. If you're late starting and everyone is up and working... OMG you better have the most original story cooked up. Something along the lines of a friend being jailed, robbed at gunpoint by the taxi driver or an emergency back home could work.

- I Did Learn This In School! Dealing Drugs -
But don't let the crack heads on the yacht

It is not uncommon for larger yachts to ask for a drug test to be performed before hiring a crew. This is either done as a blood sample or hair follicle test. Captains can also ask for a drug test to be completed any time during your employment. Drug testing kits are easily purchased at Wall Mart and online. I know of captains that keep a drug testing kit in their cabins and threaten to test the crew around the dinner table. It usually happens the night of pulling into St Maarten.

Funny, what does one do when the captain is the one with a drug abuse problem? There are terrible captains out there with hidden drug abuse issues and conspicuous drinking habits. You'll experience the violent mood swings, the nonsensical verbal abuse of crew, anger management issues and the copious amounts of alcohol to calm their nerves. What comes around goes around. Captains that think they're God, have a long way to fall and when they fall, they fall hard.

If the crew is not secretly doing drugs, then we'll have dim witted guests who can't keep their shit together. The millionaire multi-store owner who was sketchy as fuck on his phone, cutting deals and then running off to score in the car park. Then coming back, ready to pound another bottle of gin. He was embarrassing to watch, dropping all his drugs on the main deck aft while calling out to passing celebrities and trying to pick up women from the dock on the main port in Ibiza. His wife was watching, also high as a kite, helping the cause by suggestively posing on the outside couches.

We quite enjoy the madams that snort coke on the vanity tables. They're such a mess, they can't even do their drugs right. You'd think it would be a simple matter to rack some powder into a thin straight line. But no, they get the white stuff everywhere! To tidy it up, the housekeeping team have a specially labeled mini hand-held vacuum cleaner called ABUSE DRUG and they only use it for that purpose.

The celebrities that you see on the covers of magazines, looking their best, are the ones doing drugs in their gilded cages. We've seen one very unhappy, now pregnant Princess, repeatedly visiting the bathroom and drinking straight vodka all night. She was so beautiful to look at, with her perfect hair and immaculate outfits, yet so miserable. We also get the high profile celebrities that have to be held up during photo shoots on the yacht. One singer was so out of it her head was lolling around but they succeeded in getting the cover shot in the few moments of lucidity. We enjoy watching the shenanigans of messy crew, owners and especially charter guests on yachts, it's illegal to possess drugs. Even if your boat is under a foreign flag in international waters, state border control can board and enforce the global zero tolerance policy. Upon boarding the yacht and finding drugs, the captain and crew will lose their licenses, potentially face jail, and the yacht will be seized.

How to deal with drugs!

If you have charter guests on board and happen to see something naughty like the guests doing coke off each other in the main saloon, the best solution is to report it to the person above you and let them make the call. When it's the captain doing the dope, call the designated person on shore or the management company. He is putting your life and everyone else's on board in jeopardy. You could die!

Follow Your Heart.
At The End Of The Day,
It Is You That Has To Live
With Your Decisions.
- My Mum

- Gee, I Hope You're Tough -
You may find yourself on the dock, with all your belongings in black garbage bags

Be prepared to have thick skin and many shoulders to cry on. The road to success in the yachting industry is a long one, filled with asshole captains, wanker first officers, bitchy hormonal, lazy chief stewardesses, jealous fat wives, mean owners and back stabbers. During any time of the day, no matter how secure you feel in your employment, one of these people may decide they don't like you anymore. BOOM! You've got one hour to vacate the yacht. Gee, hope you're tough.

Don't laugh, it's true! That dickhead chef that keeps picking a fight with you? Turns out to be more important than you are! You've just spent the past charter working your guts out, covering for the lazy chief stew and fending off the chef's abuse when you're called to the bridge.

- Mistakes Not To Make When You Know Someone Is Going To Be Fired -
Shall I spill?

No. Never. Any gossip that is overheard or told to you in the hope that you will pass it on should never be repeated. They are trying to catch you out. Promise! If you hear that a crew member is about to be fired, it's already too late for them. You'll see the warning signs through fighting, screaming and lack of communication.

Getting fired is not a bad thing, it just means a lesson is being taught and it's time to move on. The person who is being fired will no doubt hate the entire crew for about six months. But, their life will move on and so will yours. Do yourself a favor and don't be the person who spilled the beans. Stay out of it. It's none of your business.

- What If The Universe Is Just Waiting To Give Me More? -
All the best stories begin with jumping ship

Ok, it seems that the positions to-be-filled ads are a little scarce, and competition is fierce. It's scary, the funds running low and you've been turned down for yet another dream job. You're scraping the bottom of the barrel when a captain offers you a position with less responsibility and less money. What the heck, you'll take it until something better comes along.

You then find yourself in this scenario:
The captain is a dickhead, complaining about you all the time behind your back. No leadership, which is evident when he comes down to find you, while working, to scream at you. You have never met a worse person in your life and you want him dead. There is nothing that anyone can say to make you feel better. Your level of misery and hatred for all those around you can result in violence. You want this bastard fucked up.

How to make a leaving statement: (preferably, mid charter, while the guests are onshore eating dinner)

1. Book a flight for the night that you are planning on leaving and a taxi for the appropriate time. A quick getaway is needed here
2. Find a way to get your hands on your passport, seaman's book and original documents. Say that you've applied for a stewardess course and you need to have original documents verified.
The passport also needs sending off for a foreign visa. Get all your documentation and keep it tight. You never want to see these people again
3. That night, while everyone is having dinner, pack all your belongings in black garbage bags. If you ask for the luggage you came with, it'll be a dead giveaway, resulting in not having the satisfaction of screwing over the captain mid charter
4. Take out all of your belongings in the black garbage bags while everyone is eating. Stack your stuff in trash bags next to the skip on the dock. If anyone asks, tell them that you were cleaning out your cabin

5. Eat a last bite with the crew, refraining from smiling like an idiot
6. Help the crewmember on watch, clean up the crew mess and offer to take out the garbage
7. Take out the garbage. Grab the last of your gear in the black garbage bags from your cabin as well
8. Walk off the boat and walk directly to the garbage skip with your gear and pre-arranged taxi. Put your garbage bags in the taxi's boot and jump straight in. Be warned the captain will get the police involved looking for you. Fly out on the next flight and get wasted on as soon as you can. You deserve it. #triedandtestedmethod

How to leave the yacht with class

You're ready to move on. The captain has enforced a dry boat policy. Which means the job is driving you crazy with sober boredom and no playtime. Time to find another a working environment, where everyone is encouraged to behave like adults. You've put the hours in, tried not to drive the rest of the crew crazy with your complaining, and have been applying for a million other jobs. Your bank balance is now topped up, freedom! It's time to move on and jump ship! From here on you can choose your next adventure!

1. Resist the urge to boast about your new position. Keep your enthusiasm under control
2. Try not to gloat about the bigger salary, more responsibility and amazing benefits in your next position. It's just not fair
3. Do not encourage the other crew to leave and under no circumstances are you to make them feel bad for staying. For many of them, leaving is not an option
4. In the days leading up to your departure, ensure a smooth transition. Are all your logs up to date? Paperwork filled? Emails responded to? Don't leave a mess for the next person to clean up. They will bitch about you to the other crewmembers
5. Upon your departure leave on the same high that you came in on

It's tough sticking out jobs and taking positions for less money. Whatever happens, don't worry, you'll get another job soon enough. Just remember, you're going to see these same people in the same ports, year after year. Go out with your head held high.

- Tried and Tested Sure Fire Ways To Receive Your Termination Notice -
Please God, get me outta here

Dude this job sucks. I'm tired of the whingeing owners who are never happy, the captain who treats everyone like shit and a miserable crew. If I stay any longer, all this misery is going to leech into my bones. I know they're going to fire me, I've seen the emails, heard the gossip and the captain has stopped communicating with me. The thing is, if I leave, I give up my termination pay, as per my contract, and I've been here for two years putting up with this crap. I need to get terminated… now.

Gotcha! Work your way through the list to get fired:

1. Get drunk with the guests on. No specific time, while they're out having dinner, while you're serving them dinner or after they've gone to bed. Collect the empties from dinner service and leave them lying around your cabin for the other stewardess to see, then gossip about it

2. Systematically sleep with other crew members on board if there is a no couples policy. Touch people in inappropriate places too, when they least expect it

3. Turn up delightfully offensively hung over. Check your breath can kill a goat all day

4. Pick fights with the other stewardesses, the chief stewardess and/or the first officer. The captain will try and keep you. Crew longevity looks better to the management company. Be consistent. Continuously wear all of them down

5. Sleep in and keep turning up late for work

6. Don't follow orders. Just do whatever you want

7. Refuse to eat with the crew. Instead plate up and eat in your cabin

8. Spread rumors that the captain is fiddling the books or stealing tips

9. Start smoking cigarettes with guests on

10. Be miserable. Don't talk to anyone and when a team member talks to you, look at him or her like they are stupid.

Remember if the captain offers a mutual consent on leaving, don't do it! It means he's trying to skip out on your termination pay. Same goes if you quit.
Remember to keep at least one HOD on side. You're still going to need a reference. Best of luck.

STOP THOSE ENDLESS SUMMERS

You'll probably spend more days hating your life and trying to top yourself, than enjoying it. It's a constant grind, with long hours, wishing you were somewhere else.

- The Ugly Truth About Beautiful Reference Letters -
Yes, you need them

The first thing recruitment agents, captains and department heads will ask for, is reference letters from your previous positions held. A good reference letter is a hard copy stating the following: the period of time you were employed on the yacht, what your role was, your behavior on the job and a recommendation for your next position. In our industry, reference letters are a strong positive reinforcement that you did a good job and worked well as a team player. To receive a reference letter, captains and HODs are very choosy about who they give them to; they are putting their reputations on the line. They will not write one if they dislike you or you showed poor performance.

Reference letters don't have to be big and elaborate. If you've already left the boat, a copy of a simple glowing emailed reference will suffice. Other good reference letters are photocopied thank-you notes from guests, charter guests and emails from the owners, thanking you for a job well done. Recruitment people will never ask for an original hard copy. With all of the above, make e-copies, saved to your email in case you lose everything else such as your laptop, hard drive, etc. You can then attach all references when sending off your resume.

14.

THE DELICATE POWER GAME OF YACHTING

The Biggest Noise Is
In Your Head.
-Ivan. MY Katina

- Pretty Sure I Can Learn That On The Job -
The truth about the different positions on board

So you want our job, congratulations! With all the crazy people around, all ships need to establish the chain of command and responsibility. This hierarchy is the same from small lasers to cruise liners and every seafaring vessel in between.

To begin, there is only one leader to direct the maneuvers for the rest of the crew. You, my friend, are going to start at the bottom like we all did. The yacht's crew is divided into three departments: deck, engineering, interior and are as follows:

CAPTAIN (Oversees all ship's operations)

He is our fearless leader, our beast on top of the food chain, our head of the wolf pack. Respect must be given to him at all times, as he takes ultimate responsibility for all the dramas that happen on board. No back chatting, no questioning his authority or muttering into your beard when orders are given. If the yacht is sinking, the captain is sinking with it, not you, hence the level of respect insisted upon! The easiest part is driving these big things. The hardest part is that on any given yacht the captain has three to sixty-three crew demanding his leadership, instruction and personal attention, daily. He is the role model that sets the tone for the yacht. If he is happy, everyone is happy.

This superstar role also covers the following professions on land: hotel manager/ driver/large company administrator and project manager. His role is mostly paperwork and foreseeing the organization of forthcoming projects. He also oversees crew hiring, trip scheduling, itineraries, overseeing the general maintenance of the yacht and making sure guests are happy.

A captain's three main objectives:
1. Safety of all those onboard
2. Continuously maintaining the yacht to a brand new standard
3. Guest service.

FIRST MATE/OFFICER

When the captain needs some R'n'R time or is incapacitated, the first mate is the second in command and steps in to fill the captain's big boots. You'll find the first mate is as busy as the captain. His key responsibilities are ensuring the yacht is seaworthy at all times and coordinating the outside maintenance of the yacht. Further accountabilities are passage planning, navigation, organization of crew regarding watches, upholding standards and procedures on board. He should work faster, harder, longer and better than his deckhands and be a champion at motivating his team.

The first officer's three main objectives:
1. Ensure the yacht is seaworthy at all times
2. Ensure the yacht is immaculate at all times
3. Ensure the safety of all those on board by checking standards are adhered to.

BOSUN

This guy is the leader of the deck team. He fulfills the wishes of the first officer in prioritizing exterior work to be completed. In this role, the bosun has more skills and knowledge than his deck crew and has a clear vision of the bigger picture regarding the maintenance of the exterior of the ship. The bosun will organize all deck operations, crew safety, storage use, maintenance of tenders and toys, exterior cleaning inventories and knowledge of all storage areas. He may also help other departments when necessary in the name of good teamwork and maintaining moral.

A bosun's three main objectives:
1. Carrying out the requests of the first officer in the required time
2. Have the ability to foresee problems before they arise, ensuring the safety of all crew
3. Keep the exterior team happy and motivated.

DECKHANDS

These good-looking dudes and babes carry out the physical labor of cleaning, maintaining, prepping surfaces for varnishing, painting, repairing all surfaces and exterior equipment as well as all technical spaces of the yacht. The duties of the deckhands are as ordered by the first officer, although this authority may be passed onto the bosun. If deckhands are not outside scrubbing and cleaning they will be doing bridge watches, harbor watches, anchor watches, completing standard yacht operations, administration work such as chart corrections and safety management. It is imperative for their own safety and all those on the yacht that he/she has a full understanding of the safety procedures and equipment.

A deckhand's three main objectives:
1. Always ensure the safety of those on board
2. Fulfill the tasks outlined by the first officer and bosun in required time
3. Keep the yacht maintained to the highest imaginable standard.

CHIEF ENGINEER

On the same level as the captain, the chief engineer is responsible for the running, maintenance and repair of all mechanical, electrical and water systems. This includes everything from the engine room, fuel, steering plus navigations systems, ballast, refrigeration, air-conditioning, grey and black water, anchor windlasses, boat cranes, tender launching equipment, tender engines, as well as the AV systems on the yacht. If there is an ETO on board, he will absorb the electronic side of the engineer's duties.

You'll see the chief before the start of trips, testing and running machinery, securing movable objects and familiarizing fellow crew members with the layout of the engine room and all emergency and safety items. At the end of the trip, they'll be filling in logs, ordering parts that need replacing, cleaning gear and changing out engine oils. Needless to say, yeah, he's busy! Try not to wake him in the middle of the night to find cable TV in the main saloon for the guests. Engineers are like bears!

A chief engineer's three main objectives:
1. Keep the boat floating
2. Keep the boat running
3. Keep the boat pumping.

SECOND, THIRD & TEAMS OF ENGINEERS

Their job is to assist the chief engineer as per his direction to keep the yacht running to the highest standard.

Three main objectives:
1. Fulfill the requests of the chief engineer within the time frame
2. Fix things, don't break them
3. If you don't know, ask.

ETO (electronic technical officer)

An ETO's responsibilities cover yacht navigation, controls systems, power generators, electrical distribution, automation, alarm systems and lighting systems. He reports directly to the chief engineer and captain.

A ETO's three main objectives:
1. Know how to use and maintain all electronic systems
2. Keep the electronic systems working and up to date
3. Ensure backup systems are in place and accessible.

PURSER

Busy little bees these pursers are. Often, they come from a cruise liner or business management background. This is not an entry-level position as the role carries a heavy responsibility. They are required to assist the captain in the financial management and administration of the yacht. Day-to-day tasks will consist of bookkeeping, overall management of crew (employee benefits, holidays, visas), dispersing and accounting funds for each department, purchasing of onboard supplies and provisions, organizing guest activities and reconnaissance missions for owners. It's a pretty stressful role when you have twenty-two kosher New York Jews on board with their security, and they change their mind more than the wind changes direction.

A purser's three main objectives:
1. Keep track of all accounts
2. Meticulous record keeping for all departments
3. Personal administration for all guests and crew.

CHIEF STEWARDESS

The chief stewardess is responsible to the captain for providing front of house service to guests. Her primary role is organizing the interior department to ensure that the owner and guests' needs are always delivered efficiently, above standard and in an unobtrusive manner. No guest should ever receive anything less than the best service and produce possible, and this is facilitated through the chief stewardess and the interior team. At all times the chief stewardess is to maintain the interior of the yacht to the highest standard, ensure the crew are neat and in the correct uniform, have control of the stocktaking plus inventories, take charge of provisioning, maintain immaculate accounts of all items purchased and train all stewardesses to the highest standards attainable.

To get here, this job requires skills:
- ✓ Ability to delegate
- ✓ Good communication, organization, and diplomacy
- ✓ Vast knowledge of wines, service, and housekeeping.

A chief stewardess's three main objectives:

1. Don't trash the boat
2. Keep the guests happy
3. Keep the interior team happy.

SECOND STEWARDESS

The chief stewardess is dependant on the second stewardess as her backup. She must lead by example in training the other stewardesses to create, prioritize and complete job lists to the highest possible standards. She may be called on to implement interior routines and scheduling. The ability to think ahead, anticipate the daily running of the yacht and guest needs is highly valued. The second stewardess must have the ability and confidence to orchestrate service as per directions, foreseeing any problems that may arise and be able to fix them.

STEWARDESS

To carry out the duties of the chief and second stewardess as requested. She must be able think clearly, adhering to time limits and have the willingness to complete goals set by the department heads. Stewardesses may be required to assist with lookout duties or help on deck when the yacht is underway. When the yacht is not underway, she will be required for extra duties such as watch keeping. She is that smiley person who gets up every day with a smile on her face, greets everyone like a long-lost friend and fulfills your every whim and command. Nothing is ever too much or too difficult. Don't get confused, just because this girl cleans your toilet and serves your food, she may also hold two degrees, international stocks and a lovely house somewhere. It's a lifestyle choice.

A stewardess's three main objectives:

1. Back up the chief stewardess in service and housekeeping to provide the maximum standard in guest satisfaction
2. Be consistent in the level of service that is executed
3. Be a team player.

HEAD OF HOUSE-KEEPING

This is one of the hardest interior jobs there is as they are busy all day long and work within tight time frames. There is no point having immaculate service if the cabins look like a kid tidied up. The head of housekeeping must be able to motivate her team in the following duties: detailing all guest/crew areas, proper care of wood, leather, porcelain, stain removals and inventories.

The HOH three main objectives:

1. Lead and motivate a team for maximum results
2. Keep the interior of the yacht maintained to a 7-Star standard
3. Prioritize the workload and work within a time-managed framework.

HEAD OF SERVICE

The head of service girl is the front of house when it comes to guest services, as she leads the team in providing 7-Star services and reports directly back to the chief stewardess. The whole experience of guest satisfaction and superior yacht ambiance will depend on her and her ability to confidently represent the yacht because she spends the most time with the guests. The head of service oversees all food and beverage service for guests and crew, including table settings, meal service, bar tendering and provisioning.

The HOS three main objectives:

1. Provide outstanding service for guests by keeping them happy, fed and watered
2. Clear, consistent communication with all crew on guest movement and locations
3. Keep the service team happy.

CHEF

Dude, these guys are the hardest working people on the yacht and do not rest for anything. To be a yacht chef, you need stamina, high energy to see the day through, immense flexibility and maturity to take the pressure … and the ability to keep smiling as adversity will keep on knocking at the galley door! This position is not for the faint hearted, you need to bring magic to the table, meal after meal. It is impossible to fake the years of training yacht chefs are required to have. Your top priority in the first week of joining a new yacht is to make friends with this crew member. Chefs are hit and miss – they're either perfectly charming and will cook all day and night and never complain — usually the ones who get paid the big bucks — or they're miserable and hate their life — underpaid and tired.

When chefs are not cooking, they're completing inventories, provisioning, maintaining the cleanliness of all walk-in fridges and working hygienically at all times. Please note, while it is their job to cater for crew, chefs do not operate a fine dining restaurant to satisfy your every whim.

A chef's three objectives:

1. Keep the guests happy
2. Keep the crew happy with options that will not make them fat
3. Maintain personal and food handling hygiene at all times.

SOUS CHEF

Sous (second/under) chefs and teams of chefs are hired on larger yachts over fifty meters. The sous chef reports directly to the head chef regarding prepping and producing food for guest and crew. He'll end up doing the grunt work such as chopping and prepping, baking, basting and mixing, and as the final production of the meal sent out to guests rests on the shoulders of the head chef, second chefs and chef helpers are left in charge of cooking crew meals and plating guest meals as per the directions of the head chef.

COOK/STEW

The role of a cook/stew covers both departments, wherever she is required. You'll find this position on smaller yachts where the style of the boat is more relaxed. Breakfast will be prepped by the cook/stew, moving into housekeeping afterward, then cooking lunch service, more housekeeping, dinner service and then turndowns. This role could also be crew/chef/stew as needed, helping in the interior when one has free time.

A cook/stew's three main objectives:

1. Guests' needs come first
2. Don't crack under the quest for perfection. If the owners wanted heaven sent perfection, they could have hired another stew
3. Be happy.

15.

HAND OVER MY HEART, IT'S A TRUE STORY

YACHTING
What Happens When
The Whole Crew Has
Fun?
You Get Fired.

- Yachting Is The Glitz and Glamour Industry -

Read between the lines for the ugly truth about your beautiful ideal stewardess

1. We play a game called what's that smell and where is it coming from? Why does this room smell so heavily of cologne? Is that poo? Did they wipe their ass with a towel and then hide it? Is that smell coming from the air conditioning vents? Nope, a charter guest put the showerhead up his bum to flush out his piles. When the guest came back to the cabin and found a stewardess cleaning the showerhead, he backed out with a, "One moment, wait right here." The guest then returned with a crisp handful of €500 — hush money. Sometimes this game can end up worth while.

2. Bigger boobs equal more money in this industry. We have one owner who tipped the chief stew for getting bigger boobs. With the owner's arm around our girl Michelle, he looked down her blouse as they were chit chatting. "Michelle, you got bigger boobs? Here have some money and I'll see to a raise." The same owner didn't like the squidgy-ness of the newly installed one-inch carpets. "Michelle, come here, feel this carpet, it is hard underneath my feet. Your boobs need cushioning while you're working too. Rip it all out and replace it with something thicker." This was all said to Michelle's new ladies, not to her face. Michelle's new boobs helped her keep her job, as she knew better than to lay cheap carpets, and Sabrina's in Monaco made €55,000 replacing the main saloon carpet

3. We are committed to our jobs. Many times, we have leant our heads against the wall and fallen asleep whist doing dishes in the upstairs pantry at 01:30 in the morning

4. When buying new cleaning products, we love to break down the smell as if it's a fine wine. "I love it; it reminds me of hot summer days in Asia after traveling for three months. The top notes are New England roses, then after, I get lilies with a base note of sandalwood. The lingering smell is a synthetic clean laundry fragrance similar to L'eau D'issey perfume. You could never overload on this stuff, but it definitely needs a fabric softener to boost up the smell. I like it; I could do it every day"

5. You stop complaining about the nineteen-hour days when there is a big fat tip involved. The smell of a tip gets everyone electrified and happy. Mama needs a down deposit for a house!

6. Sometimes the only thing to get you through the day is getting high first thing in the morning. Since alcohol smells on your breath, the next best thing is the rubbing alcohol that's used to clean windows. Spray, sniff, wipe. It takes the edge off a hangover but be careful, too much will give you stomach ache

7. We become a little obsessive and attached to our cleaning supplies. After weeks of cleaning, we have a favorite microfiber cloth and it's marked with our name. Yes, we have also developed a preference for cleaning caddies too

8. We know that dating apps are the quickest way to scope out the town. After being at sea and pulling into a new port, our entertainment is to get onto Tinder just to see who's around. Experience has taught us not to say that you are a yachty, as boys won't invest the time. "Come on, do I have to go out with the crew again? All I want is a dinner date with a good looking local!"

9. Dress ups are way more fun when you're pretending to be a wealthy aged Miss World winner. It's Tuesday and we've been cleaning this boat for weeks. Come on, time to try on all of the owner's clothing. Wigs are our favorite. We're not stressed about ruining anything either. It's common knowledge the yacht is a dumping ground for all the madam's clothing that should have been given to charity

10. When drinking, bored or hiding in the master cabin, we find ourselves talking with the other stewardesses about who we would do out of the crew. A breakdown on their physique is required, followed by our favorite body part and mannerisms. This always leads to how we would do them

and in what secret spot on the yacht. Sassy's favorite spot was the engine room with the second engineer till the perverted captain busted her

11. When guests are royal assholes, we accidently drop their toothbrushes down the toilet. That will teach you to mind your manners, mister. You can stay in bed sick now

12. We are revolted with all the washing and choose not to re-wash the bathroom towels after the guests have showered six times a day. Dryer please!

13. We're a bit sneaky — making friends with the chef is our top priority. Our clear aim is to become his favorite. Yep, I'll buy you drinks, give you a shoulder massages and listen to your stupid jokes, if it means first dibs on tasting guest food and extra desserts put aside for me. When there is caviar involved, I'm a slut for food

14. No one is safe! Once on shore, everywhere we go, we mentally undress men. Do you know how hard it is to act normal when you pull into St Barts and the sailing regattas are on? Why don't we have hot deckhands like that? My vajaja is hungry

15. Detailing cabins with ear buds that come up dirty gives us great satisfaction. Finally, a spot I haven't cleaned a million times!

16. As a stewardess, preparation is essential. A stash of water is always kept in our cupboards for when we come home trashed

17. Yes, we lie and say we can drive the tender. There is no way we're going to say no to a chance to drive the $40,000 tender with 700 horsepower on the back! Pretty sure Mr. Google can teach me that

18. There is no hesitation in complaining about how expensive the real world is when returning home. But provisioning the boat? A minimum of six trolleys should cover us for a week. "Oh, that was only $1,200? My allocated budget was $3,000"

19. We secretly taste (drink) the dregs of the €3,750 bottles of wines we serve. Deals are also cut with our wine supplier to chuck in a few bottles of the same. After a non-yielding charter, it's a pleasure drinking a bottle in the peace and quiet of our cabins

20. If you piss us off we have no hesitation in using the Taser gun or pepper spray that we picked up cheap in LA on you while you're sleeping. By this stage we don't give a fuck and want to get out of this jail. #Kristenididit

- Rubbing Shoulder With Millionaires And Getting Free Life Lessons -
Everyone has a story and if you listen closely you will gain a wealth of knowledge

My favorite rich old crony had to be Mr. Warmers, ranked 517 on the Forbes richest list with 2.7 billion. He and his family graced us with their presence and chartered our yacht for €750,000 for two weeks in the Balearics.

Got to say, I admired Mr. W from the moment I opened his suitcase. No one I have ever met had traveled so lightly. The ten guests before him brought eight pieces of hard shelled Globe-Trotter 2017 luggage collection each, for a seven-day trip. This guy only brought five shirts, three swimming shorts, three pairs of basic nondescript shoes, some underwear plus a change of clothes and jacket for the airplane, all in one carry one piece of luggage. The personal beach bag that he took everywhere was a cloth shopping bag from 120 Lino, an upper-class linen store. He was so happy, content and proud to show this bag off, grateful for the free gift. His watch was a Swatch with a leather strap, and the most fantastic item that he owned was his sleeping eye mask, handmade in Africa.

"Do you think that's too much? Did I go crazy?" Mr. W asked me. I wanted to hug him for being so minimal and not having one show-off possession. How refreshing! I wanted to emulate him by not being a heavy consumer but by living simply — by being grateful for every little gift and act of kindness shown to me.

For every meal, while all of his guests tucked into the organic, vegan, grown-by-virgins-in-the-rainforest food, he would bow his head, cross his thumbs over each other, bring them to his forehead and pray. I haven't seen anyone do this dying ritual for years. The thought of him bowing his head amidst the chaos and cacophony made by his aggravating daughter and annoying son-in-law still humbles me. It's a beautiful gift to see one of the richest men in the world be grateful for the food placed in front of him.

Without a doubt, the best part of this trip was not the ease of this family but the eavesdropping on their lunch and dinner conversations. I can wholeheartedly confirm that once you have the formula for making money, the easier it gets. The method is simple. You've got to love it, the process of making the next million, investing, trading and the thrill of closing deals.

The next lesson I learned is that your personal mission should be to become a world-class philanthropist. Nothing is more satisfying than being able to help people on a grand scale. Imagine if you had more than enough money to build hospitals in Africa, educate underprivileged girls in India and save the rainforest in the Amazon. This guy was doing exactly that. He once said to me, "All of this means nothing if you don't give back and help those less fortunate." When I was in this elderly gentleman's presence I could feel that his calling was to tread lightly on this earth.

The third lesson: be calm and grateful. Having an even temperament shows emotional control and intelligence.

Fourth lesson: plant the seeds, water the plants so that the crops may grow. Get up, be present and make your dreams come true by working consistently every day.

Dear Mr. W, I sincerely thank you for teaching me so much. Out of all the millionaires we've had on board, you are one who has had the greatest influence on me. You're an inspiration to all those around you.

DID YOU KNOW?

If your guests are genuinely rich, like mind-blowingly wealthy, you won't find them listed on any Forbes rich list. The billionaires of the globe do not advertise their net worth. They will put their money in offshore bank accounts under the name of a company. That company might be based in South Africa or Switzerland, and another company, located in Cayman Islands or some other tax haven owns this company, and then yet another trust or organization owns this one and the one located in Ireland or the Virgin Islands, or who knows where. It's a merry-go-round.

Lost you? Good, that's the idea. These billionaires have teams of full time accountants who work for them, to make their money virtually impossible to trace, and therefore, pay taxes on. If you're legitimately rich, chances are you've never heard of them or found them on the internet. These are the people who own countries, the internet, the media and the companies that feed and heal you.

- Imagine Dealing With Crazy Requests & Loving Every Minute Of It -
There is nothing more satisfying than spending other people's money

Yachts are a pretty outrageous hedonistic bubble. You're going to see and hear bizarre mind-blowing conversations and requests. Everything is said with confidence. Ridiculous requests are part of our profession. It is your job to say, "YES, I'll get right onto that," without a discussion to make it happen. When we have fabulous eccentric guests on, we love, love, love to actively encourage these obscene requests and up the ante.

"Yes, sir, I heard you mention a massage. Can I go ahead and organize that on the sun deck aft with the world's most highly sought after massage and energy clearing expert?"

"Madam, we know you love sashimi and sushi so we went ahead this evening and set up a fresh Japanese carving station on the main deck aft, complete with the most highly skilled *itamae* (sushi chef) this side of the Mediterranean. We selected the finest grade A salmon with the perfect amount of marbling and belly fat from Tasmania this morning. It will melt in your mouth (and mine.) May I suggest an aperitif time of 20:45? That way the temperature will be perfect and the sunset will be setting on our stern."

"You love fresh lychees with homemade coconut ice cream?" (secretly, me too!) "We'll source this a.s.a.p." Guarantee lychees are not in season, but I can have them flown in. "Anything is possible."

Madam: "Can you please organize for my private hairdresser to arrive from London day after tomorrow?"
You: "Yes, madam, too easy." The reality is the hairdresser has to cancel all his appointments, and it's a huge inconvenience for him. There is no publicity that he can generate from the Madam and he loses his regular clients.

While at anchor in front of the Monaco Grand Prix
Owner: "I'd like to go there."
You: "Where, Sir?"
Owner: "Over there."
You: "You mean the Monaco Grand Prix."
Owner: "Yes"
You: "You mean tomorrow? Tickets for the Grand Prix? Yes, sir, we can arrange that."
Owner: "No, let's take the boat over."
You: "I'm sure we can organize that." You look across and it's packed. Boat to boat and you know these people have bribed their way in months ago. €45,000 and eighteen hours later you're docked at the Monaco marina. Some other boat got bumped out and now you're in!

Theres a high profile celebrity who came to fame as a model, then her clothing line and reality TV show… following up with several kids with a three different baby daddies. The media loves her! I think she's done unquestionably well marrying up. For each time she has, she's received a larger yacht. She's not bothering trying to date the captains, let me tell you that! This lady has a reputation of hiring and firing nannies more than we get takeaway. Some of them have only stayed a day, none have stayed longer than three months. On the last trip she tormented the poor nanny so much that she snuck off in the middle of the night, slept on a park bench and paid for her own ticket from St Barts to Canada. This same high maintenance madam wanted a full buffet prepared at all times. Fried chicken, smoked BBQ ribs, hamburgers, shrimp, coleslaw, sweet potato fries, bruschetta, disgusting amounts of food! This madam never touched anything though, she just wanted to look at it and have it on offer should her friends drop by. During lunch service one day, while the lead service stewardess was pouring waters, the madam, in front of all her friends, commented the water levels were not even. We're talking a couple of millimeters out here, not half full and half empty. The madam was not happy. She made the stewardess take all glassware away, replace them and refill them again. The same day her youngest child broke his leg jumping between the yacht and tenders un-supervised. She just couldn't deal.

We've also worked for the man that insisted on keeping his dead mother's wardrobe onboard, and he had crew wash selected items every week. Also:

157

- ✓ The billionaire owner that has three custom made yachts but barely even uses one. The crew are constantly on stand-by to keep them on their toes. One of the yachts and its crew were ordered to sail around the world to scope out potential dive sites. Last summer while this particular yacht was off the coast of the Maldives, the owner used the yacht for the first time in five years. It was easier for him to use the head on the yacht then to tender into the 5-Star hotel he was hiring out

- ✓ The owners that insisted on bringing dogs, to have them spew and poo all over the pure silk white carpets

- ✓ The eighteen pieces of large hard shell Louis Vuitton, for one person, packed to the brim with garments, all hand washed and folded with tissue paper. This was for a one-week trip!

- ✓ The ninety pieces of luggage that filled four cabins for an Arab Prince on a two-week charter

- ✓ The pretend models asking for her designer gowns to be dry cleaned. Serious lady? All we've seen is rocks for the past three days!! Do you know where we are? No, neither do I!

  More 'whatever floats your boat' silly requests:

- ✓ Instead of saying, 'You're welcome, we would appreciate it if you said, it's my pleasure'

- ✓ Never look the principal host in the eye

- ✓ Ensure the whole yacht is fragrance free, no use of chemicals and the crew have to refrain from using any perfume

- ✓ Can the fumes always blow downwind?

- ✓ The actor/singer/model on board who insisted on always having her bottle of Grey Goose on her at all times

- ✓ Owners that only eat a particular type of flat pita bread. We had to fly it in from mainland Spain to the Greek Islands

- ✓ My personal favorite ,"Can you do something about that?"
  Me: "I beg your pardon?"
  Guest: "The sun!"
  Me: "Oohhh, looks like we're in trouble here. Not sure where I should put it?"

- ✓ Don't forget the beach BBQs for charter guests that take five hours to set up. It's a nightmare for crew that go through this routine once a week. All the furniture and equipment is sent over at 06:00. Designer rugs are laid out, custom made marquees are tethered, chairs are covered with contrasting long bows, white table clothes are steamed beach side, massive vases with candles are strategically placed and table decorations positioned. A reconstructed tiki bar is also built, complete with a fully stocked bar. To complete the scene, crates of off-white pebbles are carefully laid (and picked up at the end of the night) so charter guests don't have to get sand on their feet

- ✓ Our yachty favorite is the owner seeking very specific crew. Australian/New Zealander, 168cm tall, blond hair, size ten, no drama, well-mannered, happy, quietly spoken, delivers immaculate service and will not drink all the wine. Come on, are you looking for a stew or a girlfriend?

Quickly learn that everything can be solved with money. Nothing is too extravagant, out of season or unattainable. When in doubt we prefer to use the local marina concierge services, and we highly recommend signing up to at least one worldwide concierge company. It will save you the hassle of spending hours on the phone and trying to convince the person on the other end that you are serious. Use them for restaurant reservations, late night requests such as more champagne, special cigars, or getting on the short list for a particular handbag. Whatever it may be, make it happen, the word NO is no longer in your vocabulary.

- The Proper Way To Hang Lametta -
Some of the best moments are the unexpected

What continues to astound me is how welcoming yacht families are. They entrust me with their kids, their other 'baby' (the yacht), have taken me in, treated me like one of their own and confided in me like a long lost relative. If the gift of being a part of their family was not enough, they have made my bank balance fat, gifted me with diamonds, designer handbags, expensive watches and memories that beat any movie ever created.

Our fairytale and busiest time of year on a yacht is Christmas. You're there to facilitate their dream family Christmas, to be a part of their handed-down traditions and be welcomed into their story world. I'll never forget this year for as long as I live. I picked up a sweet little freelance gig that I was very excited about. Sixty-five meters, a team of decorators, eighteen crew and a four-day Christmas event for thirty passengers. Boom! I was going to get in there, plan the shit out of it, train up the girls (I had a third, fourth, fifth and two day workers) and throw a Christmas event to compare with the best of the best in Monaco. I was in my element. Let me at it!

It took a week and a half straight for a team of decorators to 'titivate' the yacht. Fresh Christmas trees were brought in, boxes of decorations were hung and costumes were custom-made for the crew. My team was a group of girls burning the candle at both ends. We had balls in Cannes to attend, service training at Michelin star restaurants and dates with the sexy local French/Italian/Monaco men. Giddy up!

Now, it must be said: I am not a big fan of Christmas. As a child, we spent our Christmas breaks on our boat, caravan or in some weird third world country. Our father was adventurous and sought to pass it onto his kids by throwing the TV away and telling us to get out of the house. We had a busted plastic Christmas tree forty cm high, that got pulled out every year after being squashed into some random hiding place, (and still does) to be un-twisted and put in any old corner. Christmas in the tropics is different to the rest of the world. Us Aussies don't have snow, we wear as little clothing as possible, drink champagne, and eat lychees under the waterfalls. Go to the beach, eat BBQ prawns and drink beers while watching the sunset. Even if I'm in the Caribbean, we'll just put up some fake tree and double check there is enough mosquito spray on board. What I'm saying is, I'd never experienced a full-blown movie-like Christmas until I joined this boat.

It was straight from a movie set. Million-dollar wood finishes, heated exotic marble finish, handmade tapestries, gold everywhere and paintings to die for. You can imagine the pressure to get things right. The two daughters had flown over from England to see how the fort was holding up, every day for a week, leading up to the event. They were happy, but needed more! More decorations *titivating* the bar, the ones we already put up were getting lost amongst the other knick-knacks, the hallway decorations were not evenly spaced and the tree —aagh! stop me dead in my quest for perfection. Who knew there was a perfect way to hang tinsel and lametta? I just threw it at the tree, like fairy dust. Thus began my education into the lametta art form.

The two daughters just stared at the oversized tree in the 'Rose room.' Oh, this tree was beautiful, it was real! It had tiny little pine-corn buds forming at the ends, perfectly formed leaves and a fresh pine smell. All the decorations matched the room, there were beautiful big blue hand-blown glass baubles with delicate, intricate designs, little angel figures, dressed in matching robin's egg blue silk outfits and gold beading hung in falling cascades all around the tree. It was nothing short of a real dream. The owner's daughters were not happy though. The lametta had to be perfect, just as their mother had taught them.

To hang perfect lametta: take one piece at a time of real gold lametta (try sourcing that now). Start on the tip of one leaf, hang it over the leaf. Check that it is even on both sides. Take the next piece of lametta, space it approximately four cm from the first piece. Repeat this process till you cannot fit any more on that branch. Stand back, check your work. Is all the lametta evenly spaced on both sides?

Choose the next branch and repeat the process. Stand back and check if it works. If not, redo. It took us three attempts on five seperate trees to get it right.

After the first late night party with all the children around her and copious amounts of wine, the owner's wife pulled me aside and with pure delight, told me how much she loved the trees. It was all worth it. If she was happy, everyone was happy and it was going to be a successful Christmas. They also gifted the whole crew Louis Vuitton bags on Christmas Day… so the crew was happy too!

- Don't Give Into Hookers' Demands -
Stories from our all expenses stay onboard hostel M/Y Mariah

Our mantra is: "Don't give in to hookers' demands." Hookers, after spending one night aboard these grand yachts will get too comfortable and think they own the place. They will boss you around and make you run ragged to show off to the other hookers. Their requests make us laugh. Freshly cut pineapple cores and kiwi fruit juice at 04:00 to make their vagina smell sweet. Multiple requests for strawberries (again for their vagina. Lady, the buffet is still up, help yourself) and a constant supply of tea. You try doing personalized teapots for twenty-four girls who order five minutes apart, and want it replaced when it is cold. "Oh come on, it's not like you are going to tip me, and you see how hard I'm busting my chops."

She's not the best boat on the French Riviera. The story goes…

I picked up what I thought was going to be a sweet little freelance gig. They flew me to Imperia, Italy to join a Saudi 120+ meter yacht for her maiden voyage. Brand spanking new, straight from the shipyard. Out of this world! The boat had glass elevators, multiple welcome areas finished in thick cut marble, sweeping staircases with white carpets, ostentatious chandeliers, tenders as big as the largest private yachts in Australia, and guest-area finishes so beautiful it made you cry with the perfection. This trip was going to be a walk in the park with one of the largest crew in the yachting world and a multi-leveled playground for me to disappear into. Surely with all that crew, no one would be keeping tabs on me. A game plan was formulated. Eat as much expensive imported gourmet food as I could, make friends with everybody, don't work too hard, and chill.

The guests enjoyed our impressive arrival show. All the crew had to stand to attention in their perfectly pressed white uniforms with epaulettes. There were sixty of us out there in the hot summer sun, along the railings on all three decks with our left hands saluting from our foreheads and right hands tucked in tight behind our straight backs. No one was to move until the guests had reached the interior. The six crew delivering our guests on board the 100ft tender, were standing in the same upright position on their back deck. As the two ships lined up stern to stern, a signal was given from the tender and the lines were thrown at exactly the same time. Both lines were perfectly caught and tied off in exactly the same way. Very quickly the six crew on the tender lined up to help our guests off, their right arms lifted in front of them to form a human handrail.

Our guests consisted of a United Arab Emirates Prince, his entourage of five from-another-mother brothers and twelve of the most beautiful models in the world. It cost a fortune catering this small party. We spent €10,000 on each buffet (€30,000 for breakfast, lunch and dinner) which no one ever ate. They chose instead to order cheese pizza and liquid gold bouillabaisse soup from a famous local restaurant. You cannot imagine the coordination it took for the purser, galley and deck crew to get hot food back to the yacht on anchor.

Drama! This was all, of course, as per the hookers' requests.

All the drop-dead sexy food we had flown in was wasted on the hookers. The size two skinny bitches barely ate. Shame. The caterers followed my request to have each canapé look like well executed art pieces. Tiered buffet stands were arranged with tiny bowls and crystal shot glasses of layered amuses bouches. Plates were painted with vintage port gravy. Sitting on top, like a scallop shell, were two flaky savory pastry biscuits and a divinely generous serving of Eduardo Sousa's ethically farmed creamy and sweet foie gras. The Baie de Bourgneuf oysters were perfectly nestled in their bed of shaved ice. The still-alive-two-hours-ago painted crayfish from Queensland was de-shelled, keeping the meat intact and displayed on large, flat, grey pebbles, on a bed of seaweed in a sawn off wine barrel. Of course, there was New Zealand lamb, Wagu beef and organic vegetables from France but all this was nothing compared to the dessert section!

Have you ever dreamt of living next door to an expensive Parisian bakery? Well, I have. One with perfectly lovely little petits fours patisseries and cakes finished with fresh thick cream icing, wild strawberries glazed with St Germain elderflower liqueur and gold leaf balanced on top of towers of cake ecstasy. Have you ever dreamt of sweet, elfin chocolate rolls, covered in Valrhona ganache chocolate with well-positioned disco-themed handmade decorations? Are you like me and wished for lavender and lemon cake with the finest layers of lemon cream cake finished with a thick sweet and sour white chocolate glaze? Well, we had it all. It blew my mind. Never have I seen such amazing desserts. I put every one of them in my mouth! We took the prize of having the best of the best that season. Handmade and hand caught, flown in from all around the world in the previous twelve hours. This was a feast fit for a king and their hookers to revel in with their eyes. We didn't take it personally that our guests couldn't put a dint into this first class buffet. The service girls and I got stuck into it pretty hardcore after they'd all given up.

Saudis enjoy top-shelf luxury foods and goods as much as they enjoy their women. Never, in all the high-end places and good-looking company I have kept, have I seen such drop-dead stunning women. They all had the new season's YSL handbags with gold tassels and insanely-tailored gorgeous cocktail dresses. I wanted to be them and was embarrassed to be in the same room dressed in my cheap synthetic uniform. I wanted to be surrounded by expensive things too but there was nowhere to go except the level five pantry to wash their lipstick off their used martini glasses.

Can I tell you about my day? 10:00 start. Hit the pool deck bar to relieve Jacqueline (super fun, down to earth, wholesome New Zealand chick) and stayed there till I could convince another crewmember at 15:00 to cover me for a toilet break. Not kidding. Five hours, behind a bar, in the sun, unable to leave!

Escaped from the pool deck thinking setting up the lunch buffet would be better. Pure chaos. In the middle of setting up the buffet, one of the Sous Chefs says, "That's it I give up." To this, the second stew, who looks like an off-duty model replies, "Who the fuck are you to give up? I've been here for seven months." These four service girls carried everything up on their backs from the shipping containers sitting on the wharf, up five flights of stairs (lift wasn't in service) to the main dining room. That means all the finishings for guest areas, chairs, boxes of linens, table decorations, buffet set-ups, crates of wine and table decorations. Took them weeks and it broke them. The chef then shut his mouth and went back down to the kitchen with silver metal walls and no windows.

The days seemed stupidly long. On day five of seventeen hour shifts with guests on, our head chef breaks out into a hives-type rash.

"Could be anything mate, looks like an allergic reaction."

"Maybe it could be Chikungunya, you just came Costa Rica, right?" (Chikungunya is a mosquito disease that's been kicking around the Caribbean for the past couple of summers.) It turns out he had RUBELLA. German Measles! A highly contagious, airborne disease, that is infectious two weeks before the symptoms start to show. HOLY FUCK!!

The Aussies and Canadians got agitated and could not keep the volume down in the crew mess. As one does when a contagious disease breaks out in a tight, confined space and the head chef has touched everything that you have put into your mouth. AAAGGHH!

Everyone was on their phones calling their Mums back home. "Mum, find my vaccination card, there's been a deadly outbreak on the boat." We were all told to keep it down to not scare the other crewmembers. Dude, half the crew hadn't been vaccinated for this! They couldn't afford it in their third world countries!! We'd all had contact with the head chef. He was cooking for us and prepping for the hookers' arrivals. I even had a moment with him in the walk-in fridges. The slut in me couldn't help talking sexy-food-talk about his outstanding cheeses and caviar. No, I'm not much better than our guests.

We wanted to scream, disinfect the yacht! Disinfect the yacht! This could be the end of our killer #bitchesbemakingmoney Med season. Thankfully, our contagious disease scenario ended the same way everything does on private yachts. Very hush-hush, with everyone sworn to secrecy. The incident was swept under the rug, just like that. One minute it's here, the next, quarantined along with another girl from housekeeping.

With Arabs the dramas are never ending. By far the best bit about this trip was not setting up the hidden casino and nightclub which was <u>not</u> drawn up on the general arrangement plan to avoid hurting the young princess's feelings. We were pleased to be swapping our youth for such a noble cause. The best part of this owner's trip was when our model friends got locked in their cabins when far more fabulous people such as high profile dignitaries and royalty come to visit. You see, the Prince felt it necessary to keep both of these parties separate in order to have his needs met. Always during on of these visits, the international models decided it was worth the risk to escape from under the watchful eyes of the palace security dressed in Armani. They would stealthily prowl the corridors looking for a stewardess to command. It was highly entertaining when we found they had escaped. Security, security! "Miss, please return to your cabin. You can only demand it via room service! Yes, we are rushing to bring your organic buckwheat cereal, three poached egg white omelet, Irish semi-skimmed yogurt with Manuka honey, freshly squeezed organic grapefruit juice and double shot Sri Lankan coconut milk latte."

Morning Highlight: Seeing the Chief Stew freak out because she didn't know how to put together a room service tray for all the hookers locked in their rooms. Lady — placemat, cutlery, napkin, plate, condiments. LoL

Late afternoon highlight: Caught my new favorite guest dining alone in the main dining room. He tried to schmooze me by asking if I like foie gras. YES!! I LOVE FOIE GRAS!! The older, generously built, charming man beckoned me over, took my hand and fed me a bite of the most delicious, divine foie gras I have ever tasted in my life. Perfectly seared on the outside, smooth, creamy and fatty on the inside… This is what foie gras dreams are made of. Served on a small saucer-shaped savory biscuit with blackberry gravy jus and garnished with a spiral pith of orange. Life does not get any better than this.

As much as we can't stand being bossed around by a lady who makes her money by opening her legs, it's a constant entertainment having hookers on board. They always think the grass is greener on this side of the yacht and, once we've all become friends, the hilarious stories come thick and fast.. Pretty hard not to like them and be on friendly terms. It is then, to our great disappointment, our model friends get rotated on and off the same way fussy woman change handbags. Oops, she didn't smile or use her manners when the Prince asked if she would like some tea. She's out! These men definitely did not give into hookers' demands.

DID YOU KNOW
Even if the captain promises, gratuities are never guaranteed.
If the captain knows it's going to be a particularly tough season, he will keep half your tips and passport …
until the very end. There is nothing that you can do about it as tips are not written into contracts. If you bail,
you'll lose your entire gratuity.

- Everyone Thinks They Can Be The Chief Stew -
You just can't help it; You think you can do a better job. Prove it!

Tough, you're going to have to put in the hard yards just like the rest of us. One season's experience on a hardly used private yacht does not cut it!

You're ready to be a chief stew when you can tick all these boxes:

1. Your level of OCD is unbelievable. People at home think you've lost your marbles with how obsessive your cleanliness is. You have a technique, a system for cleaning each room and you're ready to preach it to whomsoever will listen. The sermon begins with, 'Dust is the enemy'

2. Walking into any room, you can spot wrinkles and objects out of place straight away. Your mindset is fluffing pillows and removing wrinkles from fabric surfaces instantly improves the room. "Ah, that's better"

3. You are a laundry expert. Dry cleaners are for amateurs. There is no stain you cannot remove or garment you cannot steam to perfection. You can handle all fabrics better than the professionals. In fact, you teach the professionals when they come on board

4. You handle criticism well. Nothing is too much trouble. You have the smile (not the fake one) and the standard reply down pat, "Thank you so much for bringing that to my attention, I'll fix that now," if something is amiss. Because it does not matter how experienced one is, there is always someone else riding your ass

5. You no longer mind long days and late nights. The lack of sleep has become normal and getting more than eight hours a night is a blessing. You can sleep through alarms, bow thrusters and dropping/pulling of the anchors. It's a fine art. When you have a chance to sleep, you take it; nothing will ruin it for you

7. You haven't had a boyfriend for God knows how long. You tell friends and family the reason is that you can't deal with another heartache. The reality is you have a man in every port but are ashamed to welcome them into your Facebook world for fear of being judged a slut

8. You've stopped senseless spending and are working towards putting a deposit on a house. Or you already have a house and are already paying off the mortgage

9. You have dealt with crazy stewardesses who are hormonal, bi-polar, unpredictable and reactive. You've had death threats, been backstabbed and worse of all, had your personal laundry ruined

10. Nothing bothers you anymore. You've already been degraded by the following scenarios:
    A: Have been caught cleaning feces out of a showerhead because a guest has shoved it up his arse as a home remedy for his piles
    B: You have walked into a cabin to find poo and blood wiped over all the walls and curtains. Then said, "How the fuck did they get blood on the ceiling?"
    C: Cleaned up used condoms, tampons and filthy sex sheets and then served the same people lunch with a smiling face.

11. You're a people person and are constantly charming. Everyone wants to be on your team.

- Finally, A Yard Period And We're Moving Into The House -

Never EVER forget this is a working environment

Yes, a bit of down time you say! We're moving into a 4-Star hotel while the ship is in dry dock. Bring it on!

It was a shit twelve-hour trip from Monaco to Marseille. The sea was bumpy, we were hung-over and coming down with the flu. Maybe the previous four-day bender in Monaco for New Year's Eve could have been to blame. All the crew had gotten on a bender, had too many drinks and spewed from the tables at The Brassiere. We then tried to make out with everyone and ended up slipping on the tiles and pissing off all the well-mannered, local French people. Happy New Year!

We arrived at the Marseille shipyard, holding it together just long enough for the captain to bugger off back home to go horse riding with his kids. Shipyards, no matter how much you try, are the most unglamorous playgrounds in the world. They are classified as construction sites crossed with naval base camps. Marseille's reputation is terrible as well. An influx of immigrants has turned the place into the armpit of France — a long way from being a tourist destination. The police have issued a 22:00 curfew, with warnings not to travel after dusk due to the high crime rate. Our new home scared the bejesus out of us.

However, like all fairy tales, while there are misfortunes, there are also happy endings. We moved into the best castle in all the land. One hour outside Marseille city, our nine-bedroom house stood on the edge of the cliffs overlooking a scene to rival Hollywood movies. The two balconies overlooked the opposite coast of steep, horizontal cliffs with waves crashing over the bottom rocks and a small enclosed harbor filled with colorful two-man fishing boats. To our left were the holiday homes climbing up the hills to the overbearing arch of the train station. It may have been a hike to get here from work, but the views were spectacular!

Now, the crew. A good bunch of English, a few South Africans, token Australians, a couple of crazies from Serbia and Turkey and our fun-time Dutchman. Everyone was fit and capable of putting his or her body weight away in liquor. After the captain had said he intended to use our new home as a party house, it was on! He caught me late one evening, returning from the first of many trips dropping off stuff to the house, and invited me to join him for a glass of wine. One drink turned into a few bottles of Puligny Montrachet Colin bought from the Wine Palace in Monte Carlo. Our business chat transformed into party plans. Yes, a shipyard, mid-January blues party was in order! Themes were thrown around — Zanzibar, disaster party (where everyone comes as their favorite disaster), madams and pimps and tight Lycra. The general idea was that everyone dressed in the smuttiest, most revealing costume they could find and make it a party to remember! I got a little excited and as usual went as big as possible. "I'm thinking fireworks, a Ferris wheels, sparklers, strobe lights, smoke machines, Jacuzzi and the balconies lit with gold tiki lamps." BOOM! IT'S HAPPENING!

All shipyard stories begin with, "Didn't you know this is the perfect time to drink!" In the lead up to our first big winter event, the crew did not let me down with stories. I found condom wrappers outside the bathroom window and used condoms in the used condom bin (recycling bin for beer cans.) In my excitement, I called all the girls to check it out too. Someone's doing something naughty! I realized everyone had boyfriends except for two members of the internal team. One of them was dead set straight and would never do that. The other girl, Sassy, was the life of the party and always up for a bit of fun. Girl, it must have killed you to be quiet and cold doing it over the bathroom sink! I'm not going to even ask with whom.

There were used tampons found under a tree next to the jacuzzi. Apparently, the crew were having too much fun sitting in the jacuzzi, throwing their beer bottles onto the grass and peeing behind the tree. Obviously, a soggy tampon is too much to deal with when you're drunk. "I'll just leave it here!" I found it the next morning whilst doing sun salutes.

The night of the big party. Big handclaps to the engineering department for making it happen! Now yachting is all in the details, and of course, we forgot balloons to tie to the street signs to let our guests know where our house was. So, the green deckhand came with me and we blew up condoms instead. We considered the party a big success. There was all you can drink alcohol, naked people in the jacuzzi, dancing on tabletops and secret making-out in the many rooms. The biggest highlight? The smoke machines, strobe lights, disco ball and fireworks! We were way better than Monaco will ever be!

- Highlights Of The 2017 Charter Season -
Confessions after a mental breakdown back-to-back season

✓ My start of the summer was a rude introduction to how cruel this world can be.
The dramatics started with intense interviews with the purser, captain, yacht manager and PA to the owner of a notorious yacht. I was finally flown from Miami to London to meet the owner. After making all the right noises in this short, commanding *owner's* plush eighty-second floor office, I got the green light to fly back to Miami to join the yacht. With me came his company's black Amex with no budget, in my brand new red Chanel quilted lamb skinned purse that I bought to celebrate the new job. The first charter was demanding with the constant rotation of all the gay males in a 200-mile radius and bitchy drag queens on coke. On the last day of the charter the interior crew was called to the main saloon. We thought it was for a "job well done speech" and a bit of pocket money. Turns out the owner (biggest gay billionaire on the Persian coast) called us because he thought Ryan (our hot gay purser) was stealing from him. A little argument broke out between them with poor Ryan not knowing what to do. The owner then demanded that Ryan kneel in front of him, his gay entourage and the entire interior crew. He then backhanded Ryan square in the face. The force of the slap crumpled him sideways to the ground. It was devastating to watch. All the interior crew quit on the spot. Come on Chanel we're going too, lets find a better home.

✓ After the sorry start to the summer, my new team and I took part in the most legendary charter. Our new owner rented us out to one of his friends, who turned out to be the leading member of the Russian mafia. We were one of three boats upon which the Russian and his friends rotated. They usually lunched and hung out on the largest boat with the infinity pool and waterfall. For dinner they could never decide where they would dine. Therefore, all three boats prepared a banquet feast for forty-eight people every night. If they didn't show up on the other two boats, buffet stations heaving with food were thrown out. Can you image the heart break of binning twelve different types of designer handmade canapés, vats of made-from-scratch oyster bisque, fresh chilled Maine lobsters, platters of Kobe wagu beef, whole roast lambs, ginormous salads, platters of delicious French cheeses and freshly made light-as-air creamy desserts? We didn't have the fridge space to keep it all and there's only so much food the crews can eat

✓ Found in the master cabin waste basket; the receipt for Lio's (Ibiza's VIP theater show and nightclub) was €32,000 for dinner and drinks for eight people in a six-hour period. You know how it is, when nothing less than a €6000 bottle of champagne will hit the spot!

✓ Refueling cost of a 120-meter yacht (owned by an Emirati Prince) = €750,000 to fill her up!

✓ After a summer on a heavily used back-to-back charter yacht taxiing some of Forbes richest 500 people around the Balearics, I can attest that money cannot buy you designer individuality. They are all wearing the same oyster tier love bracelets, Hermes tropical Perpetua Rolexes, Cartier scarves and $2000 Balmain sweaters. Argh! You've ruined it for me!

✓ The most beautiful girls/models/hookers being rotated in and out daily. Reasons why they had to go? There was a queue of innocent ladies waiting every time the boat pulled into a different marina. Our male charter guests would lean over the side and pick out the ones they wanted like choosing shoes. The funny thing was we couldn't distinguish between the European hookers and temporary stewardesses that came to help out when they boarded. It may have been the temp stews were welcomed on board with scented face towels and champagne, just like the hookers

✓ Witnessed a decrepit multi-million-dollar couple (who made their money running £1 shops) hitting on I-have-no-brains models in the Jacuzzi at 05:00 in the middle of the Ibiza Marina. It all got too much for the girls, so they left the unfit couple to go for it. Their mates were still around but didn't really pay much attention. They were either in the same swingers' club together or too fucked up. Shame, the night girl had dignity and retired. Would have been nice to know how messy it turned out

✓ We had a super, super, large set, muscular and very famous New Zealand male actor on board. He kept complaining to the nurse of the difficulties he was having down there. We think he wanted her to fix it without seeing his johnny. Finally, he couldn't stand it anymore and paid a visit to our friend, nurse Austin. While Austin was on her knees in her favorite position in anticipation, he unzipped his pants to reveal his foot long johnny. We swear! Turns out our superstar had herpes so Austin was in no position to benefit

✓ Had the opportunity to drop off laundry to Tim Jefferies (well-known for dating all the famous supermodels) and caught him in his underwear. He thought he was God's gift to women when he opened the door, fresh from the shower and only a hand towel covering up his privates. Sooo not the case

✓ Being rich is not an excuse for bad parenting. You must invest in your children to stop them from being drug addicts. It starts now, while we're stern to at Atlantis Marina, Bahamas. Ya hear me? No, you cannot leave them onboard by themselves while you go shopping for a new wardrobe at Versace and drink forty-dollar cocktails in the private Japanese themed bar. When your kids are screaming at you to take them swimming — take them swimming!

✓ We observed an alcoholic stew doing the captain and engineer at the same time. She would sit between them during meals taking turns to shower them with her witchy affections. What a hussy! It made us sick when we caught her secretly getting it on with both of them. It didn't end there though. On one round of dropping off laundry on crew beds (when everyone should have been working) we caught her giving head to the engineer. She did not care at all — she was on her way out anyway

✓ Death threats from a fellow short and mean Serbian stew. Stay on your meds. Dude, is it so hard to do as I say and use gloves to handle the glass and silver wear? Yes, everything I ask is necessary and not because I'm making you work for the hell of it

✓ One stewardess declared she was only showering every two days because she would rather sleep. Gross. It's a Mediterranean summer and we're sweating buckets. Have a shower now. The same stew wore the same uniform for a six-day charter trip because she thought she didn't smell

- ✓ We set up a secret nightclub and casino for the biggest high rollers in Monaco and the world's most beautiful women. To celebrate opening night we flew in Benny Benassi. His all night private set was enjoyed by forty people on the LED dance floor while they enjoyed watermelon Cristal Brut cocktails garnished with gold-foiled pink Phalaenopsis orchids as garnish

- ✓ After a boozy lunch with a famous designer, I bought a €20,000 four-meter, red, resin crocodile (for a pool feature, of course) and €10,000 worth of handmade candles (for table settings) on the service department credit card. I don't know if I was busy showing off or completely wasted when I lost the receipt. Just by pure luck the owners loved it and asked me to go back and buy another crocodile for their house in Aspen. Candles are easy to justify — I got away with that one, too!

- ✓ We had a random day charter in Miami. The main charter guest called to say that he was sending down his girlfriends while he and his buddies went to play a couple of rounds of golf. Seven exceptionally fit girls arrived on board and proceeded to strut around in nothing but shiny G-string bikini bottoms. They ended up posing on the bow doing leg raises and drinking Dom Perignon champagne with strawberries. By the time we got to the end of the channel where the cruise ships leave from, we had a gaggle of smaller boats keeping abreast with us and the action. At the same time, both the Carnival and Royal Caribbean cruise liners were tooting their horns in anticipation of departure. Instead of being modest in front of some 4000 passengers on their own cruise ship balconies, the girl with the biggest, jingliest breasts wedged herself against the aluminum railings on the front of the bow. She then threw her arms up in the air to call attention to herself. All the passengers on the cruise liners and the gaggle of boats behind us cheered. All the surrounding ships tooted their horns and we were left with our mouths open watching from the bridge. The shenanigans only stopped when the water police pulled up alongside and told the girls to cover up. The day didn't end there though. After picking up the boyfriend and his mates, it turned into a cocaine and champagne strippers' tour of Miami waters. On the whole, the group was very polite and friendly. The next day they invited the crew over to their rented house on the Miami waterfront for the Superbowl. When we arrived, a tall blond girl announced she was going skinny-dipping and who was coming with her? Our deck hands raced for the pool! Turned out the girls were running the biggest prostitution ring in NYC and were on holidays, courtesy of their boyfriend

- ✓ The end of the summer ended on a massive high. The billionaire American owner and wife had a exceptional trip and chose to show their gratitude a little differently. They rented us a villa in St Barts for four days with views of the most delicious beach you ever set your eyes on. Included in our stay was a all inclusive, unlimed spa package at the 5-Star hotel down the street, a credit card for food and drinks and two black Jeep Wranglers for crew transportation. The wife really loved us and also went out of her way to procure gift vouchers for the local Hermes boutique for the girls too. Score!

They say what doesn't kill you makes you stronger. Agreed. I'm looking forward to the next season. Grind up that Valium and sprinkle it like fairy dust on top everyone's coffees. It's time to chill out.

STEW PRAYER WHEN GETTING ON A NEW YACHT

"Please God, make sure the chef is lovely, with no temper, handsome and flirt-able would be amazing so that we can have sexy food conversations.
Please God, make sure there is at least one hot deckhand who makes my day with his smile and a stew which is my size so we can swap clothing. I promise you if you for fill this, I'll… this part I always get stuck on!

Flybridge. Sometimes a wanker mentality takes hold of them. These guys love doing nothing and giving orders.

"Welcome back to "The Slums" West Palm Beach 2013.

YACHT. note: money does not always buy you taste.

Master cabin where I hide & watch movies. Sometimes have a nap in the wardrobe.

Hello Detailing

Galley. Sometimes you feel the love.....

My cabin that I share w Bobbi. She snores, gets home late, Drunk. But always up for an adventure!!

LOCKED OUT:

DUDE THESE YACHT DOORS ARE A WHOLE DIFFERENT WORLD.

RULE: LEFTY LUCY RIGHTY TIGHTY

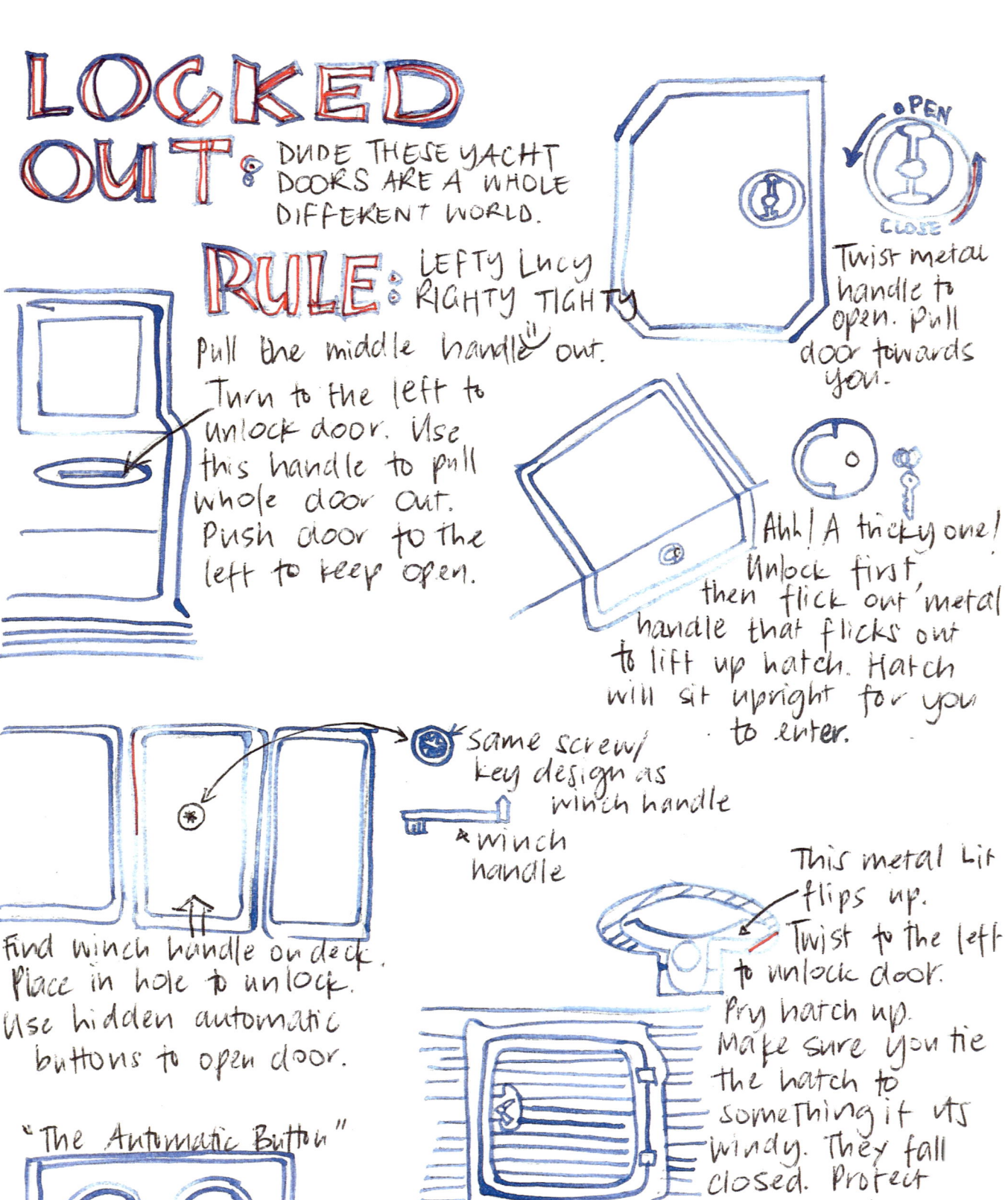

Pull the middle "handle" out. Turn to the left to unlock door. Use this handle to pull whole door out. Push door to the left to keep open.

Twist metal handle to open. Pull door towards you.

Ahh! A tricky one! Unlock first, then flick out metal handle that flicks out to lift up hatch. Hatch will sit upright for you to enter.

Same screw/key design as winch handle

↖ winch handle

Find winch handle on deck. Place in hole to unlock. Use hidden automatic buttons to open door.

This metal lit flips up. Twist to the left to unlock door. Pry hatch up. Make sure you tie the hatch to something if its windy. They fall closed. Protect your head.

"The Automatic Button"

OPEN   CLOSE

Hopefully your crew buttons are labeled. Most of the time there will be more than 2 buttons.

EPILOGUE

Chief Stews Be Saying

This book is not for the faint-hearted. We're preparing you for real life at sea with the most expensive lipstick and sunglasses one can buy.

The Business of Billionaires & Superyachts is the survival guide for fun loving people who aspire to become industry leaders in the field of 7-Star luxury yachting. To begin your new journey, we want to give you as much knowledge as possible, to quickly get you on the water to be a highly sought-after interior manager. This book utilizes real-life skills that are required in the ultra-professional world of superyachts. It is written from experience. The information contained within these pages comes from years of perfecting the best days of guests' lives, it's expertise doing twenty-two hour days on charter yachts, late nights running 7-Star hotels, and organizing international events with high-profile celebrities. This is the book that will tell you how it is, keep you ahead of the game and strategically place you to win.

What started as a just-for-one-season stint has seen many of us become addicted to the travel, money, fun and freedom! We love our life and lifestyle. Can you imagine being paid to live the life of the super wealthy and getting tipped a Mini Cooper (inspired by Goodwood), a Submariner Rolex and this season's must have Louis Vuitton handbag for your efforts? The responsibility of managing superyachts, being flown to Italy for a purchasing trip (you don't go anywhere else and it's all on the owner's black Amex, darling), attending once-in-a-lifetime events in Cannes and living the privileged life of the rich and famous, is all available to you too.

When the going gets tough one really appreciates fabulous friends with humorous personalities. I would like to thank these inspirational and gorgeous souls; Jason Laan, Kristen Kearns, Joseph Nguyen, Noemie Deeds, Emilija Atanaskova, Christy McDonald, Craig Boorman, Benny Goodguy and John McMartin. Team, you always have the best stories! Thank-you for all the wonderful nights in random locations and pep talks when the going got tough. So much love! To all the great crews, captains and amazing owners I've had along the way, you've made this a fairytale story to be repeated again and again around the dinner table. Thank-you!

It hasn't all been Hermès designer bikinis in perfect tans, St Germain cocktails and heaven scent pink peonies though. Along the way, we've had to learn on the job — under old hands — and give our utmost with no clear goalposts. Yachting is the only business that doesn't push for greater leadership training making it a unique industry to get into, to survive and to get out of. One moment you're the flavor of the month, the next, crying on the dock with all your worldly possessions in black garbage bags. This life is not for the faint-hearted: the chef may hate you on sight, there'll be days where the chief steward rips apart the bed that you just made, the girls in your team will back stab you, and then you get screamed at because you had one drip at the dinner table when pouring Dom Pérignon vintage rosé.

Remember to smile, talk sexy food with the chef and drink all the expensive champagne you can. Most importantly, laugh as much as you can and don't get caught!
#chiefstewduties #bitchesbemakingmoney #makepaperavoidjail #allthestoriesaretrue #nameshavenotbeenchanged

- REFERENCE & BIBLIOGRAPHY -

Adventure Travel Checklist. https://www.rei.com/learn/expert-advice/adventure-travel-gear-checklist.html

How to pack for yacht week. 2015, June 25th. https://www.zizoo.com/en/magazine/how-to-pack-for-the-yacht-week

Julie Perry, October 1st 2006, *The Insiders' Guide to Becoming a Yacht Stewardess: Confessions from My Years Afloat with the Rich and Famous.* Morgan James Publishing

Jobs on Yachts – Crew Hierarchy, http://super-yachtcrew.com/useful-information/crew-hierarchy/

Rolf, Potts, 2003, *Vagabonding, an uncommon guide to the art of long term world travel*, Villard Books, New York.

Ten reasons to never date a yachtie, http://www.browardpalmbeach.com/music/ten-reasons-to-never-date-a-yachtie-7482318/2

What does a superyacht chief stewardess do? http://stewardessbible.com/what-does-a-superyacht-chief-stewardess-do/

Lois P.Frankel, 2014, *Nice girls still don't get the corner office,* Hachette book group, New york.

4 Steps For Taking Your Networking To The Next Level, https://www.workitdaily.com/4-steps-networking-level/

How Leaders Create and Use Networks, https://hbr.org/2007/01/how-leaders-create-and-use-networks

How to make friends with anyone in five minutes, http://www.wired.co.uk/article/how-to-make-friends-with-anyone-in-five-minutes

Caitlin Fredman and Kimberly Yorio, 2006, *The girl's guide to being a boss (without being a bitch),* Random House Inc, London.

How Much Does A Superyacht Really Cost? http://www.forbes.com/sites/aliciaadamczyk/2015/04/08/how-much-does-a-superyacht-really-cost/#2299c3bd26eb

A to Z Guide of manners & etiquette, http://www.a-to-z-of-manners-and-etiquitte.com

Peggy Post, 2011, *Emily Post's etiquette, Manners to the new world,* 18th Edition, Smallword & Stewart, New York

Table manners, https://www.etiquettescholar.com/index.html

27 Etiquette Rules For Our Times, http://www.forbes.com/sites/robasghar/2014/04/22/27-etiquette-rules-for-our-times/#6622926761dc

Signs That Your Manners Need Work, http://etiquitte.about.com/od/Manners/fl/Why-You-Need-To-Learn-Proper-Etiquette.htm

Asian Manners and Etiquette, http://www.pitlanemagazine.com/cultures/asian-manners-and-etiquette.html

Watchstanding, https://en.wikipedia.org/wiki/Watchstanding

Avoiding Seasickness, http://www.cruisecritic.com.au/articles.cfm?ID=48

Whats a dead give away someone comes from money? http://www.reddit.com/r/AskReddit/comments/4kq18y/whats_a_dead_giveaway_that_someone_has_come_from/

How to Identify the Fake Rich From the Real Rich, http://www.moneymozart.com/how-to-identify-the-fake-rich-from-the-real-rich/

5 Telltale Signs That Someone Is Rich, http://thoughtcatalog.com/ryan-oconnell/2012/06/5-telltale-signs-that-someone-is-rich/

How Can You Tell If A Guy Is Rich If He Displays Little Material Wealth?, http://www.financialsamurai.com/how-can-you-tell-if-a-guy-is-rich-no-display-of-wealth/#sthash.UyPhCMS3.dpuf

Superyacht silver service, http://superyachtcrewjobs.com/silver-service.html

A fabulous bag of tricks for planning an unforgettable party, http://rubyconnection.com.au/insights/lifestyle/a-fabulous-bag-of-tricks-for-planning-an-unforgettable-party.aspx

How to throw a unforgettable destination party, http://www.nextavenue.org/how-throw-unforgettable-destination-party/

Types of service, http://www.hbirbals.com/servicetypes.htm

Russian service, http://fnbclasses.blogspot.com.au/2010/08/russian-service.html

Different Types of Table Service That You Must Know About, http://www.buzzle.com/articles/different-types-of-table-service.html

Serving the Meal, http://www.cookingnotes.org/howto/servingmeal.htm

7 Steps To The Perfect Dinner Table, http://www.housebeautiful.com/entertaining/table-decor/tips/g994/how-to-set-dinner-table-1110/

How to Set a Pretty Table, http://www.realsimple.com/home-organizing/how-to-set-a-pretty-table/special-occasion-dinner

Boat theme parties, http://www.pintrest.com/explore/boat-theme-parties

101 party themes that will make your party rock, http://www.hexjam.com/uk/news/101-party-themes-that-will-make-your-party-rock

How to store wine – and other temperature issues, https://montalto.com.au/right-wine-temperature/

How to serve wine 101: Tips on the perfect serving temperature, http://www.winespectator.com/webfeature/show/id/how-to-serve-wine-temperature

White wine descriptions, http://www.vintnerscellarwaterloo.com/article/84/white_wine_descriptions.html

Red wine information & basics, http://www.winemag.com/2015/10/27/red-wine-basics/

40 wine descriptions and what they really mean, http://winefolly.com/tutorial/40-wine-descriptions/

An easy explanations of wine types, http://www.primermagazine.com/2011/learn/an-easy-explanation-of-wine-types

The only 8 things you need to know about rosé wine, https://www.buzzfeed.com/rachelysanders/what-you-need-to-know-about-rose-wine-facts?utm_term=.mtz4kzPB4#.hirDK0l3D

A complete guide to drinking rosé wine this summer, http://www.epicurious.com/expert-advice/a-complete-guide-to-drinking-rose-wine-this-summer-article

A bullshitter's guide to champagne, http://www.gq-magazine.co.uk/article/how-to-drink-serve-champagne-bullshitters-guide

Glossary of wine terms, http://www.winemag.com/glossary/

Wine terminology & vocabulary, https://www.vinology.com/wine-terms/

Match food with wine, http://www.bbcgoodfood.com/howto/guide/match-food-wine

Your wine and beer pairing guide, http://www.sunset.com/food-wine/wine-pairings/wine-pairing-101

A-Z Stain Removal Guide Over 100 Pages Of Instructions For Removing Stains, http://www.stain-removal-101.com/stain-removal-guide.html

Stain Removal Guide, The General Rules for Removing Stains, http://www.clothingdictionary.com/stain_removal_guide.htm

Leaving Your Job? Don't Be a Jerk About It, http://www.thehippocket.com.au/leaving-job-dont-jerk/

Fending Off the Creeps: How to Avoid Sexual Harassment, http://www.inc.com/stacey-epstein/5-ways-to-handle-sexual-harassment.html

David Jacobson, 2007, *Get me out of here,* Elwin Street Limited, London

For couples in close quarters, squeeze-y does it, http://www.today.com/id/43399930/ns/today-today_health/t/couples-close-quarters-squeeze-y-does-it/

Confused by Nautical Expressions and Other Boating Jargon? http://www.sailboat-cruising.com/nautical-expressions.html

Lightning Source UK Ltd.
Milton Keynes UK
UKRC010855120821
388463UK00009B/85